Legal Translation Outsourced

OXFORD STUDIES IN LANGUAGE AND LAW

Oxford Studies in Language and Law includes scholarly analyses and descriptions of language evidence in civil and criminal law cases as well as language issues arising in the area of statutes, statutory interpretation, courtroom discourse, jury instructions, and historical changes in legal language.

The Legal Language of Scottish Burghs: Standardization and Lexical Bundles (1380–1560)
Joanna Kopaczyk

"I'm Sorry for What I've Done": The Language of Courtroom Apologies
M. Catherine Gruber

Dueling Discourses: The Construction of Reality in Closing Arguments
Laura Felton Rosulek

Entextualizing Domestic Violence: Language Ideology and Violence Against Women in the Anglo-American Hearsay Principle
Jennifer Andrus

Speak English or What?: Codeswitching and Interpreter Use in New York City Courts
Philipp Sebastian Angermeyer

Law at Work: Studies in Legal Ethnomethods
Edited by Baudouin Dupret, Michael Lynch, and Tim Berard

Speaking of Language and Law: Conversations on the Work of Peter Tiersma
Edited by Lawrence Solan, Janet Ainsworth, and Roger W. Shuy

Confronting the Death Penalty: How Language Influences Jurors in Capital Cases
Robin Conley

Discursive Constructions of Consent in the Legal Process
Edited by Susan Ehrlich, Diana Eades and Janet Ainsworth

From Truth to Technique at Trial: A Discursive History of Advocacy Advice Texts
Philip Gaines

Discourse, Identity, and Social Change in the Marriage Equality Debates
Karen Tracy

Translating the Social World for Law: Linguistic Tools for a New Legal Realism
Edited by Elizabeth Mertz, William K. Ford, and Gregory Matoesian

Conceptions in the Code: How Metaphors Explain Legal Challenges in Digital Times
Stefan Larsson

Legal Integration and Language Diversity: Rethinking Translation in EU Lawmaking
C. J. W. Baaij

Legal Translation Outsourced
Juliette R. Scott

Legal Translation Outsourced

Juliette R. Scott

OXFORD
UNIVERSITY PRESS

OXFORD
UNIVERSITY PRESS

Oxford University Press is a department of the University of Oxford. It furthers the University's objective of excellence in research, scholarship, and education by publishing worldwide. Oxford is a registered trade mark of Oxford University Press in the UK and certain other countries.

Published in the United States of America by Oxford University Press
198 Madison Avenue, New York, NY 10016, United States of America.

CIP data is on file at the Library of Congress
ISBN 978–0–19–090000–7 (pbk.)
ISBN 978–0–19–090001–4 (hbk.)

9 8 7 6 5 4 3 2 1

Paperback printed by WebCom, Inc., Canada
Hardback printed by Bridgeport National Bindery, Inc., United States of America

CONTENTS

LIST OF FIGURES, TABLES, AND BOXES

Figures

Tables

Boxes

ACKNOWLEDGEMENTS

Dr Carol O'Sullivan, without whom this enterprise would simply not have been possible.

Professor Vijay K. Bhatia, for being such an inspiration, and for having very kindly taken the time to give me his invaluable views on my project on several occasions.

Professor Jan Engberg, for his constructive comments on my methodology, and generously discussing issues on several occasions.

Advocate-General Eleanor Sharpston at the Court of Justice of the European Union, for her vocal championing of professional attitudes toward working with legal translators.

Professor Laurence Solan, for his insights on my project plan at its initial stages.

Dr Gianluca Pontrandolfo, for his idea on triangulating the survey of commissioners by questioning translators.

Ben Meeham of QDA Training, for his invaluable assistance with the software NVivo.

Sahar Bhaimia, for her assiduous proofreading of this manuscript.

Pam Juden, my aunt, for her quiet support during difficult times.

John Scott, my uncle, Emeritus Professor at The University of Western Australia, for his unstinting support and love, together with Dr Simone Scott, my aunt and a respected scholar.

All of the anonymised participants, both in the legal profession and the translation profession, who, by so kindly answering my surveys, gave me such rich data to work with.

Legal Translation Outsourced

Introduction

I.1. Background

Legal translation has come to the fore in recent decades. This is partly a result of globalization, which has led to significant increases in cross-border transactions and litigation; and migration, whether the movement of workers or retirees, or the displacement of persons; and partly stems from the development of multilingual legislation, whether supranational such as in the European Union, or national as in Switzerland, Canada, or Hong Kong.[1] Legal translation may facilitate international business, or it may be required to uphold various types of rights, to combat organized crime,[2] or to provide access to justice.[3] Certain academic disciplines—for example, comparative law—are taking an increasing interest in legal translation.[4] Growing volumes mean that more and more translation of the law is outsourced and is no longer the preserve of in-house translators. In turn, this means that the training of legal translators should be of prime concern,[5] as should quality control.

Within academia, legal translation studies, having emerged in the 1970s with momentum from Canadian initiatives towards bilingual legislation (A. Wagner & Gémar, 2015, p. 1), have burgeoned, fostered by, in alphabetical order, precursors such as Claude Bocquet (1994, 2008), Deborah Cao (e.g., 2007), Gérard-René de Groot (e.g., 1987), Jan Engberg (e.g., 1999 onwards),

---

[1] Switzerland (e.g., Dullion, 1997, 2007), Canada (Gémar, 1982), Hong Kong (Cao, 2010); and for an analysis of how globalization is affecting legal translation, see Megale (2015).

[2] See Scott (2017d).

[3] E.g., as a result of the transposition of Directive 2010/64/EU of the European Parliament and of the Council of 20 October 2010 on the right to interpretation and translation in criminal proceedings.

[4] For example, a conference entitled 'Comparative Law: Engaging Translation' was held in the UK from 21–22 June 2012, and the University Toulouse 1 Capitole, France, held '*Justement traduire: L'enjeu de la traduction juridique*' from 11–12 May 2017. See also the work of Pommer (e.g., 2005, 2008), Glanert (2011, 2014), Engberg (2013, 2017), and Husa (2017).

[5] Scott (2017a).

Jean-Claude Gémar (e.g., 1979), Anne Lise Kjaer (e.g., 1994 onwards), Rodolfo Sacco (1987), and Susan Šarčević (e.g., 1997). It is striking that translation has been virtually ignored within legal scholarship,[6] with the exception of Rose Kennedy (2000)—her paper on 'Problems in the Legal Translation Industry' was both wide-ranging and highly relevant. Recent years have seen 'Legal Translation Studies' evoked as a discrete field within Translation Studies,[7] and one may take a positive or negative view of such a separation: on the positive side, for example, there are more and more dedicated conferences and journal issues,[8] which offer opportunities to deepen knowledge, understanding, and co-operation in our specialist area, while on the negative side, one could argue that an already diminutive discipline might do itself a disservice by further dispersal and forfeit potential cross-fertilization with other specialized translation areas.

In any event, the highly interdisciplinary intrinsic nature of Translation Studies, and, by extension, Legal Translation Studies, ought to argue in favour of its permeability. In addition to the intersecting disciplines and subfields singled out by Fernando Prieto Ramos,[9] I offer the following that are of particular relevance: Business Studies, Discourse Analysis, Forensic Linguistics, Genre Theory, Language for Special/Specialized Purposes (including the teaching of non-native speakers), legal drafting, and Socio-Legal Studies. The discipline of Legal Linguistics is also of great relevance.[10] In sum, with the range of intersecting fields and subfields, nomenclature issues,[11] and the sometimes restricted communication of scholarly work among language communities,[12] it is surely possible to facilitate and improve cross-field knowledge sharing.

---

[6] There is a small body of work which embraces the translation of legal information sources (e.g., Somers, 2007; Yates, 2006; Peruginelli, 2006, 2010)

[7] E.g., Biel & Engberg (2013); Prieto Ramos (2014).

[8] A non-exclusive sample of conferences: the Centre for Research in Language and Law (biennial since 2010), http://www.crill.unina2.it/crill/conferences-and-seminars/; the Institute of Linguistics at Adam Mickiewicz University, Poznan, Poland, 13th annual edition set for July 2018. Dedicated journal issues have been published by, for example: *FACHSPRACHE, inTRAlinea, JoSTrans, Linguistica Antverpiensia, Meta, Perspectives*, and *The Interpreter and Translator Trainer*, while *Comparative Legilinguistics – International Journal for Legal Communication* has appeared several times a year since 2009, the biannual *Language and Law Linguagem e Direito* was launched in 2014, and *HERMES – Journal of Language and Communication in Business* has included relevant papers since 1988.

[9] Prieto Ramos (2014, p. 266). He sees 'Legal Translation Studies', which he refers to using the acronym 'LTS', as the intersection between Law (including in particular Comparative Law and Legal Hermeneutics), Translation Studies (specifically Translation Methodology, Sociology of Translation, Translation Technology, and Translation Pedagogy), and Linguistics (for which he notes Text Linguistics, Contrastive Linguistics, Terminology, Corpus Linguistics, and Pragmatics). His examples are non-exclusive.

[10] Heikki Mattila (2006); A. Wagner & Gémar (2015); Prieto Ramos (2014, pp. 267–268).

[11] E.g., 'legal terminology' versus 'legal lexicography'; 'legal interpreting' versus 'legal interpretation' (which further runs the risk of confusion with 'statutory interpretation'); 'juritraductologie' versus 'traductologie juridique'.

[12] In particular the strong communities working on the triptych of language, translation, and law in Danish, English, French, Polish, and Spanish.

It is also important to remember that a key role of Translation Studies is to both study and advise the profession. Steps have been taken to close the gap between academia and practice over the years. Some nonlimiting examples are the work of Christina Schäffner (e.g., 2012), Maeve Olohan (e.g., 2007), Andrew Chesterman (e.g., Chesterman & E. Wagner, 2002), and Janet Fraser (esp. 1996, 2000, 2001). These need to be extended in the legal specialism, to the benefit of all. The previously mentioned 2010 Directive stimulated EU-funded research projects that closely involved the judiciary and police services before and after its entry into force.[13] The publication edited by Anabel Borja Albi and Fernando Prieto Ramos (2013) is worthy of special note insofar as it embraces many areas of practice, and is even priced at a level and drafted in a register that could make it attractive to professionals outside academia.

To conclude this necessarily abridged account of the discipline and its interaction with the profession, I will cite some of the areas in which research has latterly been most intensive. These include the application of corpus linguistics techniques in order to analyse legal language in and for translation,[14] including international projects such as ECPC;[15] further affiliations with comparative law (e.g., Dullion, 2015); legal translator training (e.g., the work of Esther Monzó Nebot, 2015; Łucja Biel, 2010b, 2011, 2017; Catherine Way, 2016; Aleksandra Matulewska & Karolina Gortych-Michalak, 2014), translation and interpreting in judicial settings, as well as sociological and knowledge-based approaches. The future has yet to be written, but seems likely to consist of a blurring of interdisciplinary boundaries in order to consolidate a rather fragmented research community, and of an even greater engagement to embracing and fostering practice.

As noted by Biel and Engberg (2013), the study of translation at international courts and institutions has dominated legal translation studies for many years. This book seeks to address the lack of empirical data on translation as it is carried out in the commercial world.[16] It looks at what happens in the market, and constitutes practitioner research aimed at potentially improving practice. It also seeks to make a theoretical contribution by unpacking how outsourced

[13] E.g., Grotius I & II, Agis I & II, Building Mutual Trust I & II, AVIDICUS 1, 2, & 3, TRAFUT, ImPLI, Qualitas, QUALETRA, LIT Search.

[14] E.g., the work of Stanisław Goźdź-Roszkowski (2004, 2006a, 2006b), Łucja Biel (2010a, 2017), and Gianluca Pontrandolfo (2011, 2015, 2016).

[15] The European Parliamentary Comparable and Parallel Corpora project, coordinated by Dr María Calzada Pérez at Universitat Jaume I, Spain, with members based at different universities in Europe, funded by the Spanish Ministry of Education and Science, http://www.ecpc.uji.es.

[16] This issue is not confined to Legal Translation Studies and arises throughout Translation Studies (see, for example, the work of Anthony Pym (e.g., 2012) and Maeve Olohan (e.g., 2015), as well as Angelelli & Jacobson (2009).

legal translation is performed, by drawing threads from satellite disciplines into a model of the legal translator's textual agency; by modelling constraints on performance; and by illustrating the outsourced legal translation process in practice. Finally, an informational/contextual tool (a briefing template) is offered for use by practitioners—both those procuring legal translation and those providing legal translation services.

The research described in this book was based on a hypothesis that performance of outsourced legal translation was less than ideal, and that there was scope for improvement. That hypothesis was based on extensive personal experience in the market, to be investigated by means of a qualitative global survey. My underlying aims in undertaking the research were and remain as follows: first, to achieve a better understanding of legal translation practice, by those performing this complex task, by their clients, and by intermediaries; and second, where possible, to make suggestions for improvements in the form of concrete practitioner and client tools. In so doing, I had a third goal: that of bridging gaps between academia and practice, and between legal and translation practitioners, to the benefit of all.

The book further aims to address some of the points made by Biel and Engberg in their landmark paper on developments in legal translation studies (2013, pp. 1–11): by being both process-oriented and function-oriented;[17] and by having a strongly interdisciplinary core (see also Prieto Ramos, 2014). Thanks to my language combinations,[18] my references to the literature delve into more than one of the field's 'language-specific enclaves' (Biel & Engberg, 2013, p. 2). By proposing a number of theoretical models for the area of outsourced legal translation[19]—as contrasted with the more widely researched institutional or in-house contexts—I also seek to contribute to the enrichment of 'methods and approaches' (Biel & Engberg, 2013, p. 2).

I.2. Key Definitions

For the sake of clarity, I provide below some definitions for terms used throughout this book. To disambiguate my use of **agency, agents**, and **agencies**: I discuss the translator's 'agency' from several perspectives: (i) textual agency—mediated action on the text; (ii) capacity to act; and (iii) relational

[17] The terms 'function' and 'purpose' are both adopted in the literature, and I follow suit. However, I mainly use intended 'purpose' when referring to my own work for the following reasons: (i) links with the concept of 'fitness-for-purpose'; (ii) I draw from Bhatia's work on communicative purpose (e.g., 1987); (iii) the term may speak more clearly to market actors. I nevertheless adopt the terms 'functional', 'functionalist', and 'functionalism'.

[18] French and Italian.

[19] Some initial versions were presented in Scott (2015c).

agency, understood to be 'working with others to strengthen purposeful responses to complex problems' (Edwards, 2008).[20] I use the word 'agent(s)' as an alternative term for translator(s), who can, in different ways and to differing extents, exercise these three forms of agency.[21] The translator is also seen as an agent through the lens of the principal–agent relationship described by corporate agency theory. The plural 'agencies' is used to refer to translation service provision entities acting as intermediaries.

Outsourcing refers to the procurement of services from providers that are external to their client, as opposed to personnel based in-house, and I use it in a neutral way without the negative connotations sometimes associated with the term. Law firms or companies may outsource legal translation where the necessary expertise is not available in-house (no skills in the given target and/or source language); or where the expertise cannot be assigned to the translation task (in-house translator(s) and/or multilingual lawyers/personnel are not available to undertake the task); or because there are volume constraints (too much text with a fixed deadline, e.g., impending court appearance or service of process). I have chosen **commissioning**[22] as the most appropriate term for the action of procuring[23] the translation of a legal text from a self-employed practitioner. The translation **brief** and the corresponding action of **briefing** translators refer to the specifications or instructions given by a client when commissioning a translation.[24]

Throughout, **performance** has been construed primarily in its legal sense, that is, fulfilment of contractual requirements, as well as implying the 'carrying out' of a service. I have elected to discuss the optimization of performance rather than of 'quality', deeming the word 'quality' too highly charged. Nevertheless, to quote Joanna Drugan, 'The translation process has a significant impact on quality' (2013, p. 183).

---

[20] The legal interpretation of agency within the meaning of the 'law of agency' dealing with proxies and representatives has been excluded in this book. For a summary of doctrine, national and international legislation see http://www.trans-lex.org/911000.

[21] Agents as they are understood in the field of literary translation—i.e., intermediaries negotiating authors' rights (e.g., Buzelin, 2006)—do not participate in the supply chains of legal translation.

[22] See, for example, Bassnett (2002); Chesterman (e.g., 2009); Katan (e.g., 2009); Kinnunen (2011); the Aequitas project (Hertog, 2001); and also the Building Mutual Trust Framework Project for Implementing EU Common Standards in Legal Interpreting and Translation (http://www.building-mutual-trust.eu).

[23] The Partnership for Public Procurement, the largest procurement association in the world, makes available a glossary in which it defines procurement as: 'Purchasing [. . .] or otherwise acquiring any supplies, services, or construction; includes all functions that pertain to the acquisition, including description of requirements, selection and solicitation of sources, preparation and award of contract, and all phases of contract administration. The combined functions of purchasing [. . .] receiving, and inspection [. . .] operations' (http://www.globalpublicprocurement.org/Resources/Glossary/).

[24] There is a parallel here to the brief understood as instructions given to a barrister (in certain jurisdictions, e.g., Altobelli, 2007).

I have chosen the term **actor**[25] to describe those involved in the outsourcing of legal translation.[26] In the context of translators' agency, the term 'actor' has been used, *inter alia*, by Kristiina Abdallah (2010), Olohan (2011), and Inghilleri (2005). The term **principal,** used by agency theorists, for example, to describe the party outsourcing work, may also be referred to as **commissioner**.[27] For the purposes of this research, I focus on self-employed[28] **legal translation practitioners** who may or may not be certified, accredited, or sworn.[29] A fuller discussion of the various actors appears in section 1.1.7 in Chapter 1.

For a systematic discussion of the many areas of legal discourse, I adopt the following terms: **macrogenre** as comprising all of the different areas of language of the law;[30] in which '"**subgenres**" are grouped under "**genres**", which act thus as common headings encompassing a number of the lower level categories' (Monzó Nebot, 2008, emphasis added).

I.3. Practitioner Research

Insofar as my own professional situation was both the instigation for this research and an enabler for data collection, it is important to begin by explaining that I have worked as a legal translator for 25 years, mainly for corporations, law firms, and institutions, and always on a self-employed basis. To date, I have run my business from three European countries, working for clients worldwide. For many academics wishing to carry out research into translation practice, and particularly the legal specialism, trust and perceived issues of confidentiality, as well as simply establishing contact with the actors concerned, are significant barriers to obtaining data. By virtue of my position as a practitioner, I was able to leverage my networks and involve stakeholders with relative ease. This book should thus be framed within the body of practitioner research, also known as action research (Robson, 2011; Cochran-Smith & Donnell, 2006;

---

[25] 'A participant in an action or process' (Oxford Dictionaries online http://oxforddictionaries.com).

[26] The term 'stakeholder' might also be used as an alternative for 'actors', but I feel that 'stakeholder' implies a degree of control that legal translators in particular do not possess at the present time.

[27] Biel (2014a); Bowker (2001); Katan (2009); Mossop (2014); Nord (2007); Strandvik (2015).

[28] The practices involving translators working in institutions or in-house—in terms of briefing, access to drafters, feedback, etc.—are, as a rule, posited to be more effective in optimizing their agency than practices involving external practitioners.

[29] The terminology and legislative framework surrounding such status varies widely (see Vigier, Klein, & Festinger, 2013). Since, to date, in the majority of countries, there is no set of official criteria qualifying legal translators as such, this title is self-awarded by the workers in question.

[30] Garzone and Ilie use the term 'macrogenre' as broader than a genre (2014), while Garcìa Izquierdo and Borja Albi see macrogenre as between legal system and, in turn, genre and subgenre (2008). Also see Bhatia (e.g., 2014, pp. 65–67) on 'colonies of related genres' (2014, p. 65).

Drake with Heath, 2011). A more detailed discussion of this paradigm can be found in section 5.1 in Chapter 5.

I.4. Research Questions

The guiding thread of this book consists of the tensions between the briefing and performance of outsourced legal translation, constrained by context and contextual resources, and the potential risks involved. The overall research question—how to optimize the outsourcing of legal translation—is broken down into two questions on briefing: How does the briefing process work within the outsourced legal translation environment? Are legal translation principals and/or translators working as external practitioners satisfied with that process? And it includes two questions on performance: Do the principals express any issues vis-à-vis the performance of translations received? Do such legal translation principals and/or translators have any suggestions to improve performance?

I.5. Boundaries of the Study

The object of study is the outsourced translation of legal texts. In-house translation, whether carried out at law firms, institutions, or translation companies, and interpreting of the spoken word are not, therefore, within the scope of the research.

I explore how translation practitioners' agency might be optimized through the eyes of two groups of actors from the chain of supply—commissioners and translators. The role of intermediaries[31] was thus not a primary area of research as such, although some references are made, in particular regarding information flows.

Since the outsourcing of legal translation has hardly been studied at all, I chose not to exclude any language pair or country from the fieldwork, which therefore stands as an initial and preliminary investigation that could be followed up by more detailed regional ventures.

---

[31] In this regard, though not specifically concerning the legal domain, see Olohan & Davitti (2015).

1

The Outsourced Legal Translation Environment

> The translator does not always know whether the gadget is room size or palm size.
> 'It is not important, just go ahead and translate'.
> —Abdallah (2010, p. 21)

1.1. The (Legal) Translation Market as an Outsourcing 'Entity'

Translation services are provided in a market that is often referred to, revealingly, as an 'industry'.[1] It comprises a number of services including written translation, interpreting, and related activities, performed either as part of the translation process or as discrete occupations, such as proofreading, copywriting, localization, project management, terminology research, and, more recently, the post-editing of machine translation. These services may be outsourced by clients to a number of different types of provider, either through intermediaries such as translation agencies, translators' networks/teams, or online platforms,[2] or directly to individual translators or translation companies.[3] Of course, translation and interpreting services may also be supplied within institutions,[4] whether large corporate entities or multinational organizations such as the United Nations or the European Union.

In fact, the translation market could be described as anything other than an entity. Indeed, such qualifiers as 'fragmented' (e.g., Olohan, 2007, p. 37), 'disordered', and 'disparate' might be more suitable. In order to portray the context in which outsourced legal translation takes place, and before examining

---

[1] For an in-depth discussion of the implications of this term, see Fry (2009).

[2] Such as Proz.com, TranslatorsCafé.com, GeoWorkz.com, etc.

[3] Confusingly, agencies acting purely as intermediaries, translation companies, and individuals may all be referred to as language service providers (LSPs).

[4] As stated in the Introduction, this book focuses on non-institutional translation.

ways in which self-employed legal translators and their clients interact, and how these translators' interventions might be optimized, I present some features of the translation market as a whole,[5] wherever possible with reference to the legal field, focusing on six specific areas that typify the environment: the prevalence of outsourcing, cursory specifications, status issues, diversity of skill sets, heterogeneous quality, and a rapid rate of change primarily brought about by technical advances.

1.1.1. WIDESPREAD OUTSOURCING

In today's globalized world, we increasingly refer to the international outsourcing of services, which Kedia and Lahiri define as

> handing over of service[6] functions (that were done in-house) by firms to providers (i.e., vendors) [...] where the former does not have ownership, authority or direct control. (2007, p. 23)

In the case of translation services, outsourcing is highly prevalent, and a lack of ownership, authority, and direct control applies as much to translator-providers as to clients. Translation may be outsourced via translation companies, also known as translation agencies, or directly by end-user clients such as law firms and multinationals. The following selection from the literature gives an idea of scale. Olohan writes of 'predominantly freelance translators' (2007, p. 37), while Lagoudaki's survey of 874 'translation professionals' from 54 countries reports that 73 per cent were freelancers (2006, p. 32). In a survey of translation companies in Portugal, Ferreira-Alves reports that 'outsourcing is a common practice' for all of his respondents (2012, pp. 233–262). For Pym *et al.* (2012, p. 89), a weighted average suggests that the general proportion of freelancers is around 78.4 per cent, depending on the country and the sector, with reports of lower figures in the greater China region. For comparison purposes, in the UK digital and creative sector, Williams *et al.* (2012) found an average of 23 per cent of freelance workers in 2009—a far lower figure than translators, despite the fact that this sector is traditionally considered to have a relatively high rate of freelance workers.[7]

---

[5] Translation services are provided in many different fields such as, *inter alia*, marketing and advertising, audiovisual, literary works, technical, scientific, and medical, as well as the main focus of this study—the legal domain, which often overlaps with those of finance and business.

[6] Goods may be outsourced, too, but this field of research is generally separated by scholars from that of services.

[7] Williams *et al.* (2012) cite 13 per cent of freelance workers across all UK business sectors in the same year.

1.1.2. CURSORY ORDER SPECIFICATIONS

A notable difference as compared with other business sectors is that outsourced translation orders are often placed on an *ad hoc* basis, not through formal or long-term contracts—hence the success of online platforms[8] as intermediaries between translators and their clients (e.g., Pym, 2014). Equally, in many business sectors, specifications stating the client's requirements are an essential part of the ordering process.[9] However, when undertaking this research, it seemed that the content of an outsourced legal translation order was almost always cursory,[10] to say the least—and likely to include only the following information: date of delivery, language pair, word rate, and number of words. Furthermore, where agencies or end-user clients have regular contacts with translators, the 'purchase order' may only consist of an informal email containing the preceding information and a request to proceed. In general, orders seem to almost never include detailed instructions relating to the translation process, such as recommended terminology, style, register, reference documents for consistency, intended users, or purpose. Translation order content was therefore one of the key points that I sought to investigate in my fieldwork.

1.1.3. PERCEIVED LOW STATUS OF AGENTS

Much has been written about the low status of translators.[11] For some authors, this is due in part to the predominance of women (e.g., Dam and Zethsen, 2010). Pym *et al.* (2012) quote a figure for 'the general proportion of women' as '70% or above', whilst Sela-Sheffy and Shlesinger call translation 'a pink-collar profession' (2008, p. 80). In other sectors, too, scholars have theorized about the link between gender and professionalization—in particular in the medical field (e.g., Witz, 1992). In a global survey of translation practice, Katan (2009), whilst having a generally positive outlook concerning translators' own perception of their work as a 'profession', nevertheless found that it was a 'scattered cottage industry' (p. 111), where 'almost a third (31%) of the respondents classified the translator as having "low" status' (p. 126), and where many of them compared their status to that of secretaries.[12] A further barrier to professionalization may

---

[8] Proz.com, Translator's Café, Lionbridge's GeoWorkZ, etc.

[9] See *Principles and Practices of Public Procurement: Specifications*, as adopted by 'over 80 government agencies and professional associations' worldwide, made available by the Chartered Institute of Procurement & Supply and the Partnership for Public Procurement (http://www.globalpublicprocurement.org/Documents/Resources/public-procurement-practices/SOPSpecifications.pdf).

[10] This conjecture was based on my own professional experience, as well as market publications, forums, and debate.

[11] E.g., Dam & Zethsen (2009b, p. 2); Sela-Sheffy & Shlesinger (2008); Snell-Hornby (2006, pp. 172–173); and Venuti (1995).

[12] The parallel between translators and secretaries has been drawn by other scholars, such as Kennedy's 'bilingual typists' (2000, p. 440), and Gouadec, for whom 'translation is often seen as little

be the common practice for translators to combine translation with other jobs such as language teaching or other activities, or to use it as a part-time source of income (Katan, 2009, p. 118; Pym *et al.*, 2013, pp. 76–78).

I would disagree with Gouadec's somewhat idealistic view according to which being 'self-employed gives [translators] [. . .] "professional" status along with architects, doctors and other highly qualified practitioners' (2007, p. 186). Whilst this may be a perception of those entering the profession or outside it, I doubt that those having practised for a significant time would feel that their status is on a par with the other named professions.[13]

The issue of status is also bound up with that of the (lack of) qualifications required in order to enter the translation profession.[14] Unlike lawyers or doctors, whose qualifications, if not exactly equivalent, are certainly recognized by their international counterparts, translators, including those specializing in the law, may come from a wide range of backgrounds: holding (or not) degrees in languages; thematic qualifications in their (legal) specialism; diplomas in translation studies; or indeed, they may not be formally qualified at all.[15] The word 'unregulated' is used by Pym *et al.* (2012) in an extensive study funded by the European Commission's Directorate-General for Translation (DGT), which examined the translation profession in Europe, drawing comparisons with Canada, the United States, and Australia. The data used for their study come from previous surveys and contributions from more than 100 experts and informants (Pym *et al.*, 2012, p. 3).[16] Indeed, they found that '[i]n no country that we have surveyed is any academic qualification—or indeed any kind of formal qualification at all—required in order to use the term "translator" or its equivalent generic terms' (Pym *et al.*, 2012, p. 20).

Professional bodies do not generally act as gatekeepers to the profession,[17] partly because there are so many of them—217 associations for translation and interpreting were identified by Pym (2014, p. 467). Indeed, some countries have more than one association competing for potential members (e.g., UK and

---

more than glorified secretarial work' (2007, p. 245). See also section 3.2.6 (Chapter 3 in this volume). Katan (2011) also notes a translator-secretary collocation in the EUROSTAT NACE classification 'Secretarial and translation activities' (currently applicable 2008 version retrieved from http://ec.europa.eu/eurostat/statistics-explained/index.php/Glossary:Statistical_classification_of_economic_activities_in_the_European_Community_(NACE)). Pym *et al.*, however, note other categorizations (2013, pp. 9–10).

[13] Scott (2015a), January 9, keynote address, currently unpublished.

[14] We may ask ourselves whether translation can in fact be termed a 'profession', given its lack of regulation at this time. In this regard, see Pym *et al.* (2012, p. 14).

[15] Except in a minority of countries where the specific area of sworn or certified translations can only be performed by authorized translators (see Pym *et al.*, 2012; and Vigier, Klein, & Festinger, 2013).

[16] These figures evolved, since informants were encouraged to continue to supplement the data even after the study was closed.

[17] According to Gouadec (2007), only in Argentina, Denmark, Norway, and three provinces of Canada is access to the translation profession subject to approval by a local union of translators.

Italy[18]). Currently, to my knowledge, there are no internationally applicable regulations, whether at the governmental level or put in place by the profession, laying down minimum qualifications for legal translators.[19]

In recent years there has been a discernible downward pressure on prices, owing in part to globalization (Cronin, 2003; Gouadec, 2007), and possibly to the after-effects of the 2007–2008 financial crisis, but perhaps more importantly to signalling problems.[20] It is worth noting that the *terminology* used for and by the profession is not without significance and merits further investigation, but is beyond the scope of this study.[21] The instability of translator–client relationships in the outsourced environment could be another contributing factor.

Market disorder is viewed as a potential threat in the policy recommendations made by Pym *et al.*: they warn that 'good translators' may leave the profession if a 'laissez-faire' attitude continues to be adopted by the authorities, especially with regard to court-authorized translators (2013, pp. 109–119). Notwithstanding, when compared with other subsets of the profession, together with medical translation, the legal specialism is often held, anecdotally, to be one of the better paid. The actual situation in the legal field is difficult to ascertain. This is partly due to the complexity of the market, and partly to the fact that self-employed translators are notoriously reluctant to make their tariffs public,[22] despite regularly being the subject of surveys by professional bodies.[23] Unfortunately, most of these surveys do not break down their data by

[18] In the United Kingdom: the Chartered Institute of Linguists (CIOL) and the Institute of Translation and Interpreting (ITI). In Italy: the Associazione Nazionale Italiana Traduttori e Interpreti (ANITI) and the Associazione Italiana Traduttori e Interpreti (AITI). I refer here to associations in direct competition for membership by legal translators, thus excluding literary translators' bodies, for example.

[19] The European Legal Interpreters and Translators Association (EULITA) has put forward the introduction of a European Professional Card for cross-border services, involving approximation and harmonization, particularly of qualifications, through a 'Common Platform' or register to enable the mutual recognition of authorized/sworn translators throughout the European Union member states (Pym *et al.*, 2012). It is currently at a very early stage.

[20] 'Signalling' refers here to how suppliers communicate their services, skills, and ability to potential clients in the market. The effectiveness of translators' signalling mechanisms is examined extensively by Pym *et al.* (2012, 2013).

[21] As an illustration in English: a cline going from 'asset', 'resource', 'vendor', 'freelancer', 'supplier', and 'provider' to 'translation professional' or 'translation practitioner' transmits very different signals. To describe translators as 'assets' or 'resources' links them, linguistically, with being 'used'. At the other end of the scale, 'practitioner' invites verbs such as 'consult' and the lexically and semantically related 'consultant' and 'consultancy'—and transmits higher status signals. The same kind of negative to positive signalling applies to the cline of 'rate', 'price', 'tariff', 'fee', and the cline 'purchase order', 'translation order', 'job specifications', 'brief'; and the related verbs 'place an order' or 'instruct'. For further discussions see Scott (2017b).

[22] Durban (2010) suggests that this may be due to antitrust challenges, though she does not provide any details or references.

[23] A further difficulty for researchers in obtaining data is that some market surveys are carried out by private entities such as Common Sense Advisory, whose charges for their reports exceed the budget of all but the largest corporations. Some translators' professional bodies make survey data on tariffs

specialism, or if they do, details are not provided. Legal translators' fees will not be further investigated in this book, but would be an interesting avenue for further research.

Finally, we might hypothesize that low status and high levels of competition in the market, as well as the lack of stability of freelance work *per se*, could have an effect on translators' willingness to engage with their principals—either to ask questions or to exercise control over working processes.

1.1.4. DIVERSITY OF AGENTS' SKILL SETS

The field of legal translation forms part of a profession that also comprises many other specialisms, with very diverse subject-specific skills.[24] Within the field of law, legal translators may and often do specialize still further—for example, in areas such as contracts, patents, insurance, financial texts, or certificates and diplomas. They may have initially trained as linguists and/or as lawyers before entering the translation profession (Lavoie, 2003; Orlando, 2015), or undertake legal studies and/or qualifications during the course of a linguistic career. Later, they may also pursue additional training to develop their expertise in one or more particular areas of law. Legal translators are also required to deal with specific technical areas arising in legal texts—the genre of patents is an obvious example of texts containing highly technical terms, but consider also legislation on swine fever, or litigation involving complex financial products, or expert witness reports.

Apart from essential thematic skills, translators also need to be highly literate in the use of fast-developing information technology, for example CAT tools, also known as TEnTs,[25] information mining and retrieval, and preferably in using electronic corpora as a reference tool for terminological purposes;[26] they need to possess good interpersonal skills, such as those required for running a small business, or teamwork, and for social networking with professional aims; and they should have an excellent mastery both of their native language—the target language into which they will be translating—and of one or more source languages. Beyond language, translators also require intercultural competences.[27]

---

available to their members only, although Pym *et al.* (2013) were granted access. Their study was not specific to legal translation, however.

[24] Scott (2013, 2015a).

[25] Computer-aided translation tools, or translation environment tools.

[26] E.g., Bernardini (2016); Corpas Pastor & Duran-Munoz (2017); Gallego Hernández (2015); Garcia (2009); Rodríguez-Inés (2010); Sánchez Ramos & Vigier Moreno (2016); Scott (2012); Zanettin (2012).

[27] For further details, see the conclusions of a symposium on the translator's profile, 'What Skills for a Changing Market?' (European Commission, 2011) published by the Directorate-General for Translation of the European Commission, and the comprehensive analysis of the profession constituted by Gouadec (2007). See also the European Masters in Translation (EMT) Network publication

These manifold skills need to be maintained during the course of a career—usually referred to as 'continuing professional development' or 'CPD'—and yet there are no standard CPD requirements for translators, although professional bodies in a number of countries are starting to introduce recommendations for their members. Translators thus may have very diverse skill sets, and varying degrees of conscientiousness in keeping those skills up to date or enhancing them. For many other professions on the other hand, CPD is compulsory—for example, for lawyers, surveyors, accountants and auditors, and estate agents.[28] In recent years there have been moves towards the self-recording of CPD in all its forms as opposed to mandatory attendance at training sessions.

1.1.5. HETEROGENEOUS QUALITY AND QUALITY STANDARDS

Although there has been no major study specifically investigating *legal* translation quality in the outsourced market, Drugan provides a great deal of data on the 'industry' as a whole, collected from a wide range of sources, including 'sectors with an enhanced reputation for quality (financial, legal [. . . .])' (2013, p. 3). Her detailed examination of different quality models used in practice shows widely diverging approaches and results.

There is also considerable heterogeneity in quality standards used. Drugan (2013, pp. 74–75) lists the following recognized by her participants: the ISO 9000 series; the German *Deutsches Institut für Normung* (DIN) 2345; (C) EN 15038: 2006; the American Society for Testing and Materials (ASTM) F2575-06; and the National Standard of the People's Republic of China

---

Competences for Professional Translators, Experts in Multilingual and Multimedia Communication, as well as Scarpa & Orlando (2017).

[28] Examples of professional bodies' CPD requirements:

- Law Society of New South Wales, Australia (http://www.lawsociety.com.au/ForSolictors/practisinglawinnsw/mclecpd/index.htm),
- the Hong Kong Institute of Surveyors (http://202.65.206.164/hkis/cms/upload/CPDLink/cpdlnk20_0.pdf),
- the Royal Institution of Chartered Surveyors (RICS), present worldwide (http://www.rics.org/us/about-rics/what-we-do/continuing-professional-development/continuing-professional-development_250/requirements/), and the Board of Surveying and Spatial Information (BOSSI) in New South Wales, Australia (http://www.bossi.nsw.gov.au/surveyors/land_surveyors/continuing_professional_development),
- the Association of Chartered Certified Accountants (ACCA) (http://www.accaglobal.com/en/member/cpd/members-cpd.html),
- the International Federation of Accountants (IFAC) (http://www.ifac.org/publications-resources/ies-7-continuing-professional-development-redrafted),
- or as required, for example, of auditors by law in France (Commercial Code, Articles A822-28-1 to 8),
- and the Government of Western Australia rules for estate agents (http://www.commerce.wa.gov.au/consumerprotection/content/Licences/Real_Estate_Industry/CPD/CPD_mandatory.html),
- or the Appraisal Institute of Canada (http://www.aicanada.ca/cmsPage.aspx?id=51).

GB/T 19363.1-2003. The European Commission's Directorate-General for Translation, on the other hand, has defined its quality aim as being 'to provide *"fit-for-purpose" quality*' (European Commission, 2012b, emphasis added). Notwithstanding these various norms, I posit that there may be considerable volumes of outsourced legal translation, as well as the corresponding translation processes, that are not subjected to any kind of official quality standard, and are instead assessed by in-house criteria varying from provider to provider and/or client to client.[29] 'Quality gaps' are identified by Samuelsson-Brown: between client expectations, translation specifications drawn up, and deliveries made (2010, pp. 41–42), although his analysis assumes the involvement of a translation agency and is not specific to the legal field. I will discuss performance assessment criteria further in section 3.3 (Chapter 3).

1.1.6. THE SPEED OF CHANGE

The market is a fast-moving one—in particular, as a result of ever-developing technologies such as, *inter alia*, CAT tools and TEnTs, which in turn lead to increases in individual productivity.[30] Cloud computing is changing the way translation documents and projects are shared—in some cases used by legal translation agencies ostensibly to heighten confidentiality and more strictly control access to documents (despite the arguable security levels of the technology), or to facilitate the splitting of work. Translators are also being asked, or in some cases required, to work directly on cloud-based software or 'software as a service' (SaaS) systems. As regards terminology, there are text-mining prospects aimed at 'leveraging big data' in the legal translation field (Heylen *et al.*, 2014).

The spread of machine translation (MT) is also having a noteworthy effect, as a result of more generalized access to tools such as Google Translate by the public, and their usage by some translation clients, as well as by some translators either within or outside TEnTs. Its use in the legal field involves considerable dangers—not only in terms of quality, but also where Google Translate, or other online tools, might jeopardize client confidentiality and lead to potential breaches of nondisclosure agreements, for instance.[31] This aspect should not be neglected.

There are now some tailor-made MT systems in place at institutions and a small number of translation companies; and an increasing trend towards 'post-editing'—the revision of textual output from MT systems by human translators.[32] At present, in the legal field MT tends to be used in specific

---

[29] Some evidence of this can be seen in the survey data presented in Chapter 5.

[30] e.g., Bowker & Corpas Pastor (2014); Cronin (2013); Olohan (2015).

[31] E.g., Blake (2015).

[32] O'Brien & Simard (2014); Alonso & Nunes Vieira (2017).

circumstances, such as when dealing with very large quantities of documents for gist purposes—for example, during the discovery/disclosure process. Such translations may or may not be post-edited, according to the relevance of documents to a case, deadlines, and volumes involved. Although there is a very large body of academic literature on machine translation, it has so far been less extensive in the legal field.[33] In view of the risk potential in legal settings, further research, particularly into quality and application, could be of great interest to the legal profession. In fact, court cases are now emerging that involve machine translation and in particular its judicious use.[34]

Globalization and the Internet have facilitated contact between the various actors in the market, and at the same time increased levels of competition[35] from other service provision professionals from different geographic areas or through crowdsourcing, though this may be less relevant to the legal field. A different sort of competition is reported by Monzó in a region of Spain where crossover with the profession of notary, brought about by legislative change, has eroded market boundaries for certified legal translators (2011, pp. 26–28). The last 10 years have also seen changes in the sources of work and of providers—such as through online platforms.

1.1.7. COMPLEX ACTOR INTERACTIONS IN THE OUTSOURCED LEGAL TRANSLATION MARKET: A REPRESENTATION OF THE CHAIN OF SUPPLY

Many actors may[36] be involved in the chain of supply when legal translation is outsourced to external practitioners. Figure 1.1 seeks to illustrate its complexity, and is presented in sequential order, from the stages comprising the drafting and handling of the source text (ST) through to the stages of production and reception of the target text (TT). It is important to note that the translator is

---

[33] Until recently, such literature has focused, in the main, on general technical aspects rather than the field of application. Some exceptions are Farzindar's work (e.g., 2009); Artelsmair (2010); Kit & Wong (2008); Mule & Johnson (2010); Somers (2007); and Koehn's work (e.g., 2005), which relates particularly to institutional texts. The European Patent Office's recent *Patent Translate* service may well stimulate research.

[34] In European Patent Office decision T 1343/12 *Dust adsorbing oil/UNI-CHARM* of 10 October 2014, an ambiguous machine translation 'presented the *opportunity for two plausible, but completely opposite, conclusions*' (emphasis added): an analysis of the case suggests that '[i]f the machine translation is ambiguous at a critical point, the prosecution of an application may run into difficulties. In such a case, regardless of the principle (and cost) of procuring a human translation when it is not the applicant's responsibility' [no requirement to supply translations of prior art documents] 'it may be practical to [. . .] save the inconvenience of appeal by providing a human translation' (Smyth, Barker & Belcher, 2015).

[35] Pym *et al.* (2012, 2013); Cronin (2003, 2013).

[36] The flow chart in Figure 1.1 aims to show a variety of alternatives. All of the actors included do not necessarily participate in all instances of text production, and, equally, there may be other actors that have not been included.

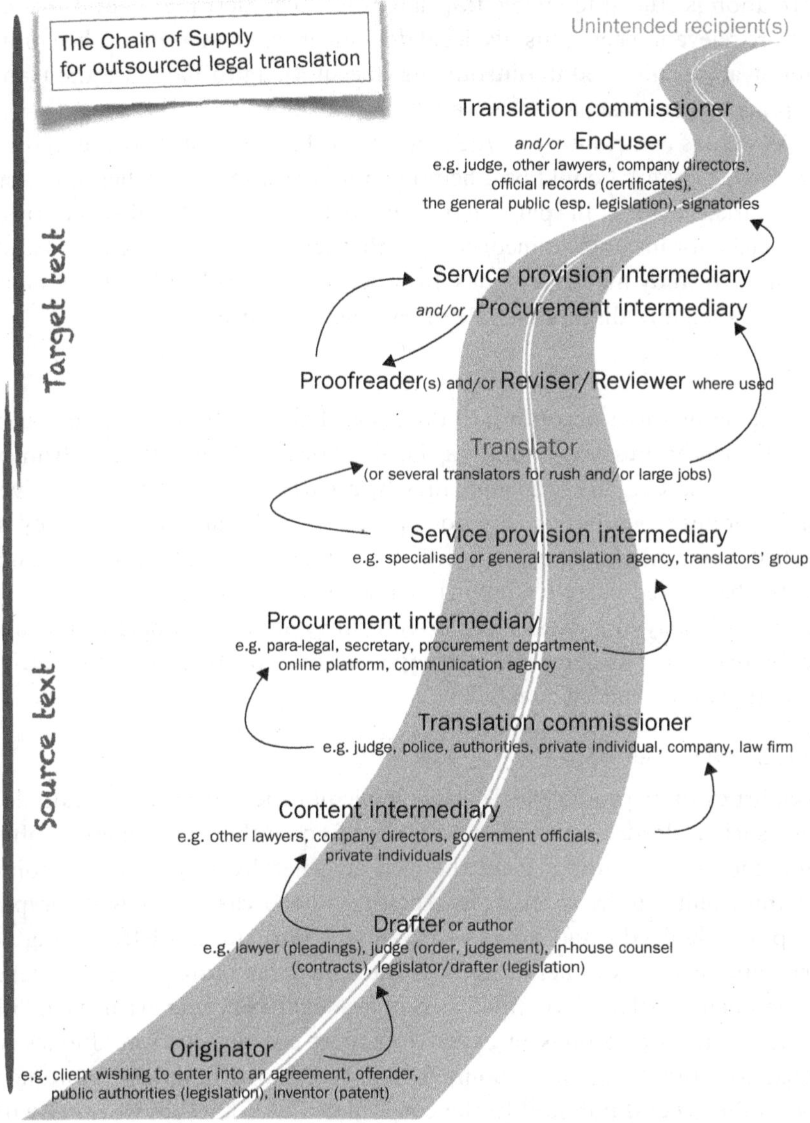

FIGURE 1.1. The Chain of Supply for outsourced legal translation.

positioned at a considerable distance from both the drafter/author and from the end-user or recipient, often with no direct contact except via intermediaries. The serpentine, meandering path followed in the drafting, translation, and subsequent delivery of a legal document shows how information flows can easily be waylaid or hampered. The situation could also be termed 'structurally unfavourable' (see Abdallah's findings in a nonspecialist translation context, 2010). It is generally accepted that contextual, intertextual, and extratextual information is crucial to enable translators to do a good job[37]—and this is all the more relevant where sensitive legal documents are concerned. The complex chain of actors involved in outsourcing does nothing to facilitate the translation practitioner's task, and it is fraught with risks.

As well as contributing to the analysis in this book of how the market is organized, Figure 1.1 could be a helpful communication tool when interacting with market actors, in particular principals, and could also be further developed—for instance to incorporate other text production scenarios and/or actors, or to study high-risk nodes. In order to further elucidate the Chain of Supply, I shall now discuss the role of each actor in turn.

1.1.7.1. Originator

The originator varies according to the genre. Public authorities, political parties, lobbyists or pressure groups may be at the origin of legislative instruments. In criminal matters, the originator may be a party committing a crime, which then generates a number of case documents. In civil matters, a company may decide to enter into an agreement with its supplier. In litigation, the originator may be the injured party (claimant) or the defendant or respondent party, or even a third party in a joinder. An inventor may apply for a patent. I shall define the originator as being the party (person or entity) whose actions trigger the writing of a given legal text.

1.1.7.2. Drafter/Author

Specialist drafters produce legislation, while notaries[38] draw up certain documents such as deeds at their client's behest, frequently constrained by official requirements on wording. Here the drafter generally stays close to content that the client wishes to express—such as in the case of a will, or property purchase deed—and adapts the content into standard legal language. Barristers or attorneys acting as advocates have far more leeway to debate, on the client's behalf, potentially complex legal concepts with each other through written pleadings in expert-to-expert communication. Judges may choose to write using either complex legal terms, or language more accessible to the general public.[39] In the corporate world, lawyers working within law firms or as in-house counsel may draft various types of legal documents. There are many different drafting styles, often depending on or constrained by the textual genre, sometimes at the suggestion of their client, sometimes placing the focus on the end-user.

---

[37] E.g., Bhatia (1997, 2010b); Cao (2007); Obenaus (1995); Schroth (1986).

[38] Under code-based systems, solicitors in other jurisdictions.

[39] E.g., the UK's Lord Denning or Supreme Court Justice Scalia in the United States.

1.1.7.3. Content Intermediary

By content intermediary, I refer to those actors that adapt or can affect the textual material produced. Junior counsel, for example, may have their writing checked or revised by senior lawyers. Non-legal professionals can also affect content—for example directors or shareholders wishing to change the terms of a contract, or individuals in the case of private deeds. Whole teams collaborate to produce legislative texts.[40]

1.1.7.4. Translation Commissioner

In judicial contexts, a judge or public prosecutor may request a translation as part of an international case either under requirements for a fair trial; as an investigatory measure; at a pretrial stage; or under cross-border procedures. Lawyers may commission translations either of documents in their own case file or of those produced by the adverse party. The police may request a translation directly or through the court, for example as part of the letters rogatory process. Official authorities may order translations either directly, or require them from private individuals in support of an application—for example, birth/marriage/death certificates, driving licence, diplomas, and so forth. Companies may commission translations of a wide range of legal genres in various spheres of their business. Many different actors may thus initiate the translation of a document. I shall refer to the actor who triggers the translation as the commissioner.

1.1.7.5. Procurement Intermediary

In the outsourced legal translation market, interaction between the commissioner and the translator providing the translation service is often indirect. Thus a paralegal, secretary, bailiff, or procurement department may deal with finding a translator. Work may even be outsourced through an online platform.[41] In the corporate world, communication agencies may deal with procuring translation services as part of their mandate.

1.1.7.6. Service Provision Intermediary

In some instances, translation commissioners and/or procurement intermediaries may contact or work with legal translators directly. Where this occurs, it tends to be the result of a long-term relationship. However, a service provision intermediary is often interposed, both before and after the translator's work. That intermediary may be a specialized legal translation agency, a general

---

[40] E.g., Strandvik (2014, 2018, forthcoming, in press); Cao (2007, p. 102).

[41] A community platform which allows clients to post job offers and obtain quotes directly from freelancers. Examples are Proz.com or TranslatorsCafe.com, Translators' professional bodies may also provide online listings, but generally only act as a 'signpost', putting clients and translators into direct contact.

translation agency, or a translators' group/team. The extent of their effect on the text itself may vary considerably—some limit themselves to in/out logistics, whereas others contribute to quality control and may provide editing services (see section 1.1.7.8. 'Proofreader').

1.1.7.7. Translator

A legal document may be translated by a single translator, or by several translators in cases of high volumes—for example, in high-profile cases or tender packages—or if there is a very short deadline. The translator may deliver 'for-delivery' standard work directly to the end-user or to the commissioner. Where contact is direct, there may also be a collaborative stage with exchanges about the text—for example, where the initial text was less than clear.[42]

1.1.7.8. Proofreader

Whilst professional legal translators always proofread their own work prior to delivery, a 'second pair of eyes', or even a third or fourth pair, may be desirable, according to the purpose of the target text.[43] Self-employed translators may engage a proofreader themselves when working with direct clients. Many service provision intermediaries retain proofreaders either in-house or on a freelance basis.[44] Those intermediaries with the highest-quality standards deploy more than one proofreader on a given text—for example, one native speaker of the source language and one native speaker of the target language, and/or one or more proofreader(s) specialized in copyediting. An ideal situation might include proofreading by a bilingual lawyer having studied and with experience in translation, preferably qualified in both source and target legal systems. However, it has been observed that translation rates would rarely allow for persons with such a profile to be involved (e.g., Schroth, 1986, p. 47). The terms 'reviser' and 'reviewer' are also used when referring to proofreaders: depending on the organization, they may or may not describe the same duties, as the nomenclature is not stable.

1.1.7.9. End-user

Once the translation has been checked, the completed translation is delivered to the end-user, who may or may not be one and the same as the commissioner. For instance, the translation of a contract may be commissioned by a secretary,

---

[42] Anecdotally, some translators report that corporate clients and lawyers express their appreciation for the translator's 'eagle eye' concerning source text shortcomings or errors.

[43] It may even be a requirement *if* included in translation service specifications—see the standard ISO 17100:2015(E), point 5.3.5. See also Mossop (2007).

[44] Owing to recent technological innovations, translators are more and more frequently being asked by translation agencies to post-edit the output of machine translation (Alonso & Nunes Vieira, 2017; O'Brien & Simard, 2014), including in the legal field.

but delivered to the company directors; or the translation of a formal notice may be commissioned by a process server, but delivered to the defendant party.

1.1.7.10. Unintended Recipients

After delivery, or in parallel to it, translated legal documents may fall into the hands of unintended recipients or receivers. By 'unintended', I refer to actors that the translator did not have in mind when producing the target text. This is highly relevant since knowledge of the intended user is likely to affect translation choices made. By the same token, the target text's purpose impacts translation decisions (see section 2.4 [Chapter 2] and section 3.2.5 [Chapter 3]).

1.2. Agency Theory as a Lens to Research the Outsourced Legal Translation Market

1.2.1. THE SUITABILITY OF THE THEORY

In order to examine more closely the somewhat flawed environment sketched out in the previous section, I suggest that agency theory, a way of exploring business and organizational relationships through the metaphor of a contractual relationship, may provide useful tools. Let us begin with a definition:

> Agency theory is concerned with resolving two problems that can occur in agency relationships. The first is the agency problem that arises when (a) the desires or goals of the principal and agent conflict and (b) it is difficult or expensive for the principal to verify what the agent is actually doing. [. . .] The second is the problem of risk sharing that arises when the principal and agent have different attitudes toward risk. (Eisenhardt, 1989, p. 58)

The preceding extract comes from a widely cited literature review, written when the theory was at the height of its development and adoption by the business world. Eisenhardt summarized: 'Agency theory is directed at the ubiquitous agency relationship, in which one party (the principal) delegates work to another (the agent), who performs that work. Agency theory attempts to describe this relationship using the metaphor of a contract' (1989, p. 58[45]). In my view, this is eminently suitable for the context of outsourced legal translation where the client or intermediary that places work can be considered the 'principal', and the translator the 'agent', and where the contract may indeed often be more 'metaphorical' than a formal documentary act.[46] Eisenhardt's second case (b) in the preceding definition is of clear relevance to translation

---

[45] Citing also Jensen & Meckling (1976), upon whose approach her statement was based.

[46] I refer the reader here to section 1.1.2 on informal outsourcing practices: 'Cursory Order Specifications'.

principals, for it is unlikely that they will be native speakers of or even understand all languages from which or into which their documents are being translated. Nor will they be able to verify translators' output. Eisenhardt's first case, goal conflict, is even more fundamental to translators in the light of functionalist translation theories and is discussed separately in section 1.2.3.

Agency theory studies may be seen as two main research streams: 'positivist' and 'principal–agent': the latter are of 'broader focus and greater interest in general, theoretical implications' and applied to 'buyer-supplier relationships' (Eisenhardt, 1989, p. 60), while positivist studies focus mainly on 'the relationship between owners and managers of companies' (Kleinschmidt, 2007, p. 44). In accordance with the scope of my research, I shall focus on the broader interpretation of the theory insofar as it corresponds to the outsourcing of translation to external suppliers. Indeed, the theory is seen by many scholars as transferable to a wide range of fields: Wiseman, Cuevas-Rodríguez, and Gomez-Mejia (2012) argue that 'agency theory's flexibility allows for its application to a variety of non-traditional settings', and as a matter of fact, agency theory has been applied since the 1980s to many areas of business and management studies.[47]

Other scholars, however, hold different views—particularly regarding the so-called positivist stream. At the extreme, Khuruna, Nohria, and Penrice assert that 'agency theory can now be seen to have led directly to many of the worst profit-maximizing abuses unmasked in the recent wave of corporate scandals' (2005, p. 56). In the light of such negative interpretations, it is essential to stress that the way in which I deem agency theory to be appropriate for the analysis of potential flaws and dysfunctions in the outsourced legal translation market is to use a careful selection of its central themes as 'anodyne' conceptual lenses. These must be taken at face value, without attaching any historical or acquired negative connotations either from the business community or from scholarship, enlisting purely (i) the metaphor of a principal–agent relationship, and (ii) a number of recurrent general concepts from the theory, discussed from section 1.2.3 onwards.

1.2.2. HOW THE CONCEPT OF AGENCY HAS SO FAR BEEN APPLIED IN TRANSLATION STUDIES

Hitherto, the broad discipline of Translation Studies[48] has employed the concept of 'agency' as human (and even nonhuman) intervention, rather than

---

[47] E.g., corporate governance; executive compensation; incentives; supply chain management; manufacturing organizations; auditing, accounting, and financial markets. For an overview see Mitnick (2013).

[48] The only legal translation studies research involving agency that I have been able to identify is a study of interprofessional collaborative practices in court interpreting in Finland by Kinnunen (2010).

applying corporate agency theory.[49,50] Whereas agency theory takes a dyadic, or even polyadic view, and focuses on agents and principals essentially as opponents, looking at ways of optimizing relationships, a collective decision was made to define agency within Translation Studies as 'willingness and ability to act'.[51] Willingness and ability to act are an integral part of the age-old tension that translators face constantly—how far can they 'intervene' in a text, how much can they 'change' it to suit the requirements or preferences of the target language or culture. Particular areas of focus on agency in general Translation Studies literature are social/sociological issues,[52] literary translation,[53] and interactions with translation technology.[54] Despite the relevance of the preceding interpretation of 'willingness and ability to act', particularly as regards textual agency when examining the technical intricacies of legal translation performance (see Chapter 2), I shall concentrate for the moment on what agency theory has to offer an analysis of outsourcing processes.

1.2.3. GOAL CONGRUENCE AND FUNCTIONALISM

Two parties to a contractual relationship generally have different goals—these may consist of achieving a lower/higher price for work, completing the work in more/less time, views on adequate quality levels, and so on. As the relationship progresses, these goals may conflict, converge, or become more or less aligned. Agency theory literature makes frequent use of the terms 'goal (in)congruence', 'goal divergence', and 'alignment of interest(s)',[55] and indeed Tate *et al.* go further, saying that 'goal congruence between Principal and Agent is required for contracts to be effective' (2010, p. 807). This tension between the principal's needs and those of the agent in the context of outsourcing is addressed by Logan, who suggests two solutions—the first, 'to diagnose the relationship from both sides of the contract', and the second, 'to engage agency theory to help design the types of contracts and relationships necessary to provide and support an environment of trust' (2000, p. 22). The benefits of developing

---

Like the present study, it also raises issues of status, lack of regulation, and insufficient formulation of requirements.

[49] With few exceptions, e.g., Abdallah (2010, 2012); Chan (2008).

[50] In order to avoid confusion, we should note a special reading of the concept of 'agent' within Translation Studies, who may be understood to be a person who is 'in an intermediary position between a translator and an end user of a translation' (Sager, 1994, p. 321), or to pertain to translators themselves (Milton & Bandia, 2009) as Chesterman notes: translat*or* studies 'covers research which focuses primarily and explicitly on the agents involved in translation' (2009, p. 20).

[51] Translation Studies symposium organized in Tampere, Finland, in February 2008 (Kinnunen & Koskinen, 2010, p. 6).

[52] An overview is provided by Chesterman (2009).

[53] E.g., Buzelin (2006, 2011); Bradford (2009); Paloposki (2009).

[54] E.g., Olohan (2011); Cronin (2010).

[55] E.g., Cunliffe & Luhman (2012).

relationships of trust in a service provision context, especially one involving highly confidential documents, are self-evident.

In the context of legal translation, the goals of the principal–agent relationship are intertwined with the 'function' or 'purpose' of the target text. Although logistic goals such as price, deadline, and quality are concerns for clients (and translators), it is likely that the primary concern will be the fitness-for-purpose of the target text.[56] This may include, according to the individual text in question, compliance with applicable law (source/target legal system or another) and/or conformity with the genre.

Generalist[57] approaches to translation focusing on the function(s) of source and target texts are presented in Christiane Nord's landmark work *Translating as a Purposeful Activity* (1997). Her contribution develops previous theory, in particular *Skopostheorie*, according to which 'the prime principle determining any translation process is the purpose (*Skopos*) of the overall translational action' (Nord, 1997, p. 27). Nord's broader interpretation of 'functionalism' is seen as far more suitable to legal texts than *Skopostheorie* by scholars such as Šarčević (e.g., 1997), and Madsen, who finds that 'the constraints imposed on legal texts by the legal reality'[58] are not taken into account in *Skopostheorie* (1997, p. 17). Šarčević goes further, and criticizes any all-encompassing application of *Skopostheorie*, focusing on one of Vermeer's examples, which, in her view, 'oversimplifies the decision-making process of legal translators to the point that it is misleading' (2000, p. 2). Šarčević later revises her position, however—she interprets *Skopos* as 'communicative purpose', and exhorts:

> the legal translator should take account not only of the *text type* and its *function* but also of the communicative *purpose* (*skopos*) of the translation, as well as the *legal systems* involved and other legal factors of the particular communicative situation. (2012, p. 190, emphasis added)

Šarčević does not further define the terms 'text type', 'function', or 'purpose'. We may hypothesize that by 'text type' she refers to genre, but the difference between 'function' and 'purpose' remains unclear. This ambiguity occurs in other scholars' work, and is further complicated by the fact that several key authors in this area write in German. Madsen suggests that we should 'allow for a more nuanced concept [than *Skopos*] of different types of situation in which legal text may be translated, which should have a bearing on the practical communicative situations within a legal universe in which the texts are to fulfil a function' (1997, p. 17).[59] The links between these concepts of function/

---

[56] On fitness-for-purpose, see section 3.3.1, and also section 3.1.1 on expectancy norms (Chapter 3).

[57] I.e., not specifically legal.

[58] Madsen does not specifically define 'legal reality', or 'legal universe', which is the title of her 1997 paper, although they seem to refer to what other authors have called 'legal culture' or 'legal system'.

[59] She does not specifically define 'legal universe'.

purpose and genre are further reinforced in Bhatia's work, and he includes 'a set of communicative purposes' as one of the elements that enable genres to be identified and characterized (e.g., 2014, pp. 26–27). The contribution made by *Skopostheorie* to furthering theoretical approaches to legal translation is acknowledged by Garzone,[60] although in the last analysis, like Nord, she takes a broader view, and refers to 'Functionalist Approaches' in the title of her landmark paper on functionalism and its suitability for legal translation (2000). A final criticism of the term *Skopos* when discussing goal congruence between principals and agents is its failure to speak clearly to legal practice: it is hard to imagine commissioners with no experience of translation theory being able or willing to adopt this term when communicating their goals.[61]

Agency theory's concept of goal congruence can usefully complement the concept of functionalism in Translation Studies. In discussing agency theory as applied to supply-chain quality, Zu and Kaynak underscore the following: 'Quality gurus have strongly suggested if firms are to provide products or services that customers want, it is essential to explicitly identify and assess customer *requirements*' (2012, citing Hackman & Wageman, 1995, p. 435, emphasis added), while enhancing agent competence through the supplementing of contractual *specifications* is highlighted by Hendry (2002, emphasis added). The foregoing elements of a (broad) functionalist approach can supplement such specifications with the 'technical goals' that are the *sine qua non* for legal translators to accomplish their task. I shall now pursue my arguments relating to market operation and relationships between actors, but will return to functionalism in Chapter 2 in discussing the various technical facets of legal translation performance.

1.2.4. SOURCES OF RISK

In the following discussion I construe risk as a negative factor[62] that may occur as a result of market dysfunctions and/or impaired relationships, leading ultimately to potential failures in the target text, or worse still to legal effects of translation error(s), that may be costly in monetary or other terms. I limit

---

[60] Garzone (2000) notes firstly that Vermeer's 'ground-breaking theoretical statements [. . .] need not be taken literally', and have brought home the idea that the 'rigid prescriptiveness of the past' should be done away with, as should 'criterion of loyalty to the ST with no regard for the use to which the translated text is to be put' (p. 2). Secondly, she notes that there is space for the 'application of functional criteria [in the legal field] even in a context of absolute respect for ST meaning and values' (Garzone, 2000, p. 2). Thirdly, she notes the 'reluctance of experts to accept the idea that a theory which is general in nature and not tailor-made should be applied to legal translation' (p. 2).

[61] Further discussion of terms for use with practitioners can be found in section 4.4 (Chapter 4).

[62] Whilst being aware that risk-taking may be construed as 'an active *positive* option' (Pym, 2015, p. 6, original emphasis).

myself here to aspects of market operation, and will discuss risks involved in translation performance in Chapter 2.

In the context of outsourced legal translation, one of the most relevant ways of encapsulating risk foregrounded by agency theory is *information asymmetry*, which occurs when one party to a transaction has more or better information than the other party. In traditional agency theory, information asymmetry is often seen as advantageous to the agent, requiring, for example, the principal to set up monitoring procedures (e.g., Melander, Rosell, & Lakemond, 2012), whereas scholars have been silent about asymmetries that may disadvantage the agent. Regarding information acquisition during the course of a principal–agent relationship, Eisenhardt stresses that information asymmetry between principal and agent is increased in short-term agency relationships (1989, p. 62), since over time they will make discoveries about each other's needs and requirements.

A subset of information asymmetry, *knowledge asymmetry*, underlines the fact that principal–professional agency exchanges involve 'information asymmetry that is particularly severe, since principals do not possess the technical knowledge to evaluate the effort invested or the outcome accomplished by professional agents' (Sharma, 1997, p. 768). This is clearly the case in translation, where '[n]ot knowing *how* the agent does a job is distinctly different from and compounds the problem of not knowing *what* the agent does' (Sharma, 1997, p. 768). In a study applying agency theory to the incorporation of new technologies, Melander, Rosell, and Lakemond (2012) focus on knowledge sharing through the concept of *black-box* and *grey-box* approaches, where the latter refer respectively (as does the *white-box* approach) to degrees of transparency[63] on the part of actors involved in the development of products or services.[64]

In the field of translation, information asymmetry is not necessarily to the advantage of the agent—in fact, it makes their job more difficult.[65] Abdallah (2010) found that 'inadequate or substandard source materials and lack of relevant information are not uncommon in the translation industry' (p. 20). She quotes from one of her interviewees as follows: 'The translator does not always know whether the gadget is room size or palm size. "It is not important, just go ahead and translate"' (p. 21), and concludes,

> translators are not always able to perform, post-contractually, their work adequately due to the restricted flow of information between the various principal-agent dyads. (p. 22)

---

[63] Where black is opaque and white is the most transparent.

[64] Gawn deplores 'black-boxism' in relation to the 'isolation of the translation act' (1988, p. 459) in his discussions of bilingual legislation, financial, and business texts.

[65] Knowledge asymmetry can also have negative consequences for a translation agent [translator], because of a lack of understanding of their work by the principal. This will be discussed further in my conclusions, in the light of the triangulated survey.

To summarize, in the case of legal translator-agents, in order for them to apply their *knowledge* effectively (knowledge held by agency theorists to be asymmetrical in their 'favour'), they need more contextual *information* from their client—in other words, the information asymmetry favouring the client-principal must be rebalanced towards the translator.

In addition to risks involved in failures to share information and knowledge, issues may arise regarding the roles of the parties to the contractual relationship. In the context of agency theory, 'moral hazard' refers to the risk of 'lack of effort on the part of the agent' (Eisenhardt, 1989, p. 61),[66] and may arise when the principal cannot fully monitor the agent. In other words, the agent may pursue their own agenda rather than acting in the principal's interests. I would hypothesize that moral hazard in the case of legal translation could be alleviated by longer and stronger relationships between principals and agents, and indeed Melander, Rosell, and Lakemond (2012) note that the length of buyer–supplier relationships is important. A translator could potentially put more effort into their translation—for example, creating tools for consistent terminology—if they felt that they would work for the same client again in the foreseeable future.

In the same vein, 'adverse selection' traditionally refers to the 'misrepresentation by the agent of [. . .] [his or her] skills or abilities' and occurs when 'the principal cannot completely verify these skills or abilities either at the time of hiring or while the agent is working' (Eisenhardt, 1989, p. 61). However, Perrow (1986) accuses agency theory of not having a balanced view of both sides of the principal–agent relationship. Shapiro goes further, and notes that 'agency problems on the agent side of the relationship are often mirrored on the principal side' (2005, p. 268). She cites Perrow (1986), observing that adverse selection may occur where agents are 'unwittingly drawn to principals who shirk, cheat, and opportunistically seize perquisites for their own use; who deceive and exploit their agents' (Shapiro, 2005, p. 268). In the case of legal translation, agents may offer languages in which they are less competent, or work in specific areas of the law where they have little experience. Less scrupulous translators may even perform legal translation without any experience or specialized knowledge. Legal translation principals, on the other hand, may place work without stating issues that will affect the time required—such as heavy formatting to be recreated from documents in PDF format,[67] or highly technical content.[68]

[66] Here we see, once again, agency theory's tendency to interpret situations and problems from the principal's viewpoint.

[67] It is common practice in the legal translation market for source documents to be provided in PDF format. One may hypothesize that this is to avoid documents being tampered with. However, it considerably increases the amount of work required from the translator.

[68] For example, litigation involving a fire on a yacht may contain highly technical chemical, electrical, and shipping terms.

A hotly debated issue in the last few years is the use and ownership of translation memories[69]—whilst obtaining discounts from translators for repetitions in source texts, principals often do not pay any extra for translation memories that they may either request free of charge from the translator upon delivery, or later create themselves in-house without even consulting the translator.

One of the basic assumptions of traditional agency theory is 'risk aversion' on the part of the agent. As Eisenhardt puts it,

> The argument behind a more risk averse agent is that agents, who are unable to diversify their employment, should be risk averse and principals, who are capable of diversifying their investments, should be risk neutral. (1989, pp. 60–61)

The preceding focuses on the agent's fear of losing a business relationship with his or her principal. However, the claim that principals should be risk neutral[70] does not seem at all appropriate for the legal translation environment. In most legal genres, it is hard to imagine how translated documents might carry little or no risk for those commissioning them, or that principals might be indifferent to those risks.

To place risk aversion in the context of legal translation: a translator may not wish to jeopardize their client relationship by 'bothering' the client with difficulties encountered in a source text, such as unclear passages, inconsistent use of terms, or errors. This is likely to have negative consequences for the principal in terms of target text quality. Similarly, the ability of principals to diversify may actually lead to increased risk in the case of legal translation: where clients employ several translators on one large project, there may be more likelihood of inconsistent translations of the same terms, incompatibilities in style or register, and so forth.

Hence, it may very well be in the interests of the principal (the translation commissioner) to be more concerned with the risks involved in supplying the agent (translator) with incomplete information (an insufficient translation brief) as regards the outcome (translation quality), in particular because the translation may then not be performed with the aim of meeting the principal's goals—simply because the translator is unaware of those goals. I would therefore argue that, in the case of outsourced legal translation, the mono-directional and rather negative view taken by agency theory of agents' behaviour up to now, whether in terms of information or knowledge asymmetry or risk aversion, should be broadened—to the benefit of both 'sides'.

---

[69] E.g., Troussel & Debussche (2014); Smith (2009).

[70] Risk neutral: indifferent to or balanced with respect to (financial) risk (www.oxforddictionaries.com).

1.2.5. REGULATING MECHANISMS AND BALANCE OF POWER

The traditional agency theory approach pertains to a dyadic relationship between principal and agent, or buyer and seller. This does not correspond to the majority of legal translation outsourcing contexts, which are far more complex. Shapiro, the agency theorist, introduced the idea of multiple principals and agents, citing the 'Hydra factor'[71] first put forward by Adams (1996), when referring to the following problem: how can agents 'understand and reconcile the duties delegated to them when they are receiving mixed messages and conflicting instructions [. . .] from multiple principals?' (Shapiro, 2005, p. 267). The latter view is far more relevant when studying outsourced legal translation, as is the work of Abdallah, who applies the preceding to translation production networks (e.g., 2010, 2012).

Agency theory puts forward two types of mechanisms that may govern contractual relationships: outcome-based and behaviour-based.[72] While 'behaviour-based contracts are more likely to foster creative solutions' and 'outcome-based contracts encourage an emphasis on compliance [. . .]', in fact 'a hybrid solution is often needed' (Tate *et al.*, 2010, p. 8; discussing Oliver & Anderson, 1994). Sharma, unlike most scholars working with agency theory, focuses on principal–*professional* exchanges, and maintains that behaviour- and outcome-based contracts as a means of control are not appropriate for agents with specialized knowledge (1997)—which, of course, aptly describes translators. The contractual basis used in translation practice, however—since translation is, as a rule, paid by the word, line, or character—is predominantly outcome-based. Some related tasks such as proofreading may nevertheless be paid at hourly rates (behaviour-based).

Let us now consider the distribution of power in principal–translator relationships. Through the lens of agency theory, Bergen, Dutta, and Walker note that 'most agency models define efficiency from the principal's point of view. The assumption is that the principal is the dominant party in the relationship' (1992, p. 2). However, interpreting the theory as it could apply to professionals, Sharma asserts:

> The greatest distinction of principal-professional agency exchange is its violation of a key assumption in agency theory that principals have the power to design and enforce contracts. (1997, p. 766)

---

[71] Hydra factor: principals engaged in joint enterprises aiming at goals that were 'contingently compatible at best' (Adams, 1996).

[72] Examples of outcome-based contracts might include quality provisions relating to product inspections; profit sharing; golden parachutes for CEOs; or piecework. Behaviour-based contracts pertain rather to supplier processes as opposed to outcomes—such as technical assistance, sales calls, or hourly pay rates.

Further, Sharma holds that because of their expertise, professional agents wield power over what he terms '*lay principals*'.[73] However, he mitigates this by adding that whether 'professional agents can and actually do take advantage of their power' (1997, p. 770) will vary. In a relationship involving self-employed professionals, there may be less independence between agent and principal as compared, for example, with relationships between contracting parties that are both firms. Where the agent is an individual, the principal–agent relationship may thus be more hierarchical or power-driven than a formal contractual relationship, and as a result there may be greater scope for principals to punish, control, or reward agents (e.g., Rigdon, 2005). We shall see in Chapter 5 to what extent this power distribution applies when the professionals concerned are translators.

[73] Sharma defines 'lay principals' as non-experts, where professionals hire other professionals to 'perform services for which they themselves do not have expertise', and where a professional in one area is a non-expert in another and is dependent on such other professionals (1997, p. 759).

2

Facets of Legal Translation Performance

Legal translation: 'the ultimate linguistic challenge'.

—Harvey (2005, p. 57)

I shall now explore the legal translator's textual agency—his or her intervention—seen as the negotiation of a number of facets: language aspects, legal system(s), textual genre, and text purpose; leading to the presentation of a multidimensional model[1] that aims to encapsulate the complexity of legal translation performance in practice. I would stress that although these four facets are discussed separately and in a certain order owing to the format restrictions of this book, this does not mean that I consider a sequential ordering of the translator's intervention to be appropriate—the following cognitive negotiating processes are likely to be handled quasi-concurrently and contingently in performance of the task.

2.1. Negotiating between Languages

At a first level, the translation of a legal text involves the natural language in which it is written. This dimension of the legal translator's work may be likened to the work performed by translators in all specialized and nonspecialized fields. As in all fields, the language variant(s) should be specified—and it is perhaps even more important in legal texts owing to the related problems arising out of differences in legal systems, styles, concepts, and terminology between two jurisdictions—which appear with "similar force even when two [or more] jurisdictions share the same language', such as German in Germany, Austria, Switzerland, Belgium, and Italy (Kischel, 2009, p. 9).[2]

---

[1] Further discussion of this subject can be found in Scott (2017c), which draws from the work presented in this volume.

[2] Kischel (2009) refers in this regard to 'sublanguages', while I will use the term 'language variants' and reserve the term 'sublanguage' for the language of legal genres and subgenres, following García Izquierdo & Borja Albi (2008), for example.

2.1.1. TRANSLATION 'EQUIVALENCE'

Whilst equivalence as a term applied to translation seems to have its origins in the 1950s from various sources (Pym, 2010, pp. 9–10), in 1959, Jakobson introduced the idea of 'equivalence in meaning' (2003, pp. 113–118). Building upon Saussure's work on the signifier and the signified, he focuses on the gap between terms and semantic fields, based on the theory that humans' perception of and terms for objects and concepts differ through language. It is revealing, with regard to the themes addressed in this book, that such arguments are also central to comparative law, in particular when discussing differences between legal concepts across (legal) cultures (e.g., Bogdan, 1994; Constantinesco, 1983; Platsas, 2008).[3]

In Translation Studies, equivalence is regarded in many ways: as a prescriptive or descriptive method for translation;[4] rejected as inappropriate (e.g., Gentzler, 1993; Snell-Hornby, 1988/1995) or considered to be neutral and adopted 'for the sake of convenience—because most translators are used to it rather than because it has any theoretical status' (Baker, 2001, pp. 5–6).[5] Many of its aspects revolve around mapping source and target text relationships, types/typologies of meaning, and some interpretations even extend beyond the text to equivalence of language itself (e.g., Catford, 1965; Koller, 1979, cited from the German by Nord, 1997).

In the field of legal translation, Šarčević (1997) refocuses discussions of equivalence in its various forms on the legal systems applying to the translation in question, and hence on legal equivalence, while Biel (2009) provides an analysis of literal, descriptive, and functional equivalents and demonstrates their practical application in legal translation contexts. The term 'equivalence' itself sits uneasily within a legal translation context: its inherent duality is (i) at odds with the multidimensional nature of the task, and (ii) needs to embrace the basic tenets of comparative law (e.g., De Groot, 2006, pp. 423–433). Indeed Cao claims that 'no exact equivalence or complete identity of understanding can be expected or is really necessary' (2007, p. 35), while Kjaer observes that '[e]stablishing equivalence between legal texts across languages is as impossible as squaring a circle' (2008, p. 67). It is for these reasons that I have chosen the verb 'negotiate' in this chapter in describing translation performance—when we negotiate we can reach solutions, but they may require compromise. Glanert and Legrand, among the main proponents of the 'impossibility of legal translation' (2013, p. 524), admit the paradox inherent in such a position: 'the fact that the translation is impossible does not imply that it must not be done and

---

[3] I will tackle legal equivalence in the section on negotiating legal systems (section 2.2).

[4] E.g., Nida (1964); Venuti (1995); Vinay & Darbelnet (1958/2000); and, as an overview, Pym (2010).

[5] It may nevertheless be useful to reflect on how the term is received by translators' clients.

indeed does not mean that it cannot be done' (2013, p. 518). Cao asserts, moreover, that 'law is translatable despite various inherent difficulties, and despite the often-heard claims to the contrary' (2007, p. 5). I echo Kjaer's concern that '[t]heories that cannot account adequately for what actually happens each and every day at the office should be challenged' (2008, p. 72).

An alarming connotation of the equivalence paradigm for legal translation would be for it to be seen as 'not only the goal of a translation but the yardstick by which language sciences could analyse translations' (Pym, 2009). By extension, in an outsourcing context which involves legal professionals and/or the judiciary—that is, nonspecialists as regards translation and translation theory—we must be circumspect about using the term 'equivalence', for were it to become a criterion for quality assessment, it might place translators in danger of incurring their liability should their translation not be deemed 'equivalent'.[6] As Gémar, whose work on the theory and practice of legal translation extends over several decades, recounts:

> Alors, existe-t-il une méthode de traduction garantissant l'équivalence totale à recommander?
> De toute évidence, *non*, et en traduction juridique, *encore moins*. (2012, p. 71, original emphasis)[7]

We may surmise that Gémar refers in the preceding extract to his view of equivalence (1998) as a vague notion capable of being interpreted in different ways by different actors, which, moreover, like human communication, is never absolute or perfect, and must remain subordinate to the legal effects of the translated text in the relevant jurisdiction. In the light of all of the foregoing, and in the context of outsourced legal translation, I hold that 'equivalence' is damaging—not to Translation Studies as held by Gentzler (1993), but, as a term, to effective communication with the market. In section 4.3.3 (Chapter 4), as part of reflections on briefing, I discuss an alternative term that has been proposed by Ng (2014).

2.1.2. LEGAL LANGUAGE/DISCOURSE(S)

First and foremost, legal discourse is not singular in nature but plural. The discourse of legislation differs from that of contracts, and from that of court proceedings, and so on. There are also considerable differences between spoken and written discourses in this field. Rather than 'discourse', some scholars have

---

[6] E.g., in this regard Monjean-Decaudin (2012) has reported on situations in the French courts where translations have been challenged.

[7] My translation, maintaining original emphasis: 'So, is any translation method to be recommended that guarantees full equivalence? Clearly *not*, and in legal translation *even less so*.'

used the terms 'legal register'[8] or 'legal language' (e.g., Tiersma, 2000), as well as 'variety' (Bhatia, 1983). Indeed, Kurzon spoke of 'a substantial amount of terminological uncertainty' (1997, p. 119) in his detailed examination of the various terms employed. In this book I shall mainly refer to *discourse* as a unifying framework of communication for the community of legal professionals, and *genres* as a pragmatic way of collecting together groups of texts in the light of their communicative purpose (Bhatia, 1987). I also use the term *sublanguage(s)* to stress the 'exclusive' nature of legal communications and to describe the lexis encountered in a particular (sub)genre and the way it is assembled.[9]

In most cultures, legal language is a 'language for special purposes' that is frequently used by restricted groups of experts such as lawyers, the judiciary, and so on, but may also be used by the corporate world and by the general public. In his reference work on legal linguistics, Mattila points out that, whilst being based on 'ordinary' or 'natural' language, it exhibits: 'linguistic norms (phraseology, vocabulary, hierarchy of terms and meanings)' and specific 'morphosyntactic, semantic and pragmatic' features (2006, p. 3). Given the limitations of space and the focus of this book, I will discuss a small selection of features with particular relevance for legal translation and for the survey reported in Chapter 5, in order to illustrate the complexities of negotiating these aspects of legal language.

2.1.3. LEGAL LINGUISTIC FEATURES

Whilst the examples of general linguistic features of legal discourse in this section are mainly taken from English, there are parallels in other languages (e.g., Galdia, 2009; Mattila, 2006). I first consider lexical features and then briefly review syntactic, stylistic, and rhetorical features.

I use the term 'collocations' to refer to 'recurrent word combinations' (Goźdź-Roszkowski, 2006b, p. 139), also called clusters, lexical bundles, word partners, compound terms, n-grams, or colligations.[10] I include phrasal verbs in the same group. Collocations are not only recurrent, they are quite inflexible. To stress their significance in legal discourse: 'collocations with a specialized legal sense are the types of word combinations that are most frequently found in legal texts of all genres' (Yunus & Awab, 2011, p. 159, citing Kjaer, 2007, p. 509). As well as arising in running legal text, collocations may occur in terms referring to legal concepts, such as gross negligence, *exceptio obscuri libelli* or

---

[8] I shall avoid this term here, owing to its connotations of levels of formality as used both in Translation Studies and in foreign language teaching.

[9] Since sublanguage occurs within a (sub)genre, it also falls into a 'restricted semantic domain' (Kittredge & Leyrberger, 1982).

[10] No distinction will be drawn in this book between these terms.

droit réel, or legal maxims, oft-cited in lawyers' written submissions, such as *fraus omnia corrumpit* or *le contrat fait la loi*. There is a specific type of 'inseparable' collocation in the legal domain, often known in the legal context as doublets/triplets or binomials/multinomials. Unlike many terms that can collocate with others or can be used alone, in certain contexts these cannot be used without their 'partner'. To cite a few examples—from English: 'null and void'; 'goods and chattels'; 'aid and abet'; from French: '*dommages et intérêts*'; and from Brazilian Portuguese: '*perdas e danos*'. The historical reasons for and value of such apparent redundancy will not be discussed here.[11] Metaphors might usefully be appended to this group, as they too are composed of several lexical units and occur within a close span of a word, and will be discussed *infra*.

A practical example raised by a translator participating in a previous study by the author shows why collocations are important in legal translation: a translator may know part of a target-language term, but not its collocate—such as whether to use 'hold harmless from' or 'hold harmless against' (or indeed 'hold harmless from and against'—the term often contains the doublet). Scott (2012) discusses further how electronic corpora might be a way for translators to resolve such terminological difficulties. This is a key issue, because collocations play a large part in the acceptance or refusal of translated legal texts by those receiving them (as noted by Biel, 2010a, 2010b, 2012). Results from the fieldwork in which the issue of collocations arose are reported in section 5.5.3.e (Chapter 5).

In a number of cultures, perhaps one of the most obvious features of legal discourse is the use of archaic language.[12] A related feature, due to the origins of many legal systems and some 'cross-fertilization', is the presence of Latinisms,[13] although the frequency of their use depends on the natural language or legal culture in question. Translation issues may also arise with terms that are monosemic,[14] for example, 'estoppel', 'tort', or 'usufruct'; and those that are polysemic,[15] with separate everyday meanings such as 'consideration' meaning payment, 'construction' meaning interpretation, or 'issue' meaning heirs. When translated, as Alcaraz and Hughes point out, terms may move from being monosemic to polysemic and vice versa (2002, p. 17).

While the preceding terms cause confusion because different concepts can be expressed with the same word, confusion in legal discourse can also arise, particularly when translated, owing to the use of synonyms as 'redundant'

---

[11] For further details and broader discussions of legal language, see Tiersma (2000) and Matulewska (2007).

[12] Compound adverbs such as 'heretofore', 'therein', 'herein', and so on, or prepositional phrases such as 'notwithstanding' and 'pursuant to' (Alcaraz & Hughes, 2002, pp. 7–9). Tiersma cites 'antiquated morphology' (e.g., 'witnesseth') and 'formulaic subjunctives' (i.e., 'be it known') (2000, pp. 87–95).

[13] E.g., *amicus curiae, caveat emptor, ipso jure*, or *habeas corpus*.

[14] Referred to by scholars variously as 'terms of art', 'jargon', or 'argot'.

[15] Tiersma (2000) refers to these as 'legal homonyms'.

words, occurring in multinomial expressions (often strictly collocated), or as a result of drafting style—the practice of 'elegant variation'[16]. This may cause difficulty in translation—for instance, where a synonym does not exist in the target language,[17] or problems of understanding where textual cohesion and/or the drafter's intention is not clear,[18] or where a translator elects to 'clarify' by replacing occurrences of synonyms with the same word, thus unilaterally eliminating ambiguity in the source text. Partial synonymity will further complicate matters.

Despite some authors finding evidence of a shortening in recent years,[19] long and complex sentences remain a prominent feature of some legal genres, as do unusual word order, the omission of articles, nominalization, passivization, use of 'shall', and layers of embedded clauses. I can think of no more eloquent way to demonstrate this issue than by using an example:

> 'Subordination' means, with respect to an obligation (the 'Subordinated Obligation') and another obligation of the Reference Entity to which such obligation is being compared (the 'Senior Obligation'), a contractual, trust or similar arrangement providing that (i) upon the liquidation, dissolution, reorganization or winding up of the Reference Entity, claims of the holders of the Senior Obligation will be satisfied prior to the claims of the holders of the Subordinated Obligation or (ii) the holders of the Subordinated Obligation will not be entitled to receive or retain payments in respect of their claims against the Reference Entity at any time that the Reference Entity is in payment arrears or is otherwise in default under the Senior Obligation.[20]

Such sentences may cause translators difficulty in deciphering anaphora, and in maintaining cohesion and coherence. Depending on the language pair in question, some measure of 'localization' may be needed, according to the intended purpose of the translated text.

Metaphor also figures widely in many genres of legal discourse.[21] I tend to disagree with Mattila when he holds that 'in modern legal language, metaphors in particular are rare' (2006, p. 75)—he himself asserts that '[a]dvocates in the

---

[16] 'The stylistic fault of studiedly finding different ways to denote the same thing in a piece of writing, merely to avoid repetition' (oxforddictionaries.com).

[17] E.g., 'wear and tear' translates into Portuguese as '*desgaste natural*' [literally: natural wearing/consuming]. The Portuguese expression, unlike the English, is not a doublet (Carvalho, 2008).

[18] E.g., switches in a lease agreement between the words 'owner', 'landlord', and 'lessor', used as synonyms for the same party.

[19] e.g., Kurzon, 1997, pp. 131–132.

[20] Taken from Section 2.19, (b), (i), (B)) of the Credit Derivatives Definitions issued by the International Swaps and Derivatives Association (ISDA) originally issued in 2003, in the context of the financial crisis and the legal conditions governing the ranking of Spain's creditors.

[21] To cite just three well-known examples: in legal theory, 'piercing the corporate veil'; in judgments, 'When these ghosts of the past stand in the path of justice clanking their mediaeval chains, the proper course is for the judge to pass through them undeterred' *United Australia Ltd v Barclays Bank*

Romance countries use these images fairly often' (p. 76). Vespaziani goes as far as to claim that 'there is no such a thing as a non-metaphorical legal language' (2009, p. 1).[22] Metaphor constitutes a communication hurdle for non-native lawyers and the judiciary (regarding English, see Campos Pardillos, 2016). Unfortunately for legal translators, metaphorical language is also highly challenging to translate (e.g., Schäffner, 2004).

My final point in this short selection of aspects of legal discourse that are particularly sensitive in translation concerns rhetoric and rhetorical devices—essential linguistic tools for lawyers in many legal cultures. To cite a few examples: 'paradoxes', 'deliberate stylistic faults', 'plays on words', 'surprise arguments', and 'deliberate howlers' (Mattila, 2006, pp. 38–39). Additionally, multiple negatives,[23] layered embedding of clauses, and ambiguous anaphora can all be called upon to muddy the waters (Tiersma, 2000). Such confusing mechanisms are in danger of multiplying their effects when this kind of discourse needs to be translated, particularly if the translator is not informed whether the intended end-user is 'friend or foe'—for example, whether the target text is for the adverse party in litigation or for a colleague.

2.1.4. THE EQUIVOCAL NATURE OF LEGAL DISCOURSE LEADING TO LANGUAGE RISK

'Law is language and language is imprecise' (S. A. Smith, 1995, citing Wesel, 1992). The latter phrase was not, as one might imagine, uttered by a translator lamenting their lot, but by a law professor. Harvey goes further—'Judges, like Humpty-Dumpty, create the illusion that words mean exactly what they want them to say, since they are free to define terms as they see fit' (2002, p. 183). Legislation too may contain equivocal language.[24] The extent of this aspect of legal discourse is borne out by the huge body of literature and constant debate on the interpretation or construction of the law.[25] Apart from the possibility of ambiguous meanings being conferred to terms by those *enunciating* them, we must also add the complexity of what those *receiving* them understand. This is

---

Ltd [1941] AC 1 at 29 (Lord Atkin); and in lawyers' submissions, 'If it [the glove] doesn't fit, you must acquit', *People of the State of California v Orenthal James Simpson*.

[22] M. R. Smith (2007) found that metaphor was so widely used and studied in legal discourse that he set out to identify different 'levels of metaphor', dividing them into 'doctrinal metaphors', 'legal method metaphors', 'stylistic metaphors' and 'inherent metaphors' (p. 921).

[23] 'Bendola cannot be permitted to stand on nothing more than unsubstantiated and self-laudatory statements as a basis for denying summary judgment' (Garner, 2001).

[24] As extreme examples: 'In New Zealand, the law says that a "day" means a period of seventy-two hours, while an Australian statute defines "citrus fruit" to include eggs' (Freedman, 2007, p. 3). Similarly, the Polish statute on fisheries deems that crabs are fish (Halas, 1995, p. 25, cited by Galdia, 2009, p. 99). In England, the High Court ruled that a 'village green' includes a tidal beach that is underwater for 42 per cent of the time (*Newhaven Port v East Sussex* [2012] EWHC 647 (Admin)).

[25] See Solan (2011b).

clearly explained by Engberg in the context of statutory interpretation and in a critical analysis of strong language theory: 'The problem is that the meaning of texts can only exist as a construction in the minds of individuals, built on the basis of perceived underspecified textual signs and existing mental models' and hence 'only if sender and receiver have near identical systems are they able to understand words in the same way' (2004, p. 1142).

Indeterminacy[26] may arise not only out of wording, but also out of choice of language or language variant. There is a growing area of legal research devoted to *language risk*[27] examining, for example, which party carries such risks of interpretation in contract litigation, or what happens when terms cross borders. Whilst there are legislative protections in place regarding the right to a defence, under private law where parties are free to choose their language regime, either the language of one party or the other, or a third-party neutral language may be selected, and various issues of conflicting interpretation may arise.

Such equivocacy may be exacerbated when translated, as exemplified by Salmi-Tolonen when discussing the language of contracts: 'Words are not containers whose contents are transferred from one interlocutor to another [. . .] *unchanged*' (2006, p. 86, emphasis added). In view of the reflections already set out in the foregoing sections relating to translation issues, I will not discuss ambiguity brought about by translation any further, and will simply conclude with the following observations: agency theory alerts us to the issue of risk sharing when the principal and agent have different priorities, as well as the likelihood of self-employed translators' risk aversion owing to the fragility of their client relationships, and further risks are present when the translator-agent receives incomplete information. The equivocal nature of legal discourse renders these issues all the more crucial in translation.

2.1.5. THE POTENTIAL RISKS OF PLAIN LANGUAGE

For some years now, plain language movements,[28] the impetus for which came, in English-speaking jurisdictions, to a large extent from Mellinkoff (1963), have been campaigning to 'simplify' legal language—often referred to in that

---

[26] Linguistic indeterminacy is broken down by Endicott into the following terms, *inter alia*: imprecision; incompleteness; incommensurability; immensurability; contestability; family resemblances (relating to common sets of features); and dummy standards (provisions presupposing a standard but not laying down a standard), while linguistic indeterminacy in American statutes has been categorized by Solan, using examples from case law, into areas such as 'syntactic ambiguity, semantic ambiguity, ambiguity of reference and vagueness' (2011b, p. 2). These analyses, however, draw examples mainly from the interpretation of laws by the courts, rather than from texts drafted by lawyers such as contracts or pleadings.

[27] Referred to by French comparatists as '*risque linguistique*' (e.g., Mauro, 1998), and in German as '*Sprachrisiko*'. See also the 'Socks Case' in German case law: Appellate Court (*Oberlandesgericht*) Hamm, 8 February 1995 [11 U 206/93]. See also Jayme (1995, pp. 189–191); Déal (2004).

[28] Such as the international movement *Clarity* (http://www.clarity-international.net).

context as legalese—and, *inter alia*, to render it more accessible to the general public. However, some legal scholars such as Phillips hold that 'on the contrary, the development and maintenance of the law's special language can be justified' (2003, preface). Offering a wide range of suggestions for the improvement of legal drafting, Pollman also stands in favour of an informed approach to legal jargon (2002).[29] A recurrent concern is the 'under-specification of legal scope'[30]—that is, the risk that plain language may in fact infringe rights, especially in common law jurisdictions where laws and legal documents are subject to interpretation by the courts, by handing power over to individual judges. To address calls for simplification without compromising legal robustness, Bhatia has made an alternative proposal: the 'easification' of legal language (e.g., 2010a). This aims to make legal texts more accessible to their 'intended readership' (p. 10), without compromising the 'depth of specification' (p. 13) that might occur if the text were simplified. Bhatia claims that, depending on the communicative purpose, the latter can be acceptable—for example, for information purposes only, to inform the general public.

On the other hand, whatever their own view on plain language, legal translators cannot, under any circumstances, unilaterally render legal discourse plainer and thereby potentially distort the legal meaning and legal scope of the text: it is essential that they adhere to their brief. In this sense, a legal translator cannot take the initiative to be a gatekeeper of public access to justice—in other words, if the text is dense, unreadable legalese, it should stay that way in the target language,[31] unless there has been a specific instruction to the contrary in the brief. This is an important matter to be addressed within legal translator training programs, and can often be a problem with inexperienced translators or those who accept legal work without being specialized in the field.

2.2. Negotiating between Legal Systems

2.2.1. ASYMMETRY BETWEEN LEGAL SYSTEMS, AREAS OF LAW, LEGAL CONCEPTS, AND TERMS

Unfortunately for legal translators, the world does not have a unique legal system. Experts cannot even agree on a single classification of the world's systems into families (e.g., Hertel, 2009; Monjean-Decaudin, 2010b; Samuel, 2014).[32] In fact, '[a] legal order may, for example, be allocated to a different

---

[29] See also Crump (2002).

[30] Bhatia (2010a, p. 9); Solan (2011b).

[31] Subject, of course, to a sensitive negotiation of what is appropriate in that target language.

[32] I will nonetheless tentatively cite, with reference to the triangulated survey, common law, civil law (code-based systems), mixed systems, and customary law, and Sharia law, as included by several scholars.

legal family as regards civil law than as regards administrative law. Even the law of companies may be characterized differently from the general civil law' (Hertel, 2009, p. 2). Thus in addition to the 'asymmetry of legal systems', there may be inconsistency between 'different branches and fields of law' (Pommer, 2008, p. 18).

It is important to note that 'legal terminology [and legal discourse] is system-bound, tied to the legal system rather than to language' and hence 'multiple legal languages can exist within the boundaries of a natural language, depending on how many legal orders make use of that same language' (Pommer, 2008, p. 18).[33] Equally, there are 'plurilingual states and regions with different legal systems or a mixed legal system' (Šarčević, 2012, p. 193).[34] Despite this complexity, as noted by Galdia, translations may also be carried out between closely related languages, such as Danish and Norwegian, where the countries also have similar legal systems, and issues related to legal systems/concepts may even disappear completely in multilingual states with a single legal system, such as Finland (2003, p. 2).

The discussed (lack of) systemic and/or conceptual equivalence clearly has a bearing on the legal translation process. In De Groot's view,

> the level of difficulty of a legal translation does not primarily depend on linguistically determined differences, but rather on structural differences between legal systems. (translated from the German and cited by Galdia, 2003, p. 2)

A few examples of highly system-specific concepts posing translation difficulties must suffice: the common law concept of 'equity'[35]; the French '*faute*',[36] *usufruit* (Kasirer, 2001) and '*viager*'[37]; trusts, particularly with regard to Italian law (Lupoi, 2013); or tort/delict (Schroth, 1986, pp. 57–58). An even more basic example from company law is the lack of correspondence between types of legal entity under foreign laws.[38]

---

[33] E.g., one natural language, French, is used to vehicle different many legal systems—*inter alia*, those of Belgium, France, Luxembourg, Monaco, some African countries, and Switzerland, not to mention its use as the working language of the case law of the Court of Justice of the European Communities (McAuliffe, 2009).

[34] 'such as Canada, India, Sri Lanka, Israel, South Africa, and, more recently, China (Hong Kong and Macau)' (Šarčević, 2012, p. 193).

[35] No equivalent in civil law (Department of Justice Canada, bijural terminology records, 2012).

[36] 'The concept of "*faute*", which is well known in French law, has no direct equivalent in other legal systems (in particular, English and German law)', *Joint Practical Guide*, issued by the European Parliament, the Council and the Commission for persons involved in the drafting of legislation within the Community institutions.

[37] 'The *viager* dates from the Middle Ages and, in its purest form, the mechanism is only adopted in France' (Février, Linnemer, & Visser, 2004).

[38] Rogers-Glabush (2009, pp. 514–523).

2.2.2. CONVEYING APPROPRIATE LEVELS OF LEGAL EQUIVALENCE

Several translation scholars have called upon the field of comparative law to advise how legal translators should negotiate differences between systems and concepts.[39] A number of projects are currently being developed in this regard,[40] not all of which, sadly, are accessible to practitioners who work outside institutions.

Scholars have also made efforts to categorize types of terminological equivalence across legal systems. Šarčević suggests the following three categories: 'near equivalence', 'partial equivalence', and 'non-equivalence', and holds that the preceding enable categories to be changed 'depending on the use of the term in context' (1997, p. 237). Referring to a projected bilingual dictionary of contract law, Nielsen goes into more detail (1994, p. 169)—he offers 'full equivalence' 'where an L1 equivalent has exactly the same semantic and pragmatic properties as its L2 lemma', but adds that instances of such equivalence are 'few and far between' (1994, p. 162); 'partial equivalence', which he subdivides into three subsets—'near equivalence', 'approximate equivalence', and 'remote equivalence'; and 'zero equivalence', where there is no corresponding legal concept in the foreign system in question. Nielsen adds, however, concerning this category, that a lack of corresponding concepts does not mean that equivalents or a 'suggested translation equivalent' cannot be offered (1994, p. 168).

Indeed, establishing a set of postulates on legal translation, De Groot asserts, 'In practical translation, an approximate equivalence of concepts is sufficient when deciding whether one concept may be used as translation for another' and, even more importantly for the purposes of this book and translation briefs, '[w]hether an approximate equivalence exists or not depends on the context and goal of the translation' (2009, p. 229–230, translated by Engberg, 2013, p. 15). De Groot thus renders both the degree of concepts' legal equivalence and their use (or not) contingent on the intended purpose of the translated text.

In most countries, there are no legislative guidelines providing for differences between legal systems or concepts. Some efforts are being made in this regard, for example as part of the harmonization and approximation[41] of

---

[39] Pommer (2005); Šarčević (1997, 2012); Monjean-Decaudin (2012); Sandrini (1999).

[40] The Textual and Terminological Database for the Portuguese Parliament (BDTT-AR); TermWise for the Belgian Federal Justice Services (Heylen *et al.*, 2014); Italian and German projects at the Institute for Specialized Communication and Multilingualism at the European Academy of Bolzano (Ralli, 2009).

[41] Despite the current lack of legal definition, harmonization may be summarized as the elimination of disparities between different states' legal systems, while approximation might be defined as the 'process of modifying different [...] legislations in order to eliminate differences contrasting with the minimum standard set by a framework decision' (Calderoni, 2010).

European legislation, and at the global level by UNIDROIT (the International Institute for the Unification of Private Law). In any event, the foregoing is intended to demonstrate the importance of making the translator aware, before translation begins, of the legal system applying to the text in question.

2.3. Negotiating between Genres and Subgenres

Having discussed how language and legal systems need to be taken into account in legal translation performance, the third facet of my model concerns genre. I shall begin with a brief review of the contribution to be made by an awareness of and reference to both source and target genres/subgenres when translating, and then explore their classification, which constitutes an important part of scholarly work in this field.

2.3.1. GENRE-AWARE TRANSLATION PERFORMANCE

Genre is defined by Swales as a 'class of communicative events [sharing a] set of communicative purposes', forming the 'rationale for the genre' (1990, p. 58). That rationale is enforced by the parent discourse community, leading to constraints on 'choice of content and style' (Swales, 1990, p. 58). The following statement by Gotti on the relevance of genre for discourse analysts applies equally well to legal translators: 'not only to get a better understanding of the linguistic characteristics of texts, but also of the macrostructure of these texts, which appears to be organized according to genre expectations and conventions', and moreover enabling them to learn 'how genres are constructed, interpreted, used and exploited in the achievement of specific goals in highly specialized contexts' (Gotti, 2012, p. 61). Textual standardization is 'stronger in legal genres' and is also recurrent (Gotti, 2012, pp. 60–61). It is thus vital for translators in the legal domain to be familiar and to comply with genre constraints when producing their target texts (e.g., Alcaraz & Hughes, 2002, p. 103; Bhatia, 2014, pp. 228–232; Orts, 2012). If translated legal texts do not comply with the conventions of the community receiving them, they are unlikely to be deemed fit for purpose. This is summed up by Gotti:

> The conventional use of [legal] genres also produces certain expectations among readers, and whenever the rules are broken a text may be misunderstood or rejected. (2012, p. 60)

Thus if generic norms are not fulfilled, commissioners and/or end-users, although sometimes unable to articulate their preferences and requirements, may find that target texts do not correspond to their (unexpressed) expectations.[42]

---

[42] See also section 3.1.1 (Chapter 3) on expectancy norms, and section 5.5.3.g (Chapter 5) on the subgenres reported to cause the most difficulty by my survey participants.

With the preceding in mind, and owing to the particularly ring-fenced nature of the legal discourse community[43] and the highly entrenched nature of the discourse itself,[44] we must ask the question as to how such generic knowledge can be acquired. Whilst fledgling lawyers are taught legal language at law school as part of their studies,[45] and paralegal staff undertake vocational training on legal writing, translators are rarely trained in the generic sublanguages of the law.[46] Nevertheless, genre can provide translators with insights in a number of ways, including but not limited to the following: the situation and context of a communication act; participants and the relationship between them, and appropriate structure and terms (e.g., Montalt Ressurrecció, Epeleta Piorno, & Izquierdo Garcìa, 2008). Corpus analysis is a powerful technique to obtain such insights. Its methods are of great use in providing translators with multi-perspective, fast, and reliable access to a given legal genre pool (e.g., Biel, 2010a; García Izquierdo & Borja Albi, 2008; Scott, 2012). More and more genre-based studies employ corpus techniques to investigate legal, business, and financial discourse,[47] and there are several international projects involving legal corpora.[48]

2.3.2. CLASSIFICATIONS/TAXONOMIES OF THE LEGAL MACROGENRE

I shall now give an overview of the numerous ways in which scholars have classified legal genres[49], before examining their categorization from a market perspective. Bhatia (1987, p. 227) outlines a structure differentiating the main legal genres by their 'communicative purposes' and the 'lexico-grammatical,

[43] The eminent Professor J. B. White advises entering law students: 'The law is a set of social and intellectual practices that defines a universe or culture in which you will learn to function' (1985, p. 52). See also Mertz (2007).

[44] Phillips (2003); Tiersma (2000).

[45] 'Legal education will provide [...] good training in writing, and particularly in the specific techniques and forms of written expression that are common in the law' (Pre-law Committee of the American Bar Association Section of Legal Education and Admissions to the Bar, 2018, https://www.americanbar.org/groups/legal_education/resources/pre_law.html.)

[46] Except in certain all too rare translation programmes run in collaboration with law schools or directed at entry into European Union institutions, for example.

[47] E.g., Pontrandolfo (2015) on criminal judgments; Gallego Hernández (2012) on corporate and financial genres. Some studies also focus on macrostructure, such as Garrido Rodríguez (2012) on vehicle purchase invoices for imports; and Garrido Rodríguez (2015) on Memoranda & Articles of Association.

[48] Two examples are: 'Generic Integrity in Legal Discourse in Multilingual and Multicultural Contexts' (GILD) at the University of Bergamo, Italy (http://dinamico.unibg.it/cerlis/page.aspx?p=212), examining arbitration laws from 12 countries; and the GENTT (Textual Genres for Translation) Research Group at Universitat Jaume I, Spain (http://www.gentt.uji.es).

[49] Other scholars, such as Danet, Levi, and Gibbons, have offered classifications that have been omitted here, as they do not contribute further to the present discussion.

semantico-pragmatic, and discoursal resources' used in varying legal contexts. Regarding written genres, he distinguishes between 'frozen legal documents like contracts, agreements, insurance policies, etc.' and 'formal' documents such as 'legislation, rules and regulations, etc.'; classifying them both under the term 'legislative', leading to a somewhat equivocal subsidiary connection between 'legislative' and 'contracts' (1987). The focus of this taxonomy on communicative purpose is highly pertinent in its implications for the study of translation and the intended user of a target text. In a more recent work, Bhatia offers a different view of legal genres, dividing them into 'primary' genres—legislation; 'secondary' genres—for example, judgments and case reports; 'enabling academic genres'—such as textbooks, critical essays, and so forth; and 'target genres'—for example, contracts, affidavits, insurance documents, and so forth (2006, pp. 6–7). We may align these categories with the different environments in which translation is carried out: 'primary genres' within institutions; 'enabling academic genres' often by authors themselves or in close collaboration with their translator; and 'target' and 'secondary' genres frequently outsourced.

A taxonomy in which 'language of the law' is differentiated from 'legal language', under an undefined and incomplete syntagm 'legal –' is offered by Kurzon (1997, p. 120, shown in Figure 2.1). First, I suggest that, if used when addressing non-experts such as when speaking to the translation market, there is a risk that the two second-level terms may be construed as synonymous. For Kurzon, '"language of the law" is the language or the style used … in documents that lay down the law, and "legal language" refers to the language that is used when people talk about the law' (1997, p. 120). However, the inclusion of the verb 'talk' in this definition is ambiguous, since the category includes both written and spoken media. Nevertheless, Kurzon's detailed efforts regarding the precise semantics of related terms such as 'registers', 'genres', 'varieties', and 'discourses' provide many insights (1997, pp. 119–139).

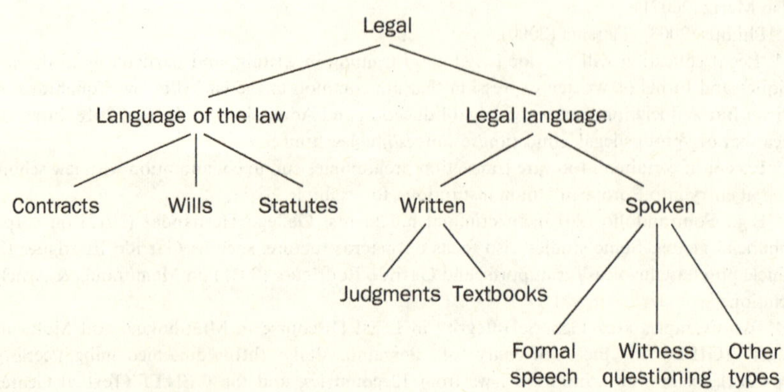

FIGURE 2.1. Kurzon's taxonomy.
Source: Kurzon (1997, p. 20).

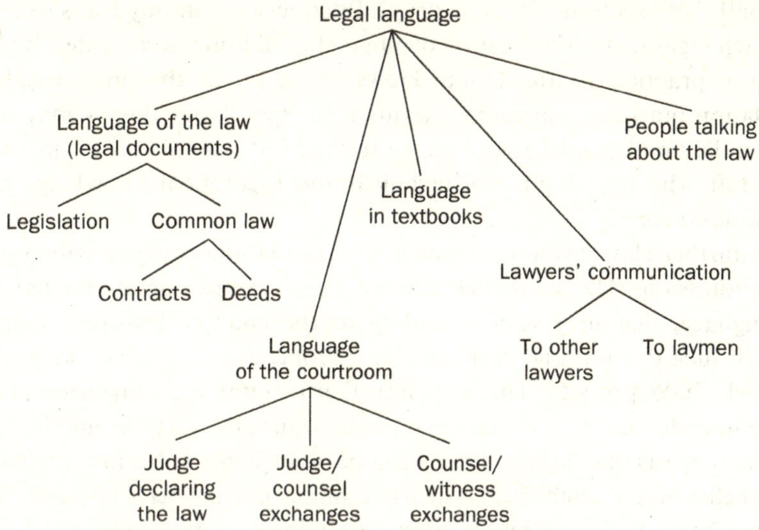

FIGURE 2.2. Trosborg's representation of legal language by situation of use.
Source: Trosborg (1997a, p. 20).

Legal language is divided by Trosborg according to 'external factors pertaining to the *situation of use*' (1997a, p. 20, emphasis added). Her categories, shown in Figure 2.2, comprise 'language of the law (legal documents)'; 'language of the courtroom'; 'language in textbooks'; 'lawyers' communication'; and 'people talking about the law' (1997a, p. 20). Some of the boundaries between the categories are unclear—for example, whether judgments or written pleadings should be classed as 'legal documents' or 'language of the courtroom'. Moreover, the subdivision of category 'language of the law' into 'legislation' and 'common law' is somewhat opaque, particularly given that 'common law' includes contracts and deeds rather than case law or precedent, for example. However, with a functionalist view of translation, we can usefully retain the idea of classifying legal texts according to their situation of use, and extend Bhatia's concept of communicative purpose (1987, p. 227).

Focusing particularly on translation in the context of the civil law system, Bocquet (2008) uses a tripartite typology of legal texts, taken in part from Cornu (1990). This typology has the particularity of using both linguistic criteria, from speech act theory,[50] and legal criteria: for Bocquet (2008), texts are '*normatifs*' [laying down norms/rules],[51] '*juridictionnelle*'

[50] The modes used by Bocquet (2008) in his taxonomy have been criticized, in particular by Greenstein (2009, pp. 2–3) as inappropriate, in particular concerning the syllogistic group.

[51] In this group Bocquet (2008) includes laws, constitutions, orders, and decrees, as well as condominium rules, swimming pool rules, or terms and conditions of contracts, which he describes as falling into the performative 'mode'.

[judicial],[52] or '*doctrine*' [legal theory].[53] Bocquet's taxonomy leads us to analyse each legal text type in terms of linguistics, adding greater depth for the technical practice of translation. However, as far as the outsourced legal translation market is concerned, terms from speech act theory may not be fully understood, whilst they may be usable, for example, in an institution with staff who have high-level technical and theoretical knowledge of the translation process.

A further classification was made by Mattila according to subgroups of legal professions. He claims that each of these groups possesses a particular sublanguage, that may vary according to the country involved. Examples given include the 'notarial profession' in Europe, 'legal authors', 'judges', and 'counsel' (2006, pp. 4–5). This gives a further taxonomical dimension in terms of the intended user(s) or receiver(s) of the translated text. As an alternative, Mattila suggests that 'legal language can be divided into subgenres on the basis of branches of law' (2006, p. 5)—such as criminal law, property law, and tax law. This has been challenged by Monjean-Decaudin, who, in discussing whether a taxonomy based on areas of law would be beneficial for legal translation purposes, asserts that division of texts in such a way has proved to be '*fastidieuse et peu pertinente*'[54] (2010a, p. 4). However, it may well be a more accessible approach for the market.

A different approach is taken by Cornu, who differentiates types of legal discourse, distinguishing '*discours législatif*' [legislative discourse], '*discours juridictionnel*' [judicial discourse] and '*discours coutumier*' [literally 'customary' discourse] (1990, p. 357). Whilst Bocquet (2008) draws parallels between the first two categories and his own typology, he describes Cornu's third group as including legal maxims and adages, and as such of little interest to translators, since they are rarely called upon to translate them. I find the latter statement surprising, as in practice such maxims do arise in written pleadings, for instance, and although the translation strategy may involve borrowings (Vinay & Darbelnet, 1958/2000, p. 85), the translator certainly needs to have an understanding of that terminological group. Cornu's taxonomy does not provide extensive depth of field.

[52] This second group covers texts from all types of court—including judgements and decisions, in addition to police reports, process server affidavits, and so on. He classes the mode for the group as descriptive, and further qualifies it as syllogistic.

[53] The third group covers texts drafted by legal experts such as comments on laws or regulations, but also includes 'comments' on orders and judgments—that we might approximate to restatements in the common law system. Bocquet describes the mode for the third group as descriptive since these texts involve indirect discourse.

[54] My translation: tedious and of little relevance.

Commissioning clients, whether from law firms or corporate entities, translation practitioners, and translation companies/agencies, do not, however, generally use the preceding scholarly classifications to describe areas of expertise. The need to embrace other text typologies has been recognized, for example, by Prieto Ramos who notes that 'subdivisions are ultimately determined by the lens through which textual realities are observed' (2014, p. 263). Therefore, to facilitate the data collection in the main phase of the surveys described in Chapter 5, some ad hoc categories were chosen. They were taken loosely from elements of Mattila's professions-based approach (2006), and form broad genre families, based on Bhatia's work on primary, secondary, and target genres (2006).[55] The categories were also selected because they are used as areas of specialization by translation practitioners.[56] The aim of these ad hoc categories was to differentiate between the types of texts that survey participants are having translated or translating, and to discern whether quality issues arising in the various categories may differ. The categories[57] are as follows:

- Corporate (e.g., contracts, terms, and conditions, calls for tender, articles of association)
- Financial-legal (e.g., auditors reports, fund prospectuses, offering circulars)
- Notarial (e.g., deeds, wills, creation of servitudes, power of attorney)
- Court-related documents (e.g., pleadings, judgments, orders, notices of appeal)
- Insurance documents
- Legislation (e.g., articles, parts of laws, whole laws, regulations, standards, treaties, whether national or international)
- Certificates (e.g., birth, death, marriage, diplomas, ID papers) for official purposes
- Patents.

The preceding categories were trialled and refined with market actors at the pilot stage of the fieldwork described in Chapter 5.

---

[55] Excluding only his 'enabling genres' (2006) since they are infrequently outsourced.

[56] With reference to translators' professional bodies and forums, as also identified by Biel (2011, p. 166).

[57] Spoken genres are not included, as the purpose of this book is to examine written translation. Several legal genres are absent from the preceding classification, insofar as they are more rarely translated by self-employed translators, e.g.: academic legal opinions; law reports; legal textbooks, dictionaries or thesauri; or public information factsheets; or because they have very specific characteristics—for example, legal fiction, the translation of which is more closely related to literary translation.

2.4. Addressing Purpose

2.4.1. THE SUITABILITY OF A FUNCTIONALIST APPROACH TO LEGAL TRANSLATION PERFORMANCE

The fourth and final aspect of the legal translator's textual agency that I shall analyse is the task of addressing the purpose of the target text. In parallel to the goal-based approach outlined in section 1.2.3 (Chapter 1) with regard to the optimization of outsourcing relationships between principals and translation practitioners, my discussion also takes a functional stance on translation performance. Concerning the suitability of this approach to legal translation,[58] Garzone concludes that

> the degree of equivalence to be achieved in the translation of a given text is not absolute, but depends first and foremost on the TT [target text] intended function as well as on the nature of the ST [source text]; the whole process is governed by a principle located at a sufficiently high level of generalisation as to be *suitable for virtually all types of legal texts.* (2000, p. 9, emphasis added)

I will not reiterate here my arguments regarding the inadequacy of equivalence as an achievable goal for legal translation (see section 2.1.1). It would moreover be irrelevant, since Garzone asserts from the outset that 'the degree of equivalence to be achieved [. . .] is not absolute' (Garzone, 2009, p. 9). Instead, I will examine how, on the basis of its reputed suitability for the majority of legal texts,[59] functionalism can assist legal translators in achieving optimum performance, and begin with the tension between source text and target text. I will assume that model contractual conditions are in place—that is, that the translator has been provided with comprehensive specifications relating to technical goals, and that unobstructed information flows operate. As Munday explains:

> knowing why a ST [source text] is to be translated and what the function of the TT [target text] will be are crucial for the translator. (2008, p. 79)

Without lessening the importance of the function of the target text, the latter assertion includes both source and target texts, as does Garzone's preceding claim, and embraces circumstances whereby translators may either have to transpose the source text purpose, or produce a target text fulfilling a

---

[58] It is interesting to note in passing that, in addition to certain translation scholars, functional equivalence has also been supported by a leading member of the judiciary—Justice Pigeon of the Supreme Court of Canada—who has agitated strongly against literal translation with regard to court documents (Pigeon, 1982).

[59] Garzone (2000) does not seem to specify which types of legal text might be *un*suitable, despite her use of the word 'virtually'.

different purpose. The target text purpose is also relevant when assessing performance, anticipating the current standard of fitness-for-purpose analysed in section 3.3.1 (Chapter 3), as Nida claims when expressing his view on adequacy:

> The relative adequacy of different translations of the same text can only be determined in terms of the extent to which each translation successfully fulfils the purpose for which it was intended. (1976, p. 64)

Nida, however, like Munday, refers to general translation theory, not specifically to legal genres.

The following selection of observations made by Pym reviews how functionalism can help with performance in practice:

> [Functionalism] recognizes that the translator works in a professional situation, with complex obligations to people as well as to texts.
>
> It liberates the translator from theories that would try to formulate linguistic rules governing every decision.
>
> It forces us to see translation as involving many factors, rather than as work on just one text. (2010, p. 56)

In sum, when deploying the various facets of legal translation performance, which are inextricably linked and dynamically connected, knowledge of the target text purpose is a crucial and indispensable prerequisite for success.

2.4.2. DIFFERENTIATION OF RECEIVERSHIP AND DIFFERENTIATION OF STATUS

The end-user of a target text is closely related to its intended purpose, and needs to be taken into consideration, as asserted by Reiss and Vermeer: 'information about the target-text addressee [. . .] is of crucial importance for the translator' (1984, p. 101, cited from the German by Nord, 1997, p. 22). Despite her 1997 criticisms of *Skopostheorie*, and whilst maintaining them, Šarčević entitled her 2000 paper 'Legal Translation and Translation Theory, A Receiver-Oriented Approach', and in that paper unambiguously claims, '[l]ike other areas of translation, the translation of legal texts is (or ought to be) receiver oriented' (p. 1). She broaches the differentiation of readership and a corresponding variation in translation strategies, and uses the terms 'addressees' and 'receivers' synonymously. Citing Kelsen (1979, in the German), she distinguishes between direct addressees (specialists) or indirect addressees (including the public).

Gémar has also subdivided readers into four groups: laymen; those who are 'lettered'; practising legal professionals; and legal scholars. He argues that depending on its destination, a translation will be constrained and informed by knowledge of its intended readership (2002, p. 168). I use the term 'end-user' in this book, firstly on the grounds that it resonates better for the outsourcing market, and second because, given the length of the Chain of Supply (see section 1.1.7 [Chapter 1]) the immediate recipient of the translation may be an intermediary or a reviser, and not its user—that is, not the reader or receiver as understood by Gémar or Šarčević.

The differentiation of translators' services according to the target text's status has been put forward, for example by Chesterman and E. Wagner (2002). In the case of legal translation we might propose the following tripartite classification as a first step:

- translations for gist;
- translations that are not to be legally binding;
- translations where the target text will be legally binding.

The triad is resolutely succinct, once more with the aim of accessibility to busy principals, and for the same reason worded as simply as possible. The proposal was tested in the fieldwork relating to the outsourced market (see discussions in Chapter 5).

2.4.3. SPECIFYING LEVELS OF COVERTNESS FOR LEGAL TRANSLATIONS

In order to further elucidate receivers' expectations, we may adopt the distinction between *covert* and *overt* translations first highlighted by House (1977)—whereby 'an overt translation is one which must overtly be a translation' (p. 106) and 'a covert translation […] enjoys or enjoyed the status of an original ST in the target culture' [… —a] ST and its covert TT have equivalent purposes' (p. 107). In this regard, Chesterman holds that '[w]hether a translation is expected to be covert or overt, and how this expectation then affects the translation itself, will be determined partly by the translation tradition in the target culture' (1993, p. 9). In the field of legal translation, I suggest that commissioners' expectations are governed rather by matters relating to generic integrity and the intended purpose of the text than by translation tradition. Whatever determines their choice, the commissioner's wish to receive either a covert or an overt translation should be explicitly stated in the legal translation brief. As a way of distinguishing between expectations, the terms 'covert' and 'overt' might speak more clearly to the legal translation market than other terms employed in Translation Studies, such as 'documentary' and 'instrumental' (e.g., Nord, 1997), which, as substantives, are almost synonymous from a lawyer's perspective.[60]

[60] See, for example, cross-referenced entries for 'document' and 'instrument' in *Black's Law Dictionary* (Garner, 2009), whilst 'covert' and 'overt' are used to collocate, representing two extremes of a cline, with a variety of words such as 'acts', 'operations', or 'surveillance' in legal contexts.

To illustrate how covert–overt positioning may be implemented in practice,[61] *covert legal translations* (e.g., contracts for signature, banking terms, conditions for publication, calls for tender being issued, etc.) must adhere strictly to a genre rationale. I see *overt legal translation*, where literal approaches are favoured and where the 'transparency' of the target text will allow the source to 'shine' through a translation, as pertaining rather to comparative law exercises (Baaij, 2014), access to foreign legislation, official translations of certificates or diplomas, and certain judicial genres depending on their destination (Monjean-Decaudin, 2012).

At the briefing stage, drafters, intermediaries, or commissioners may introduce additional constraints on or directions for the translator, making the text more or less covert/overt, such as structural fidelity to the source text (e.g., layout, whether to maintain or to split long sentences); the use of client-recommended terms; the use of 'loan words' or 'borrowings' (Vinay & Darbelnet, 1958/2000, p. 85) and/or the acceptance or not of explanatory footnotes for system-specific terms; and endorsement of paraphrasing.[62]

Levels of (c)overtness are also relevant in discussions of techniques for dealing with errors in source texts, as systematized by E. Wagner, who considers that the translator has five choices when faced with errors:

1) do nothing, just translate;
2) translate literally but put in a [*sic*];
3) correct covertly (translate correctly but don't draw attention to the error);
4) correct overtly (translate correctly and put in a translator's note drawing attention to the error in the original);
5) correct fully, translate it correctly and get the original corrected too (Chesterman & E. Wagner, 2002, p. 31).

There is another possible course of action to be added to the preceding list in the case of self-employed legal translators—that of informing their direct contact, who may well be an intermediary, of the error in *separate notes* or an *email*, since the insertion of a translator's note in a 'deliverable' that it is to be a legal instrument may be frowned upon. It is also important to stress that the (non-)action chosen from the preceding alternatives must be brought to the attention of the commissioner—that is, even if the translator has decided to correct covertly, this should be specified. The extent of dialogue between the

[61] Proposals relating to the specification by legal translation stakeholders of levels of covertness and overtness are presented in more detail in Scott (forthcoming).

[62] As an area of further research, it would be interesting to ascertain whether there is a predominance of covert or overt legal translations being outsourced or being performed by translators working in institutions or in-house at law firms.

translator and their contact person will be further explored in sections 3.2.6 (Chapter 3) and 4.3.2 (Chapter 4) on relational agency.

2.5. The Tesseract of the Legal Translator's Textual Agency

As I have illustrated in the foregoing sections, the legal translator's agency as it relates to the text is highly complex. At a first level, that of source and target *language*, the legal translator's task is analogous to that of translators in other domains, although situated within a specific segment of general language: legal discourse. At a second level, the work of the legal translator becomes even more complex, to 'negotiate' solutions between source and target *legal system(s)*. On some occasions, despite being translated into a different language, texts may not traverse legal families—for example, certain texts translated from French to Italian may both be located in code-based, civil law systems. Third, the legal translator must ensure that the given *genre* or subgenre is appropriately transposed into the target genre, for example, using the relevant sublanguage and, where necessary, macrostructure and/or layout. The fourth and final layer to the legal translator's work is to ensure that the *purpose* of the source text is correctly reflected in the target text, *if* such a reflection has been requested by the client. Alternatively, the target text may serve a different purpose. For example, if the source text is binding legislation, its translation may be requested for a public website.[63]

Let us consider this highly complex negotiation or 'juggling' of what is effectively eight multifaceted elements by the legal translator—four on the source side and four on the target side—as they progress through their work. The legal translator does not negotiate the various elements in a linear manner. They are handled quasi-simultaneously, and time is therefore a non-excludable factor.

Having searched exhaustively for an adequate model,[64] I should like to refer to a concept from mathematics—that of the tesseract. The tesseract is the four-dimensional analogue of the cube—in other words, the tesseract is to the cube as the cube is to the square (Darling, 2004, p. 316). If we accept that time is one of the dimensions, a static geometrical representation (even if it were three-dimensional) is thoroughly inadequate to model the figure. I therefore need to include here a reference to an animated video model (https://en.wikipedia.org/wiki/File:Tesseract.gif). The rotating perspective projections

---

[63] In that case, the commissioner will need to specify whether they require the translator to produce a text that is accessible for the general public, and perhaps to an extent 'redraft' the text, or whether the translation should be a literal reflection of the source, such as might be produced for study by scholars of comparative law.

[64] In choosing to present an exploratory model, I have kept in mind the points raised by Chesterman (2013) in his chapter on modelling translation processes.

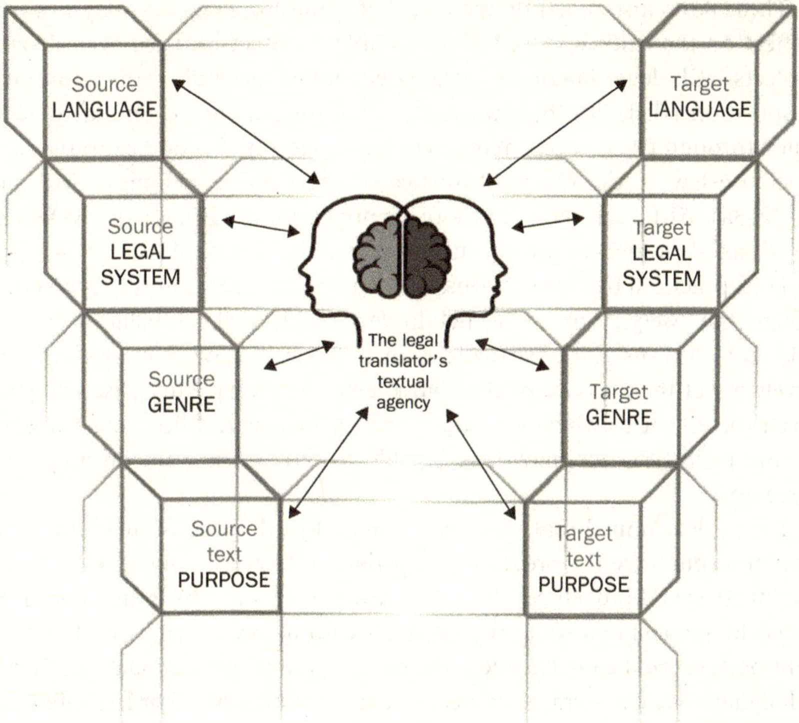

FIGURE 2.3. A simplified representation of the tesseract of the legal translator's textual agency.

as they are unwrapped and wrapped, constantly interacting with and mapping onto one another, could be a convenient way to view the legal translator's mental processes and the indissociable and synchronous nature of the fields of their textual agency.[65] I must emphasise, however, that in this case the tesseract is used purely to model complex cognitive activity,[66] and takes no account of the mathematical arguments involved. Figure 2.3 is a simplified representation of that polytope.

The flows represented by the arrowheads may be understood to correspond to the evolving quest for linguistic and/or legal systemic and/or generic equivalence, and the quest to transpose the source text purpose or to fulfil the target text's intended purpose. This *multidimensional* view of the translator's agency allows such equivalences to be free from duality.

---

[65] The shifting net of the polytope's vortices, mapping onto each other in an ever-evolving way accentuates the dynamic transformation of the text from source to target.

[66] If this seems far-fetched to the reader, it is worth noting that neural network modelling is at the heart of research leading technological advances in machine translation (e.g., Koehn, 2017; Sutskever, Vinyals, & Le, 2014; Tu *et al.*, 2017) and speech recognition. For a visualization of how billions of neurons interact in neural networks: https://www.youtube.com/watch?v=vyNkAuX29OU.

These flows also illustrate the fact that translators' agency may itself have an effect on the fields involved. For example, 'contact-induced issues' arise in Eurolects—EU legal language variants generated through translation and/or transposition (Biel, 2014b; Strandvik, 2015, forthcoming). Similarly, textual agency through translations may affect legal systems. A good example of this is the case law of the Court of Justice of the European Union (McAuliffe, e.g., 2013a). Although the practice of 'genre bending' (Bhatia, 2014) has been evoked mainly in the context of ulterior motives (Garzone & Ilie, 2014), for example, as practised by corporations, the bending of legal genres may also occur through the 'weight' of or availability/access through translation.[67] Lastly, whilst not all translators, particularly in outsourced environments, can retroactively affect the purpose of the source text, their very enterprise will greatly impact the extent to which the target text purpose is fulfilled, and translators working in institutions may even be able to have an impact on an evolving source text.

I have determined that time represents a fourth dimension in this model. In order to embrace the preceding 'negotiating flows', we may take the model a step further and introduce a fifth dimension. Consider the 'gravitational pull' exerted by planets in a solar system, each with its own specific path. The different pulls exerted can also allow the model to take into account the fact that the language, legal system, purpose, or genre may have more or less influence in different translation situations.

With regard to the relevance of, the reasoning behind, and the use of this model, which is not destined for clients and is intended for legal translation theorists, I should like to raise three key points. The first follows Bocquet's work from as early as 1994, when he asserts that it is indispensable that legal translation theory be induced from professional practice.[68] Second, my model aims to make an initial contribution to describing performance in the field of legal translation, while taking into account Toury's recommendation to balance 'the mental [and] the environmental, i.e., the situation in and for which the act [of translation] is performed' (2012, p. 67). Third and most importantly, only when we, as legal translation theorists or trainers, fully appreciate the complexity of the cognitive 'juggling' and negotiating involved, and then *communicate it to others*, will we be able to convey the importance of legal translators' task, raise their status, and, who knows, attract even brighter stars to the profession.

[67] E.g., arrest warrants (Garrido Rodríguez, 2012); Pakistani birth certificates in Spanish translation (Mayoral Asensio, 2003); or crime fiction through Nordic noir.

[68] Bocquet (1994, p. i): '*il est indispensable d'établir une théorie ou, à tout le moins, d'ébaucher un schéma théorique induit de la pratique professionnelle*'. This argument was also invoked by Šarčević (2000, p. 1).

To summarize my proposed model of the legal translator's textual agency:

i) 'General' translation techniques transferring one language to another are already not an easy task;
ii) In negotiating solutions between different systems, the legal translator enters the domain of comparative law;
iii) Genre and/or subgenre compliance must also be respected;
iv) In order to adhere to the purpose of the text, first and foremost the legal translator needs to be aware of that purpose.

3

Constraints on the Outsourced Legal Translation Process

> Legal translation is a product of a human process
> with the translator working in particular situations and contexts
> under an array of legal and other constraints.
> —Cao (2007, p. 5)

In order to explore the myriad constraints weighing upon the performance of legal translation, particularly when outsourced, I place them into three groups: those arising *upstream* of translation labours; constraints that come to bear during the performance of the translation ('*in-performance* constraints'); and those arising *downstream*, after the translation has been completed.[1] My choice of the term 'constraint' aims to embrace a number of concepts and issues. These may include norms, expectations, and restrictions or limitations relating to agency and dialogue between translators and commissioners and/or decision-makers and/or end-users.

The interaction of these constraints is illustrated in Figure 3.1, in chronological order from left to right, branching downwards for further depth of field. *Logistic* constraints such as deadlines, budget, and file formats, although less theoretically complex, can exert their effects across the board. *Briefing inadequacies* in respect of any of the norms or expectations applying can potentially give rise to information asymmetry, goal divergence, and risk at all stages of the process.

3.1. Constraints on Legal Translation Performance Arising Upstream of the Translator's Intervention

A number of obligations and impediments present themselves even before a legal translation practitioner has sight of the text to be outsourced.

[1] Further discussion of this subject can be found in Scott (2018), which draws from the work presented in this volume.

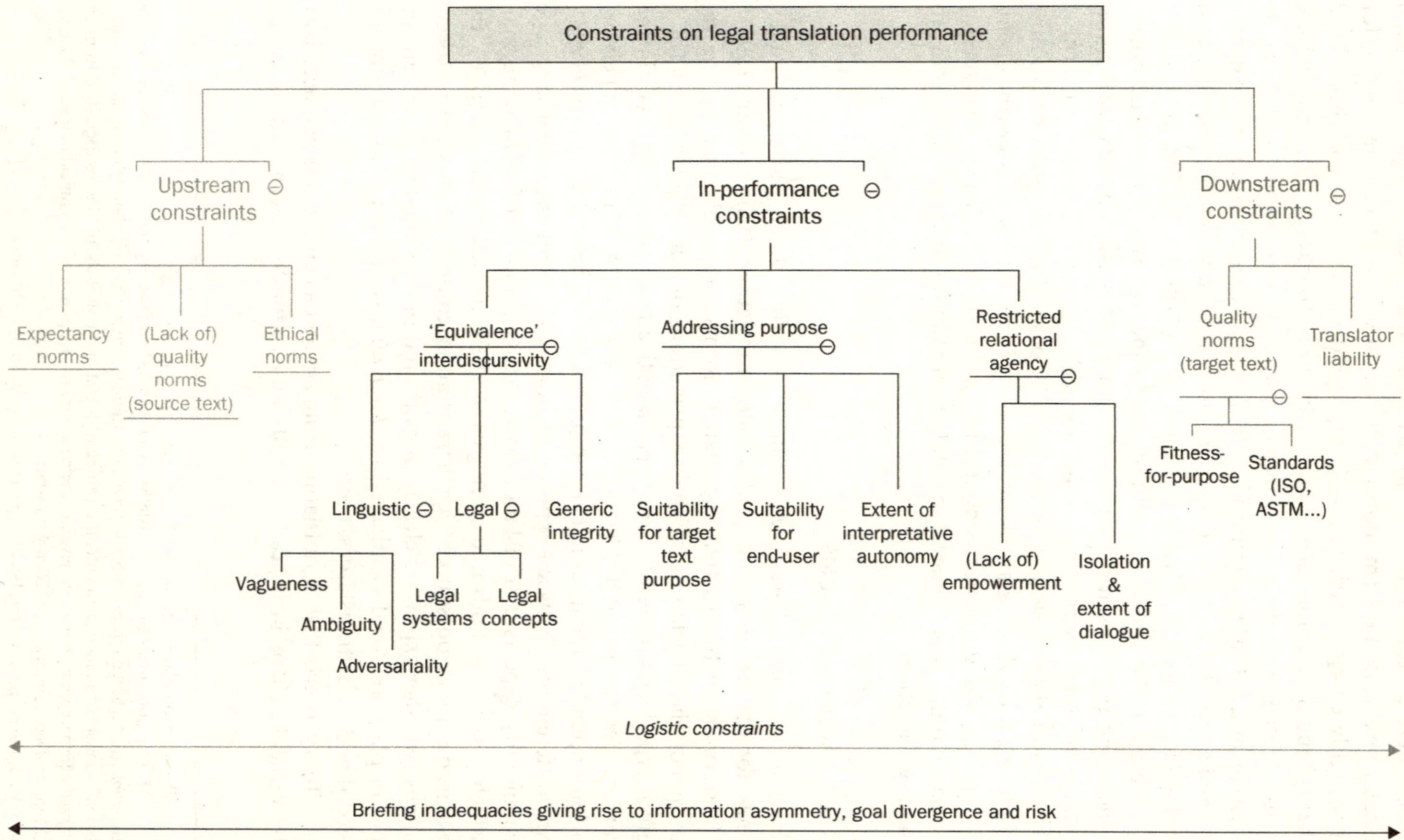

FIGURE 3.1. The interaction of constraints before, during, and after legal translation performance.

I focus here on three types of 'norms'. Any discussion in legal translation studies involving the term 'norm' must begin with a precise definition, for it is highly charged with scholarly argument in the context of both legal theory[2] and translation theory. For applications to translation, we may look first to Toury, who defines norms as a way to express values and concepts existing in a given 'community' as 'performance instructions appropriate for and applicable to particular situations, specifying what is prescribed and forbidden, as well as what is tolerated and permitted' (1998, p. 15). For Chesterman, the 'norms governing translation are: (a) professional norms concerning the translation process (= norms of accountability, communication and target-source relation); and (b) expectancy norms concerning the form of the translation product' (1993, p. 1). Regarding the constraints predating a legal translator's intervention, in an outsourced environment, I shall first discuss expectancy norms, and shall then discuss two sets of norms within a more general societal interpretation of the term, relating to quality and ethics.

3.1.1. EXPECTANCY NORMS

Translation norms have been defined as laying down 'accepted guidelines' for the production of professional translations (Chesterman, 1993).[3] Chesterman postulates that expectancy norms 'are established by the receivers of the translation, by their expectations of what a translation (of a given type)[4] should be like, and what a native text (of a given type) in the target language should be like' (1993, p. 9). The idea of 'translation receivers' is built upon by Schäffner in her comprehensive discussion of norms (1998). She differentiates between expectancy norms, or 'what the target language community expects a translation to look like', and 'professional norms', which govern 'methods and strategies of the translation process' (p. 6). By extension, in an outsourced legal translation context, clients have expectations (whether expressed clearly or not), and professional norms might be put in place and/or disseminated by, *inter alia*, translator training, professional bodies, or translators' peers.

Toury asserts that '[t]ranslating as an act and as an event is characterized by variability, it is historically, socially and culturally determined, in short,

[2] See in particular the œuvre of Hans Kelsen (1991), which sees the law as a system of norms.

[3] Translation norms for legal translation may even be laid down by the law—the French *Cour de cassation* [the highest court in France for civil and criminal matters] has stipulated that 'a "simple translation" consists of rendering the literal meaning of a text and that it should be distinguished from an *expertise* [expert appraisal] which gives an appreciation, or an opinion of a technical nature of the text' (Monjean-Decaudin, 2012, p. 226, my translation).

[4] For the purposes of this book, 'type' may be replaced by (sub)genre.

norm-governed' (1998, p. 10). In the case of legal translation, Toury's historical aspect might comprise both general legal drafting conventions accrued over time, and more specifically the law(s) applicable to the source text at the date when it was produced and/or those applying to the target text at the date when it is produced. His social norm variation might correspond to the translated legal text's receivership—whether the general public or legal professionals for example; while his cultural element might be defined as the applicable legal system or culture.

Toury also raises the issue of context, insofar as

> [o]ur words achieve the appearance of stability and regularity because we agree that certain actions are acceptable in appropriate circumstances, and others are not. (Toury, 1998, p. 14, citing Davis, 1994, p. 97)

When discussing legal translation, we may apply this notion of context-related acceptability in several ways, including, for example, to (sub)generic integrity, fitness-for-purpose, and collocations. At the very least, expectancy is a key factor in outsourced legal translation acceptance, which may relate, *inter alia*, to the expectancies of translation end-users identified to the translators before they commence work, to clients' own in-house criteria, or may be established by the wider legal community in a given geographical (i.e., state, or group of states) or specialist area of law (e.g., patents, commercial law). It is interesting to reflect whether 'guidelines' are 'laid down' as assumed by Chesterman, cited earlier, or whether in fact they are far more nebulous and for the most part unexpressed.

3.1.2. FAILURES TO APPLY QUALITY NORMS TO THE SOURCE TEXT

Much energy is devoted to examining the translation quality of *target* texts. However, *source* text quality is far less the subject of scrutiny (Molnár, 2013), and when it is, this tends to occur within institutions, such as the efforts described by Strandvik (e.g., 2015, 2018, in press), and the recommendations in the guides published by European Union bodies, *Writing for Translation* (Piehl & Vihonen, 2010) and *How to Write Clearly* (European Commission, 2012a). According to Drugan (2013, p. 22), translators are noticing 'a rise in technical texts authored by non-native speakers, presenting issues of accuracy and clarity', and she appears to include legal texts within 'technical domains' (2013, p. 3).

Despite the very large volume of literature on legal drafting quality aimed at lawyers, it seems that some source texts in the legal genre still fall through the net (see section 5.5.3.a in Chapter 5). Moreover, some legal subgenres to be translated cannot be corrected, however poor their quality: for example, evidentiary texts. Some work has been done to optimize source text quality in technical (understood as industrial/mechanical, etc.) texts in the field of controlled language,[5] particularly when the source text is destined for machine translation. Maxwell Chandler and O'Malley Deming have also broached the issue in their work on game localization—'although in some cases the quality of the source text is almost a taboo subject, [... it] should be treated just like any other asset [...]. Disorganized, uninspired and puzzling source material is guaranteed to delay the whole localization process and generate mistakes that can easily be avoided' (2012, p. 109). Indeed, they go as far as to say that the 'first guarantee' of success is the 'high quality of the source text' (2012, p. 109), and stress the importance of establishing a 'pipeline for translators to review the source material and provide feedback before translation work begins' (2012, p. 109). Whilst a 'pipeline' of review is not always feasible in the field of outsourced legal translation, particularly when a text is a *fait accompli* (e.g., evidentiary documents, court rulings) rather than in the process of being drafted, some interesting parallels may be drawn from the preceding.

3.1.3. ETHICAL NORMS

Ethical norms influence legal translation in several ways. That the translator should maintain the confidentiality of text to be translated seems self-evident, since it is embedded in professional practice.[6] However, when a self-employed legal translator receives the text via one or more intermediaries in the Chain of Supply (section 1.1.7 [Chapter 1]), precautions may be taken, such as blacking out or redacting the parties, products, dates, or places involved. Such information asymmetry will seriously hamper the translator's work—whether the subject of the litigation is a pair of sunglasses or a software package or a house, for example, or whether the party is an individual or a company. Additionally, knowing the geographical location and date of the text may well relate to the applicable legislation and therefore to standardized terms to be used.[7]

The translator's personal ethical standpoint may also come into play, not only regarding his or her choice of assignment—whether to accept a translation in a case involving child pornography, terrorism, or gruesome acts, for instance—but even at the level of the text. The issue of dominant discourse propagation is highly relevant in the case of the legal community. Whether the translator decides to act as gatekeeper or to propagate existing norms is not a trivial matter—for example, regarding plain language issues.

---

[5] E.g., Mitamura (1999).

[6] Confidentiality is generally one of the pillars underpinning codes of ethics issued by translators' professional bodies (e.g., International Federation of Translators, *Code of Professional Practice*, undated, point 1.4).

[7] See data in Chapter 5, section 5.5.3.d.1, 'Confidentiality as a Constraint to Translation Performance'.

3.2. 'In-performance' Constraints Affecting Legal Translation

In order to shed further light on the legal translation performance process,[8] we can identify two overarching taxa: the first includes aspects that constrain the legal translator's textual agency (by which I mean their mediation of the text),[9] while the second taxon comprises issues of relational agency—the extent to which the translator is able and enabled to interact with other professionals to perform the assignment in the best way possible and find effective solutions. The two intersect in the area of interpretive autonomy (section 4.3.3 [Chapter 4]), which comprises both textual and relational features.

Figure 3.2 overlays the two taxa onto the 'tree' of constraints identified earlier. I shall now explore each of the subfields of constraints identified as having an effect *during* translation performance.

3.2.1. INTENTIONAL AMBIGUITY

When we look at the practice of legal translation, the first hurdle to equivalence is the *presumption that there exists a clear, unique meaning to be transferred.* In fact, an inherent characteristic of many legal genres is vagueness and/or ambiguity. Indeed, for Endicott, 'vagueness, and resultant indeterminacies, are essential features of law' (2000, p. 1). The following neatly summarizes the issue:

> Lawyers, however, are given license to be insincere. They are trained to be simultaneously truthful and insincere. On the one hand, they are required to tell the truth in the context of legal proceedings. On the other, they are insincere in that they routinely structure their speech to lead others into drawing inferences that will serve the lawyer's goals, whether or not those inferences reflect a fair assessment of facts or law. (Solan, 2011a, abstract).[10]

Legal language may make 'deliberate use of words and expressions with flexible meanings' (Charrow, Crandall, & Charrow, 1982). The act of translation may propagate such forms of ambiguity, and, on the other hand, wittingly or unwittingly, may clarify them. Furthermore, translated legal texts may be exploited as adversarial devices.[11] Ambiguity thus severely constrains the legal translation practitioner, who must ensure that the drafter's intention

---

[8] In the context of legal translation at European institutions, McAuliffe notes that '*process* necessarily affects *output*' (2013b, p. 6, original emphasis).

[9] See also multidimensional model in section 2.5 (Chapter 2).

[10] The text cited appears in the abstract but not in the paper itself.

[11] The issue of what I shall term 'adversarial translation', whereby translated texts themselves are adduced and contested to the benefit of a party, is beyond the scope of this book but is a highly

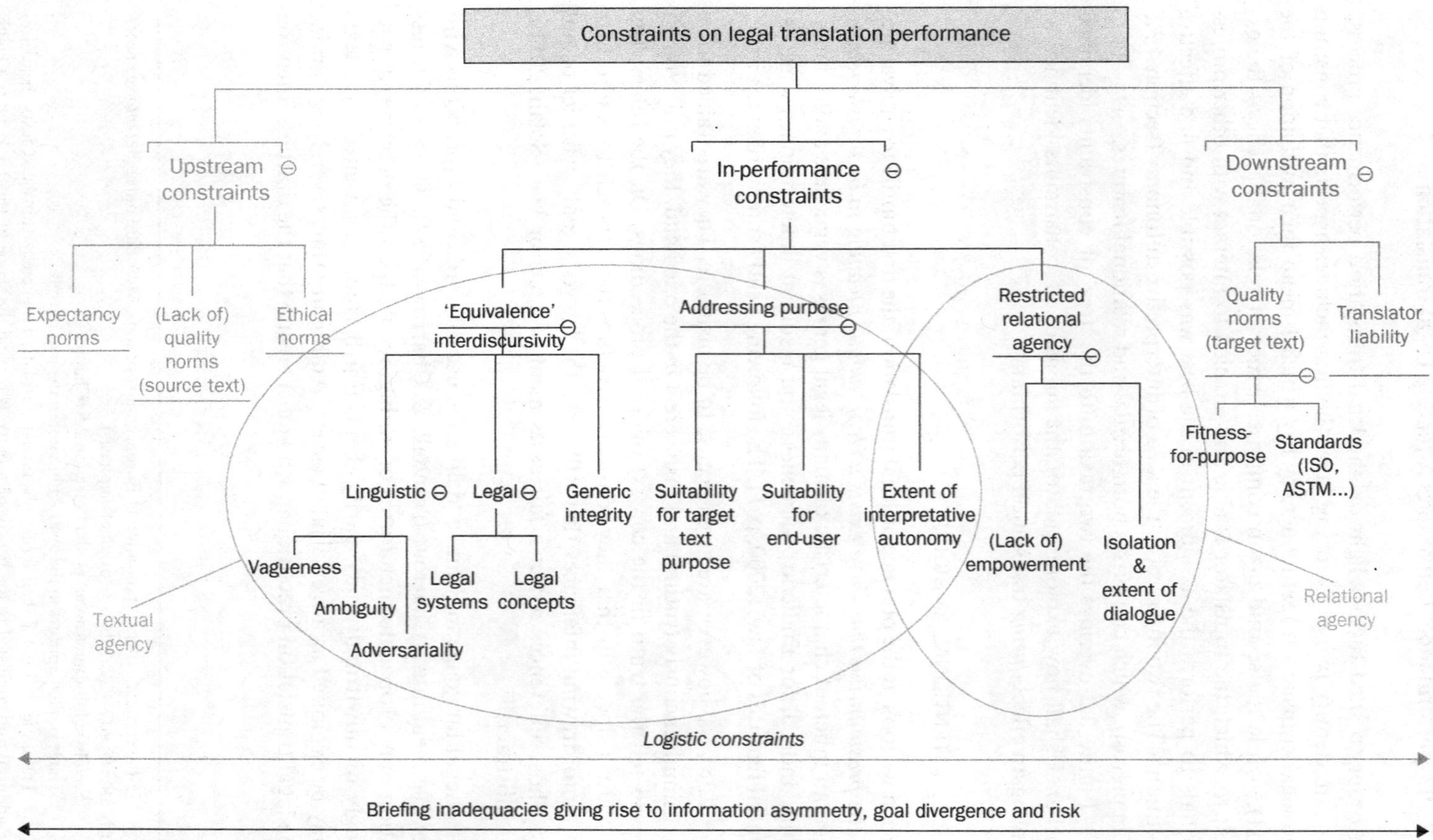

FIGURE 3.2. Constraints pertaining to textual agency, as distinguished from relational agency.

is conveyed accurately—including where that intention is to be ambiguous or vague.

I shall now give a few examples of intentional ambiguity, from different spheres. The first concerns United Nations Security Resolution 1441 relating to Iraq and weapons of mass destruction, adopted on 8 November 2002.[12] Byers, for example, holds that, although adopted unanimously, 'the document contains intentional ambiguities—in other words, that the Council members negotiated and agreed to language that they knew could be used to support arguments on both sides' (2004, p. 165). In that instance, owing to a tense global backdrop, the various signatories are held to have 'agreed to disagree', in full knowledge of 'differences in interpretative approach' (p. 166). I have been unable to obtain records relating to translation issues in this regard, but readers can readily imagine all kinds of potential complexities that could have arisen.

Whereas my first example concerns ambiguity jointly 'negotiated' by the parties involved, the insurance sector seems a good source to turn to for my second illustration—widely regarded by the general public as infamous for the ambiguity of its policies and terms to the detriment of policyholders. In this area there is specific ambiguity doctrine, for example, in 'many legal systems' (Brand, p. 105) to protect clients of insurance companies, whereby 'whenever a written contract is susceptible to two or more reasonable interpretations, ambiguities in the language should be construed strictly against the drafter of the unclear contract clause' (Burling & Lazarus, 2011, citing *Corbin on Contracts*). In this business sector, intentional ambiguity was so common as to require special legal principles to govern it. Here, too, the translation of such ambiguity may only exacerbate matters.

My last example involves the possibility that one of the parties to a contractual agreement might use an intentionally ambiguous term to their financial advantage, and has inherent translation issues. In the case of *Frigaliment Importing Co v BNS International Sales Corp*,[13] the purchaser, a Swiss company, ordered frozen chickens for roasting and frying from a New York poultry wholesaler. Having received delivery, part of which were second-class quality stewing birds, the buyer brought action for breach of contract.[14] Ambiguity had arisen regarding the definition of 'chicken'—which the parties had apparently construed differently.

---

interesting area for further research that I intend to pursue. Interested readers may consult the following cases as examples: *Rekstin v Severo Sibirsko Gosudarstvennoe Akcionernoe Obschestvo Komseverputjand the Bank for Russian Trade, Limited*, Court of Appeal, King's Bench Division, UK; *Provimi Limited v Aventis Animal Nutrition SA and Others, Trouw (UK) Limited and Another v Rhodia Limited and Others; Provimi Limited v Roche Products Limited and Others; Trouw (UK) Limited and Others v Roche Products Limited and Others*, English High Court, Queen's Bench Division (Commercial Court).

[12] http://www.un.org/depts/unmovic/documents/1441.pdf.

[13] 190 F.Supp.116 (S.D.N.Y. (1960)).

[14] For further details on this linguistically fascinating case, see Schane (2006, pp. 12–53).

> The plaintiff intends for the term 'chicken' to refer to birds no larger than broilers or fryers,[15] whereas the defendant believes that chicken includes stewing fowl as well. (Schane, 2006, p. 27)

Since the judge found no specification in the contract, extrinsic evidence was admissible. Schane notes that

> [t]he plaintiff asserts that preliminary communications were all in German, a language known by both parties.[16] The plaintiff claims to have used intentionally within its German correspondence the English word 'chicken' because of its understanding that the English word meant 'young chicken' and it was for that reason that the plaintiff had eschewed the German word 'Huhn', which includes both stewing chickens ('Suppenhuhn') and broilers ('Brathuhn'). (2006, p. 28)

In sum, the construction of ambiguous legal texts can be fraught with perils even without crossing language borders, making it all the more important to inform the translator of all intentions, whether explicit or implicit.

3.2.2. SYSTEMIC AND CONCEPTUAL CONSTRAINTS

The lack of correspondence between legal systems and concepts *per se* imposes constraints on legal translators. However, still further constraints may apply—and may be laid down by the law. In Canada, for example, the systemic and conceptual problem exists alongside that of language in the same nation. Indeed, Canadian legislation provides for just that situation in its Interpretation Act 1985:

> **8.2** Unless otherwise provided by law, when an enactment contains both civil law and common law terminology, or terminology that has a different meaning in the civil law and the common law, the civil law terminology or meaning is to be adopted in the Province of Quebec and the common law terminology or meaning is to be adopted in the other provinces.[17]

The Government of Canada provides a list of case law including decisions citing the preceding section.[18] It goes without saying how careful translators need to be in such a context.

---

[15] To avoid introducing further ambiguity: the US English verb 'broil' corresponds to 'roast' in UK English.

[16] It would have been very interesting to examine the extent of the parties' command of German. One might even hypothesize that a professional translator could have preempted this misunderstanding, if indeed it was such.

[17] See the Government of Canada website: http://www.justice.gc.ca/eng/csj-sjc/harmonization/bijurilex/interpretation.html.

[18] http://www.justice.gc.ca/eng/csj-sjc/harmonization/bijurilex/biju/case-repe1.html.

Another example of legal translation constraints indirectly imposed by the law can arise in Switzerland, where there is a federal right to use any language in legal proceedings and different Cantons and different Communes have divergent positions on officially accepted languages. In a certain case the binding law of the contract was English, the plaintiff was a French speaker, the defendant was Italian-speaking Swiss, and the trial took place in German-speaking Bern. Italian is not an official language of the Canton of Bern (German/French) and the locals use a non-uniform Swiss-German dialect rather than standard German (Wehrli, 2012). Readers are free to imagine the conceptual and systemic issues that such a situation could engender.

3.2.3. GENERIC INTEGRITY

The genre taxonomies described in section 2.3.2 (Chapter 2) may allow legal translators to gain access to and familiarize themselves with the linguistic and other features of different genres, which should include textual macrostructure. The need to take account of genre in legal translation performance is expressed by the criterion of 'generic integrity', which has been described as the 'stability of the communicative purpose across cultures' (Bhatia & Engberg, 2004, p. 8), and 'the stability in the characteristics of a genre across languages, socio-political contexts, and cultures' (Bhatia, Candlin, & Engberg, 2008). Exploring the translation of legal genres, Bhatia holds that 'one of the most crucial aspects of translation [. . .] is the concern to maintain the generic identity of the target text' (1997, p. 206), particularly in professional discourse. He further asserts that a genre-based approach to translation enables the translator to 'make relevant connection between the use of language on the one hand and the purpose of communication on the other' (p. 212). Moreover,

> failure to conform to the convention of legal discourse (to conform to the correct forms, the semantic functions, and discursive devices) could result in the entire text being invalidated or being rejected by a particular legal discourse community for failure to preserve 'the generic integrity'. (Yunus & Awab, 2011, p. 168, citing Goźdź-Roszkowski, 2004, p. 402)

Hence, maintaining generic integrity or stability is a key constraint in translation performance. Even from a monolingual standpoint, Gotti holds that 'one of the phenomena that most distinguishes legal discourse is compliance with the norms governing the construction of its different text genres' (2012, p. 60). Approaches providing reference material, such as corpora, could be particularly useful in alleviating these constraints (Goźdź-Roszkowski, e.g., 2004).

3.2.4. INTERTEXTUAL AND INTERDISCURSIVE CONSTRAINTS

I adopt a definition of intertextuality whereby 'legal texts must usually "be interpreted in the context of something expressed elsewhere"; and intertextual devices are used to point readers to that "elsewhere"' (Menghini, 2012, p. 235, adapted from Bhatia, 1998). Intertextuality may serve, for instance, to signal textual authority, provide terminological explanation, facilitate textual mapping, or define legal scope (Bhatia, 1998). We may also, however, go beyond intertextuality to 'interdiscursivity', which includes text-external factors that impact a given text: context, genre, professional practice, and legal culture (Bhatia, 2008). Indeed, 'the study of legal communication can be further enriched by taking into account inter-discursivity' (Scott, 2015b, p. 124, following Bhatia, 2008). By extension, we could view interdiscursivity as a cross-cutting relation to the three facets of legal translation performance—language, genre and legal culture/system, and even purpose.

The difficulties inherent in the interdiscursivity of legal texts when crossing language boundaries become even more severe when reference material is not supplied to the translator with the source text, insofar as the translator has to hunt down the correct, consistent, approved, or authoritative terms, legal instruments and other documents, or authority to be incorporated in their translation. Such intertextual or interdiscursive material has been referred to by Fraser[19] as 'translation resources', which she separates into resources controlled 'by the translators themselves—notably dictionaries, glossaries and other reference works', and the many resources 'controlled by the client or by the translation agency/company' (2000, p. 56). She adds that requesting such support is 'often seen as a sign of inadequate professionalism when "of course, the reverse is true"' (2000, p. 56). These 'client-controlled resources' may include, according to Gawn,[20]

> reference material, resource people, hands-on contact with whatever is being discussed in the document to be translated, access to target-language subject or writing specialists, discussion with known or possible users of the translation, and so on. (1988, p. 459)

Owing to the complexity and difficulty of legal texts, the supply of intertextual and interdiscursive resources is all the more crucial in order to ensure the best possible translation quality.

3.2.5. PURPOSE-RELATED CONSTRAINTS

The intended purpose of a legal document materially affects and/or constrains the approach to its translation. From a functionalist perspective, it comes down to the very *raison d'être* of the translation. In view of the importance of this point, I will first cite from the literature, and then provide some detailed examples from professional practice. Before proceeding, however, I must reiterate that the relationship between the target text purpose and other facets and constraints upon legal translation performance is highly complex, as seen

---

[19] In a general translation context, not specifically legal.

[20] Gawn writes in the Canadian legal context.

in the model provided in section 2.5 (Chapter 2). Hence, despite the present linear presentation dictated by the textual format of this book, the purpose is itself enmeshed, to a greater or lesser extent, with the (sub)language(s), (sub) genre(s), and legal system(s) involved. In practice, therefore, the purpose-constraint of the text in the following example—expansion in a new market—engenders and will inform various other constraints relating to specific legal concepts and status of the text. A further constraint is the need for language on the one hand complying with the generic sublanguage (warranty statements), and on the other suitable for the intended user (general public or scholars of comparative law).

The first example comes from Obenaus (1995, pp. 250–252): two alternative scenarios illustrate, primarily from a legal equivalence stance, 'both the importance of the function of the translation as the main determinant of the translator's strategy and the importance of information in helping the translator produce a text that is functionally adequate' (1995, p. 250). The subject is the translation of warranty statements.

3.2.5.1. Scenario A

> The translation of a warranty statement from US English to German is commissioned by a US corporation that wishes to expand into the German market, and 'the functions of the original and the translation are similar, the only difference being that the translation must conform to German and not to US law'. (Obenaus, 1995, p. 251)

These 'similar functions' are stated to be 'defining the seller's obligations [. . .] if the goods fail to conform to the standards expressed by the warranty'—that is, both the source and target texts are to act as warranties. It is not clear [to me] from Obenaus's discussion how or whether he defines 'purpose' as different from function. In any event, according to Obenaus, if the translation is to be legally valid in Germany, it will require a 'legal equivalence' approach.[21] In this regard, he refers to the need to address conceptual differences such as 'limited warranties' and 'implied warranties'.

3.2.5.2. Scenario B

> The translation of a warranty statement from US English to German is commissioned by a German competitor of the US company that issued the warranty, to 'gain a better understanding of the type of warranties commonly granted for similar products in the USA'. (Obenaus, 1995, p. 252)

In Scenario B, Obenaus explains that the translation will simply be a 'footnoted explanation of the original, not a translation trying to come up with

[21] Obenaus notes that in this scenario the section of the warranty relating to its interpretation in the 'various States of the United States' should be excluded as it would be irrelevant for German users (1995, p. 250–251).

equivalents' and suggests taking a different approach to the central legal concepts involved (1995, p. 252).

In these two scenarios, Obenaus shows how the translations are constrained by their purpose: by the applicable law (German [Scenario A] or US [Scenario B]); intended user (product consumers [A] or professional client from the same industry [B]); and status (legally binding as a warranty for goods sold [A] or information purposes [B]). It is noteworthy that in this instance, the stated 'information purposes' status in fact belies considerable importance—the translation will dictate company strategy in regards to their competitors. It is not 'simply' a translation for gist, which is the general understanding of 'information purposes' status.

My second illustration from the literature considers the translation of an insurance contract from the point of view of a dichotomy between a source-oriented approach and a target-oriented approach. It is Vermeer's somewhat disputed example of an insurance policy ('contract'), presented here as translated from the German by Madsen (1997).

3.2.5.3. Situation A

> If the translated contract [sic] is the object of a judicial decision and it has to serve as a 'document' of the allegations of the opposing party, the translation should be oriented towards the source language. (Vermeer, 1986, p. 34, translated by Madsen, 1997, p. 17)[22]

Madsen takes issue with Vermeer's argument whereby 'the target text always becomes an element of the target culture' because, according to her, this 'does not seem to be quite consistent with Situation A above in which the target text has to function as 'document' [court evidence]. And furthermore [. . .] does not take into account the constraints imposed on legal texts by the legal reality' (Madsen, 1997, p. 17). I would suggest that in practice the answer would be more polychromatic, and the decision as to whether the translation is oriented towards source or target language (or sublanguage) forms a part of the overall strategy produced to fulfil the translation brief, which will also take into account the legal culture applicable, as Madsen notes, and potentially also the genre [insurance policies].

---

[22] In Garzone's interpretation of Vermeer's proposal: a 'source-language oriented approach is taken if the translation is to be used only as court evidence' (2000, p. 7), whilst Šarčević interprets Vermeer's conclusions as follows: 'source language [formulae] are to be imitated if the translation is to be used as court evidence' (2000, p. 2).

3.2.5.4. Situation B

> If on the contrary, the translated contract is to be used in practice as the contract 'instrument' the translation should be oriented towards the target language. (Vermeer, 1986, p. 34, translated by Madsen, 1997, p. 17)[23]

Šarčević (2000) claims that Vermeer's suggestion 'that the translation strategy for contracts is determined primarily by function, [...] disregards the fact that legal texts are subject to legal rules governing their usage. [...] In regard to contracts, the decision whether and to what extent target-language formulae are adequate is determined primarily by the law governing the particular contract, not function' (Šarčević, 2000, referring also to Šarčević 1997, pp. 18–19, 68). Again, my argument is that the situation in practice is more multifaceted, and the translation needs to take into account the applicable law, but also genre conventions and, in particular, requirements expressed by or elicited from the client.

For my third example of purpose-related constraints, I turn to Pym (2010), whose example, like Vermeer's, is focused on source or target orientation, with a third alternative: 'word-for-word' translation.

> A legal agreement, for example, may be (1) adapted to target-side textual norms if and when it is to be governed by the laws operative in that culture, or (2) it may be rendered with the source-text form if and when the translation is more for purposes of understanding, or again, (3) it may be translated in an almost word-for-word way if, for instance, it is to be cited as evidence in court. The source text would be the same in all cases. What is different is the *purpose* that the translation has to serve. (Pym, 2010, pp. 44–45, original emphasis, my numbering added)

Apart from the information suggested earlier, the translator will also need to know what kind of legal agreement is involved, in order to comply with any specific subgenre conventions. The end-user may also affect the translation strategy: whether a professional co-contracting party; advising lawyers; authorities requiring the agreement as supporting material; the general public if the agreement is between an individual and a business; etc. In the first example, not only the legal system needs to be supplied, but ideally also references to the specific laws applicable. It would be interesting to delve more deeply into what is to be understood by Pym's 'target-side textual norms': the norms of the target legal system? Of the target language variant? Or even the norms of

---

[23] Garzone interprets Vermeer's proposal in situation B as: 'target-language formulas are resorted to if the translation is for use in practice, for the stipulation of insurance policies in a foreign country' (2000, p. 7), while for Šarčević (2000), 'target-language formulae are to be used in translations intended for use in practice'.

the target text receiver (e.g., their house rules). In the second example, it is not clear what is meant by 'rendered with the source-text form' (i.e., whether this refers to layout, or genre conventions, or something else). In the third example, the purpose of the target text is for evidence in court. One alternative might indeed be a translation in an 'almost word-for-word way', particularly in countries where this is laid down by the law (e.g., Monjean-Decaudin, 2012, p. 226). However, another strategy might be necessary if a gist translation was required at the discovery phase of evidence gathering. The issue of intertextuality is not broached either: for instance, terms and conditions that might apply to the agreement.

I shall now provide some more detailed examples,[24] drawn from my professional practice. My first example focuses on alternative translation strategies relating in particular to the **legal system** applicable to the target text. A standard lease agreement for all of the Chinese stores of a French multinational is to be translated from French to English. Some possible scenarios for the translated text could be:

a) To be signed in English as the binding version with Chinese subsidiaries, to which English law will apply;
b) To be signed in English as the binding version with Chinese subsidiaries, to which Chinese law will apply;
c) To be signed in English as the binding version with Chinese subsidiaries, to which French law will apply;
d) A courtesy translation for gist comprehension by English-speaking Chinese subsidiaries—the original French version is to be signed, which will be binding and subject to French law;
e) Translated into English as a 'pivot' or 'relay' translation for subsequent translation into Chinese, where the final Chinese version will be legally binding and Chinese law will apply.

In scenario (a), the translator must pay particular attention to the transfer of French civil law terms into English common law terms, since English law is to apply and English is to be the binding version. In scenario (b) the implications under the three, very different, legal systems (French, English, and Chinese) on any transferred concepts should be carefully weighed up. Where French law is to apply, in scenario (c), the use of footnotes or glosses including the original source term may be considered for system-specific legal concepts. The English translation (d) for gist comprehension will be subject to a lower degree of scrutiny, primarily because the French source text, not the translation, is to be signed and legally binding, and in some cases *might* be a candidate for

[24] My selections in each instance are non-exhaustive.

translation by a less experienced translator, or, more recently, by sophisticated machine translation systems adapted to language for legal purposes. Scenario (e), involving a pivot or relay translation, could make more liberal use of untranslated loan words for potentially difficult French legal concepts (section 2.4.3 [Chapter 2]), to enable the Chinese translator to bypass the pivot and refer directly to the original term, thus avoiding distortion of the original concept.[25]

My second example concerns how the intended purpose can affect how *source text ambiguity* is dealt with. A last will and testament involving large sums of money is being translated from language X into language Y, via a pivot translation in language Z, registered some years earlier as the official deed by a Z-speaking notary. The positioning of a comma, ambiguous in language Z, would affect which of two jurisdictions is to apply to the will, and one of them is a tax haven. In addition, ambiguous positioning of one word would render the will applicable to the whole estate or only to those assets on the territory of the tax haven. Alternative intended purposes for the translated text could be

a) The translation is to be sent by the interested parties to the tax authorities to determine the amount of tax due;
b) The translation is for lawyers as part of litigation over inheritance issues.

Clearly, if the translator has been informed of the intended purposes of the translation, he or she will flag these two ambiguities, since in both instances they are likely to be crucial turning points in the case.

Legislation constitutes my third example, and here knowledge of the *end-user* and/or *readership* will be crucial in developing translation strategies, which will be further informed by the extent to which the target legislative text is to be legally binding:

a) To be made available on a website to inform the public in easily accessible language;
b) So that a lawyer from another jurisdiction who does not speak the language can access relevant parts in an international case;
c) For a comparative law scholars for study purposes;
d) For transposition into another country's national legislation—either as part of a multilingual legal system or as precedent (e.g., CJEU case law).

In scenario (a), adaptation skills are required of the translator, who will essentially need to redraft the text in plain language. Unless it is an isolated

[25] In order to make the discussion as plain as possible, I have not included in this scenario considerations such as client house style, glossary, intertextual or interdiscursive material such as terms and conditions, generic conventions, and so on.

text, it is also likely that this scenario will involve high compliance requirements with reference materials—for example, to achieve consistency in a body of legislation. In scenario (b), collaboration between the translator and the lawyer may be envisaged, so as to select the most relevant sections and potentially make savings on translation costs. The commissioner in scenario (c) may request a literal translation and/or a more source-oriented approach if that is the comparatist's preferred method (see in this regard Baaij, 2014). On the other hand, in scenario (d), where the target text is ultimately for transposition purposes, in the light of the repercussions of translation errors, or ambiguities introduced by different language versions (Derlen, 2011),[26] a team of translators and/or lawyer-linguists might well be considered, in order to have the security of additional 'pairs of eyes' and to pool expertise. Here the drafters may also have some input—to take an example from the UK's National Audit Office report on transposing EU law, legislation might be 'copied-out' 'by direct translation or a simple cross-reference to the original directive', or 'elaborated' 'by adding detail in the domestic legislation' (Bourn, 2005, p. 6).

My fourth and last example raises the issues involved where there is a potentially *adversarial* purpose for the target text. Written submissions (or pleadings) may be translated in an international case:

a) For the lawyer submitting them (aimed at convincing the judge);
b) For the adverse lawyer (to enable them to challenge the arguments therein).

Pleadings in some languages, such as but not limited to English, French, and Italian, are written in a highly rhetorical style, and can even verge upon literary translation in terms of creative demands. They thus require translators able to replicate such sophistication. However, especially in 'big-ticket' cases, because of their complexity and length, they may also contain errors, not to mention the intentional ambiguity—'adversarial ambiguity' discussed in section 3.2.1. It is surely obvious that in such situations the translators' choices will be better guided if they know which of the two alternative purposes mentioned earlier applies.

3.2.6. RELATIONAL IMPEDIMENTS

Looking beyond aspects linked to the text, it is important to note that the translator is not a machine but a person, who, as such, has (or ought to have)

[26] See, for example, Case 238/84 Criminal proceedings against Hans Röser [1986] ECR 795; Case C-173/88 *Skatteministeriet v Henriksen* [1989] ECR 2763. The Court of Justice of the European Communities has yet to issue clear guidelines on differences between language versions of transposed EU law. Indeed, Derlen (2011) goes as far as to say that 'the guidelines supplied by the court are vague, sometimes contradictory and very far reaching'.

relationships and enters into (or should be able to enter into) dialogue with other actors.[27] Concerning the intersection of practice boundaries between legal translation practitioners and their principals, I focus here particularly on limited consultation, dialogue, and involvement, bearing in mind how these may affect the quality of deliverables. I suggest that in the case of legal translation, as in this example from Edwards,

> so much depends on how relationships are set up so that the *voice of the other is given weight* and the extent to which it is recognised that *all share strong motives for resourceful work* on these complex tasks. (2010, p. 77, emphasis added)

Regarding outsourced translation in particular, Abdallah and Koskainen note a change in the global supply of translation services[28] as part of 'production networks' (2007, pp. 674–675): 'With network-based production, the translator's position and role as the translation expert seem to have diminished' and 'the end client may be several links away from the actual translator, with no contact or interaction between them' (Abdallah & Koskainen, 2007, p. 676). They also suggested, quoting from a survey of the Finnish market, that 'translation companies are not keen to disturb their client' (2007, p. 676).

A study of corporate translators in Denmark by Dam and Zethsen (2011) found that their perceived influence was 'extremely low' (p. 994) and that their expertise was 'not recognized by others' (p. 989). When service provision intermediaries are involved, the picture does not seem brighter. A vast majority of respondents in a survey carried out by Fraser described translation agencies as 'merely "document shifters"', providing 'no added-value' (1997, p. 15). Whilst there are of course many types of agencies with different policies and ways of working, this tendency does not seem to have changed significantly since then—Suojanen, Koskinen, and Tuominen note in 2015 that 'the translator does not always get feedback at all, and it rarely arrives in time to change course of action in the translation in question' (p. 129). Indeed they note that

> Most translators run their own small businesses and work as subcontractors for big agencies. They are, somewhat ironically, *outsiders in the translation process,* and are typically not involved in negotiations with clients – the most *logical phase* for discussing the steps to be taken to *ensure the usability* of the future translations. (Suojanen, Koskinen, & Tuominen, 2015, p. 126, emphasis added)

An interesting comparison is drawn by Suojanen, Koskinen, and Tuominen—that in the preceding regard, 'translators differ from technical communicators,

---

27 As artificial intelligence progresses, it is likely that contextual and relational information will, in the future, also be relevant for machine translation (e.g., Tu *et al.*, 2017).

28 Their study and the others in this section do not relate specifically to *legal* translation.

who are often either directly employed by the client or physically placed in the design teams even if they are hired by a service provider' (2015, p. 126).

In sum, does this kind of isolation matter? Would the inclusion of translators in the process have positive effects as regards the target texts they produce? In order to answer these questions, we need first to embrace two somewhat incongruous views—the approach of some scholars, particularly those with a sociological gaze, whereby translators are mediators or social actors who 'play an important role both politically and culturally' in a given society (Milton & Bandia, 2009), and the market reality as described by Katan, for example, whereby translators are 'hardly empowered' (2009, p. 149), or Kennedy's review of problems in legal translation practice, in which she recommends that the role of legal translators should change 'from mere bilingual typists to highly skilled and multi-skilled professionals' (2000, p. 440). Translators are not only isolated, but they lack power.[29] Agency theory's view of the balance of power tipping towards the principal was described in section 1.2.5 (Chapter 1). According to that theory, in the case of legal translation practitioners, power would be deemed to rest with their principal, whether a direct client such as law firm, or an intermediary such as a translation agency. We have seen that, owing to the unstable and short-term principal–agent relationships currently prevalent in the market, translation practitioners are indeed unlikely to wield power within such contexts.

But how does this affect the text? Chapter 1 described some negative effects of goal divergence. Commenting on the 'scope of legal actors' agency', Carle has defined agency as the 'power of persons [...] to develop and achieve creative goals and to act effectively [...] in light [*sic*] of those goals' (2005, p. 308). Increased empowerment of legal translators, whereby, through a reduction in information and/or knowledge asymmetry and a better cognizance of goals, their textual agency is optimized, ought therefore to give rise to improvements in the quality of the target texts that they produce.

As already argued in this book, a specific and relatively common example in the field of legal translation is ambiguity in source texts. In the context of a potentially empowered legal translator, I cite Harvey's eloquent summary:

> If translators have a solid grounding in law and interact with both sender and receiver, they should be equipped to interpret the text as producer/receivers [...]. This proactive role is not incompatible with the technique of deliberate ambiguity: indeed, it requires interpretation to identify ambiguity, decide it is deliberate, and choose to retain it in the translation. (2002, p. 182)

[29] In the legal translation context, power can also be construed as knowledge or information, and in practice, as has already been mentioned, translators working in-house, whether in institutions or in law firms, generally have better access to the originators and/or drafters of texts, and thus a larger amount of 'unfiltered' information, than those to whom work is outsourced.

Whether translators are instructed, in a full brief, to go as far as Harvey suggests, or whether they engage, relationally, as suggested by Edwards (2010) and enter into a productive dialogue with their principal, ambiguity can be handled in an empowered relationship.

In a study of behavioural agency theory, Pepper and Gore (2015) note the following:

> goal setting, especially when it involves discussions between principal and agent about the appropriate level of objectives, is a pragmatic way of contracting […]. It is also a signaling mechanism, indicating to one of the parties in an exchange relationship, the agent, what is required by another party, the principal. (p. 1056)

They further state that goal setting is a way of improving quality among contractors in order to 'enhance rather than undermine motivation' (p. 1056). The relevant section of their diagrammatic representation is highlighted in Figure 3.3.

Figure 3.3 illustrates in particular the interrelationship between motivation, performance, feedback, and goal setting. I have already theorized that feedback and goal setting may well be insufficient in legal translation contexts. It follows that motivation could be affected by this state of affairs, and, even more importantly, translation performance. This hypothesis is further supported, for example, by Abdallah's study of translators' agency in production networks (2012), which noted behavioural issues such as lack of motivation, frustration, and feelings of powerlessness, resulting from information asymmetry and goal conflict.

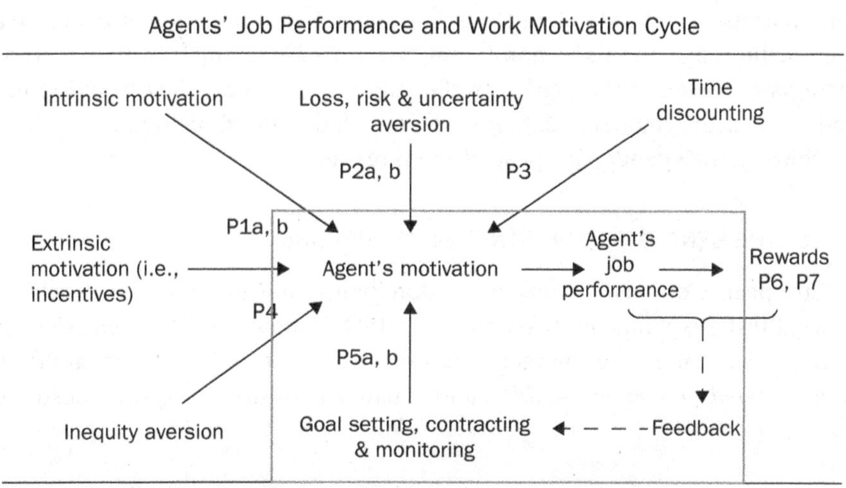

FIGURE 3.3. The effect of goal setting on agents' motivation and job performance.
Source: Pepper & Gore (2015, p. 1057).

To conclude, some of the relational impediments that may arise are translator isolation, impeded communication channels, lack of productive dialogue, power asymmetries with ensuing failure to interact, lack of involvement in goal setting, and lack of feedback. Additionally, information asymmetry can have a negative effect on the translator agent's outlook and, at the same time, affect performance and diminish the quality of the target texts.

3.3. Constraints Downstream: Performance Assessment and Liability

Once the translation has been completed, target texts in the legal field are likely to be subject to constraints—such as stringent quality norms or other criteria laid down by the client or commissioner where, if a text is found lacking, the translator's liability may be incurred. I would also posit that legal target texts are subject to high conformity expectations by recipients, in part owing to the fact that, as a rule, translated legal texts are not read by the general public, but rather by specialist recipients—experts such as lawyers, judges, consultants, corporate legal advisors, and so on.

Assessing the quality of translation services is a conundrum akin to the complexity of their performance. House provides an insight that has particular significance for the purposes of this study:

> in my view translation quality assessment means both retrospectively assessing the worth of a translation and prospectively ensuring the quality in the production of a translation. (2015, p. 2)

Hence we must not only 'firefight'[30] but also be proactive both during performance itself and, extending House's argument, also prior to performance at the briefing stage. In this section I limit myself to discussing translation assessment as practised in the market, rather than from a theoretical standpoint,[31] and in particular matters relating to the translation brief, including, still more specifically, the intended purpose of the target text.

3.3.1. THE BENCHMARK OF FITNESS-FOR-PURPOSE

A European Commission report, predominantly but not exclusively relating to legal texts, explains that: 'According to ISO Standard 8402, "quality" is defined as the "totality of characteristics of an entity that bear on its ability to satisfy *stated or implied needs*"', and 'quality is measured against customer

---

[30] E.g., *Managing Quality*, Dale (2003, in particular p. 425).

[31] See in this regard the work of House (1977, 1997, 2015), which constitutes a canon of reference in Translation Studies.

satisfaction' (2012b, p. 4, emphasis added). Indeed, the report adds that the Directorate-General Translation 'aims to provide "fit-for-purpose" quality' (p. 11). In defending 'fit-for-purpose' as a useful translation quality standard, Martin notes that the term occurs in 'charters or actual translation contracts' and in 'both the ITI's and the ATA's model terms of business'[32, 33] as well as having 'theoretical credentials' (2007, p. 60).

However, importantly, a definition from international law renders fitness-for-purpose conditional upon such purpose having been *made known* when the contract was placed:

> (b) are *fit for any particular purpose expressly or impliedly made known* to the seller at the time of the conclusion of the contract.[34] (emphasis added)

The following definition for business is given by the support lawyer Rush:

> Fitness for purpose refers to the products being suitable for the particular purpose that the [...] buyer wanted them for. *It only applies if the seller knew what that purpose was* – or it was obvious from the circumstances. (2002, p. 154, emphasis added)

In a similar vein, the consumer advice entity 'What Consumer' exhorts:

> This is the principle of fitness for purpose. There is no point claiming that paint thinner has had adverse effects if it is not being used as paint thinner! Similarly, *if you are commissioning the manufacture of a product and do not specify the purposes for which it will be used you will have no recourse* if it fails to live up to your expectations. (undated, emphasis added)

If we consider that legal translation quality may be viewed according to fitness-for-purpose, translation commissioners and/or receivers[35] who define, specify, or at the very least are privy to that purpose then become key 'quality assessors'. It follows, however, that if no purpose is stipulated in the brief, they do not have a yardstick by which to assess quality or to sanction inadequate quality. To take this argument a step further, assuming that a legal translation brief (containing the intended purpose of the target text) can be established as a procurement standard, the question of compliance with that brief then arises. Clearly, it is reasonable to expect that no recourse could be envisaged for the client if the translator has not been duly instructed. However, as long as a comprehensive brief has been provided, then the translator will have a responsibility to fulfil that brief.

---

[32] Institute of Translation & Interpreting (UK).

[33] American Translators' Association.

[34] United Nations Convention on Contracts for the International Sale of Goods (Vienna, 1980) (CISG). Retrieved from http://www.uncitral.org/pdf/english/texts/sales/cisg/V1056997-CISG-e-book.pdf.

[35] See section 1.1.7 (Chapter 1) for a discussion of the chain of supply as it applies to legal translation and the difference between commissioners and receivers.

3.3.2. OTHER QUALITY STANDARDS

International official quality standards for translation are many and varied. For reasons of brevity, I shall outline some of the most widely cited. In the context of multilingual lawmaking within the European Union, the standard EN15038:2006[36] has been tabled by Strandvik (2015) as a useful way forward for legal translation, particularly as regards 'subject-field specialization, systematic revision and *structured use of translation briefs* and knowledge-sharing among the different actors' (p. 162, emphasis added).

The ASTM (American Society for Testing and Materials) standard F2575-06 *Standard Guide for Quality Assurance in Translation*, in its Appendix 1,[37] sets out various parameters for the translation product, process, project environment, and project stakeholder relationship. The list is broken down into 40 subheadings, of which, although the standard is general in scope, the following are of particular interest for the purposes of a legal translation brief: 'target audience (especially as it differs from the intended audience of the source content) (8.3.2)'; 'purpose (especially when it differs from the purpose of the source content) (8.3.3)'; 'style relevance (is a high degree of readability important in this case?) (8.3.7.2)'; 'reference materials (8.5.2)'.

The German standard *Deutsches Institut für Normung* (DIN) 2345 on translation contracts lays down requirements for source and target texts, selection of translators, cooperation between co-contracting parties, and procedures, and is a self-certification standard (Chesterman & E. Wagner, 2002, p. 85). Indeed, it requires, in its point 4.2.3.1, that '[t]he client must explain the function of the target text to the translator and identify the target group' and in point 4.2.3.2, 'The client [. . .] must not use the translation for any other purpose' (cited by Chesterman & E. Wagner, 2002).

3.3.3. THE TRANSLATOR'S LIABILITY

Once an outsourced legal translation has potentially been assessed according to a standard, whether international, in-house, or other, a logical step, in the event of non-compliance, is either to withhold payment and/or to seek liability.

A landmark finding by the courts in a liability action in respect of the importance of briefing translators is described by Hammond[38]—a Swiss court case involving a translator who sued their customer for non-payment, the latter's grounds being that the translation 'did not resemble the source text closely enough'. In assessing whether quality was indeed lacking, the court contacted

---

[36] More recently replaced by EN-17100:2015 (May 2015).

[37] 'Historical' 2006 version, retrieved 6 January 2012 from http://www.astm.org/Standards/F2575.htm.

[38] Hammond (1995, pp. 233–245).

an expert who 'asked for the customer's product specification in addition to the source and target texts' (Hammond, 1995, p. 234). It seems that by 'product specification' the court meant translation specifications or a translation brief. Hammond refers to Holz-Mänttäri (source in German, 1987), adding that 'the real question is whether the text produced will serve its purpose, like a beer mug or an icebreaker' and concluding that '[t]he court ordered the customer to pay the translator, finding that *target texts could not be based on source texts, but had to be based on product specifications*' (Hammond, 1995, p. 234, emphasis added).[39]

As regards translator liability, Byrne's 2007 paper is a consummate appraisal of the 'legal, financial and safety implications—both real and potential—of inappropriate, incorrect, ambiguous or otherwise defective translations' (p. 2). As well as setting out some specific examples from legal, political, and commercial texts, he surveys the landscape of legislative requirements. Byrne's conclusion—that translators should beware the 'potential for litigation' (p. 20)—is still valid today. In the eight years since his paper, the general propensity to litigate, at least in developed countries, seems ever-increasing, and we see translators' professional bodies offering their members both courses on liability and specially negotiated packages for professional liability insurance.[40]

Given the impact of an inadequate brief on translation quality, not to mention flaws in source texts, it seems propitious for legal translation practitioners to render their liability subject to these two points, if not also to the logistic constraints outlined in the following section.[41]

3.4. Logistical Constraints

Before closing this section on the constraints affecting the legal translation outsourcing process, there is a last set which, although not discussed a great deal in Translation Studies literature from a theoretical standpoint, nevertheless affects both translators' lives and, crucially, the quality of their output. I use the term 'logistical constraints' to cover those imperatives not linked to textual agency, and whose impact permeates right through the process.

---

[39] I intend to carry out further case law research regarding this key finding.

[40] As non-limiting examples: ITI (http://www.iti.org.uk/become-a-member/benefits/20-membership/672-towergate-professional-liability-insurance-for-iti-members), CIOL (https://www.ciol.org.uk/index.php?option=com_content&view=article&layout=coil:norelated&id=190&Itemid=639), and, in France, the *Syndicat national des traducteurs professionnels (sft)* (http://www.sft.fr/clients/sft/telechargements/news/fichier/1415_f2_repertoire_d'organisations_professionnelles.pdf).

[41] The holding of professional indemnity cover has a potential contribution to make to the differentiation of services, to enable the profession of legal translation practitioner to be consolidated, and I discuss this in a forthcoming paper.

The first of these is the amount of *time* allocated by the commissioner to the translation task. The second is the size of the *budget*, which may dictate the extent of proofreading, for example. Third, *file formats* can also seriously affect both the time needed for translation, and even quality. Confidentiality or availability constraints lead to many legal documents being supplied in PDF format, often non-modifiable scans, sometimes handwritten. The conversion of such formats may, depending on the conditions in which the translation is performed, lead to errors in critical numerical data—this can be avoided if the text is supplied in a format from which the figures can be directly extracted.

In her analysis of the current state of the translation profession, Drugan (2013, pp. 17–25) emphasizes the speed of change in translation logistics over the last decades—from hard copy deliveries exchanged by post or courier, taking several days, to the immediate electronic exchange of files. She emphasizes expectations of 'instant' translation, and cites practices such as splitting translation among several agents, including across time zones. Drugan then examines how increased pressure on translators owing to tighter deadlines leads to quality issues, and how downward price pressure in tandem with expectations of higher productivity is reducing their income (2013, pp. 19–20).

Similar trends came to light in a 2007 survey by Gouadec of '40 translation companies and twice as many freelancers in 11 European countries plus Morocco' (p. 199). He found that

> (a) tariffs have fallen 20 to 40% on average in real terms over the past ten years – though income has not fallen to the same extent, as productivity gains from IT tools have compensated to a certain degree – (b) deadlines are becoming ever tighter, and (c) processing the 'new types of materials' tends to take more and more time. (2007, p. 199).

From a Spanish perspective, Olvero-Lobo *et al.* maintain that a demanding translation market 'sets increasingly unrealistic and short deadlines and delivery dates, and the daily volume of translation is growing at an incredible rate' (2005, p. 135).

I will conclude with some words from a UK translation business—Capita Translation and Interpreting: 'It seems obvious that quality, cost and time are interconnected and that achieving the highest level of each of these elements is near impossible, but we all still expect this to a certain extent' (2015, p. 2).[42]

---

[42] Capita Translation and Interpreting, a limited company registered under number 5122429 in Oldham, UK, apparently a subsidiary of Capita PLC (linked from the latter company's main website). In December 2011, Capita took over, from Applied Language Solutions Ltd., a framework agreement to supply the UK Ministry of Justice with translation and interpreting services. There were considerable difficulties with that contract, which led to an investigation by the National Audit Office (https://www.nao.org.uk/wp-content/uploads/2015/01/The-Ministry-of-Justices-language-services-contract-Progress-update.pdf).

4

A Comprehensive Legal Translation Brief

> Translation without clear instructions is like swimming without water.
> —Nord (1997, p. 78)

As in many professions, before work can commence, legal translation practitioners need some *instructions* to inform them 'what should be done' (*Dictionary of Law*, Bloomsbury), or as a 'direction or guideline' [1] (*Black's Law Dictionary*). The scholars at the origin of functionalist principles (see section 1.2.3 [Chapter 1]) were mainly writing in German (Nord, 1997, p. 30), and used the word *Übersetzungsauftrag*, translated at that time variously as 'translation commission', 'translation assignment', and 'translating instructions' (Nord, 1997, p. 30). The first two alternatives suffer from a lack of precision since they may also refer to the work itself and not specifically to instructions given beforehand. The term 'job specifications' is offered by Gouadec (2007). However, in her 1997 *magnum opus*, Nord makes a compelling case for the use of the word 'brief', the original use of which she credits to Fraser (e.g., Fraser, 1996a, p. 73), and adopts that term henceforward, postulating that 'the translation brief specifies what kind of translation is needed' (Nord, 1997, p. 30). I follow Nord when she argues that the term is the most apt, and with regard to its suitability for the legal translation market I note that 'brief'

> implicitly compares the translator with a barrister who has received the basic information and instructions but is then free (as the responsible expert) to carry out those instructions as they see fit. (Nord, 1997, p. 30)

In subsequent sections of this chapter I draw from the literature and from practice to provide further grounds for the use of the term, and to reflect on the content of a legal translation brief. At all times it was essential to bear in mind that if a brief was to be theorized, it would have to speak to all market actors regarding the relevance of its components and even in the terminology used.

[1] '[. . .] concerning the law of the case'.

I begin, however, with a hypothesis, grounded in extensive professional experience, that the way in which self-employed legal translation practitioners are currently briefed is less than effective, particularly with regard to the consequences of briefing on the fitness-for-purpose of their output, where fitness-for-purpose is considered to be a measure of quality. It ought to be self-evident that if fitness-for-purpose is the yardstick, then that purpose should be known. To use a simple analogy—made-to-measure clothes can only fit if the size of the wearer is known when the order is placed.

4.1. Relevant Literature

4.1.1. THE TRANSLATION BRIEF AS PROPOSED BY NORD

My discussion of scholarship on briefing must necessarily begin with Nord, for a central concept in her extensive body of work on functionalist approaches to translation is that of the translation 'brief'. Her recommendation, made for all types of text—not specifically legal texts—is that a translation brief should consist of the following components:

- the (intended) text function(s),
- the target-text addressee(s),
- the (prospective) time and place of text reception,
- the medium over which the text will be transmitted, and
- the motive for the production or reception of the text. (1997, p. 60)

Regarding the intended text function, Nord refers to the classification of language functions identified by Jakobson (1960, pp. 350–377).[2] A distinction is drawn between the target text addressees—'the prospective receiver seen from the text producer's standpoint'—and 'the receiver[,] the person, group or institution that actually reads or listens to the text after it has been produced' (Nord, 1997, p. 22). For Nord, '[c]ommunication takes place through a *medium* and in situations that are limited in *time and place*' (1997, p. 1, emphasis added).[3] Although Nord (1997) does not specifically define '*motive*', she uses as a synonym the term 'reason' for production and reception. However, in a glossary included at the end of the book, the following is supplied:

[2] Referential, aesthetic/poetic, emotive, conative, phatic, metalingual.

[3] Nord refers to layout issues in connection with the *medium*. I will not discuss the 'medium' any further in this book, seeing it as a less relevant constraint in legal translation, although it might conceivably have relevance if legislation were to be translated and by the same occasion redrafted for the general public, if space were limited on a factsheet, for example.

Brief: definition of the *communicative purpose for which the translation is needed.* The ideal brief provides explicit or implicit information about the intended target-text function(s), the target-text addressee(s), the medium over which it will be transmitted, the prospective place and time and, *if necessary*, motive of production or reception of the text. (1997, p. 137, emphasis added)

Thus her final definition in this particular work determines that the brief *as a whole* sets out the communicative purpose[4] of the translated text, and relegates the 'motive' of production or reception to being included only where 'necessary'. It is difficult for me to see a clear semantic difference between 'purpose' and 'motive' in the preceding context. This definition of a model brief does not include a reference to genre, although Nord acknowledges the importance of 'genre conventions and norms in both text production and text reception' (1997, p. 53).

Nord claims that a number of requirements for translations can be 'inferred' from the brief (1997, p. 62). The suggestion that translators can 'infer' key information they require is recurrent in an earlier work (1991/2005), in which Nord sets out a detailed model for 'translation-oriented text analysis'.[5] That model comprises what Pym refers to as 'some 76 questions'[6] (2010, p. 48) to be asked by translators during the translation process.[7] However, in a legal context, the idea of using 'clues' or 'inferred' intentions, terms that are repeated throughout the preceding questions, seems hazardous to say the least. I suggest that dialogue with the commissioning client would be a far preferable—indeed essential—course of action.

Although specifications relating to genre do not form a part of Nord's five-point brief, she underscores the need for empirical data from surveys and questionnaires on the 'way in which audiences of particular genres [. . .] react to translated texts', as well as the need to bridge the gap between theory and practice (2013, p. 208).

---

[4]The concept of "communicative purpose', was first used to categorize genre and subsequently was broadened (Askehave & Swales, 2001). Bhatia takes a more pragmatic approach to this concept (e.g., 2014).

[5]Nord offers a model for use by students when preparing translations and 'in their professional life' (preface, 1991/2005). The four Jakobsonian functions are used as a 'systematic framework for the range of possible questions which can be asked regarding the situational factors' of a text (Nord, 2005, p. 47).

[6]In fact, because many of these 76 questions consist of several parts, the number is probably closer to 100, and, as Pym notes, they may be asked twice—both of the source and target texts (2010, p. 73).

[7]As Pym points out (2010, p. 58), this method may be helpful for student translators, but is unlikely to be possible within professional time constraints—Nord herself adds that 'the model for text analysis is not meant primarily for the professional translator' (1991/2005, p. 260).

4.1.2. BRIEFING AS VIEWED BY OTHER SCHOLARS

As early as 1995, Obenaus underlines the importance of proper briefing, and proactive behaviour by translators when working with commercial law firms:

> [T]he translation process should begin with a 'purpose interview' with the client. When you walk into a lawyer's office to sue somebody for breach of contract, a good lawyer will first give you advice and inform you of any other options that may be available to you before initiating legal proceedings. By the same token, a good translator should not just take the source text and translate away but determine the function of the translation first. (pp. 252–253)
>
> The translator's ability to identify key issues and ask the right questions before performing the actual translation is vital for the quality of the translation (p. 255)

Thus, unlike Nord (1991/2005), who focuses on inference using the text as a source of 'clues', Obenaus (1995) focuses on the relational aspect of translators' duties, and their responsibility to enter into dialogue. Questions are to be asked of the client, rather than of the text.

Translator involvement in processes within EU institutions has been extensively researched by Strandvik (2012, 2014, 2015, 2018, in press), who stresses the need to ensure that 'translation is not just perceived as an add-on, applied afterwards' (Strandvik, 2014, p. 226), and emphasizes the importance of 'appropriate translation briefs' (2014, p. 225). Few other legal translation studies scholars have looked at briefing *per se*, particularly where translators are not employed in-house.

We can, however, look to general Translation Studies scholarship, in particular Fraser who, as noted earlier, was cited by Nord as the first to have coined the term 'brief'.[8] Fraser notes that her findings 'suggest that the brief for the translation and the nature of the readership are of considerable importance in professional translation' (1996a, p. 73), and in another paper of the same year finds that 'The question of the brief was, however, also crucial' (1996b, p. 93). Fraser cites Jääskeläinen (1989), who posits that 'assigning a brief does produce more adequate translations' (1996a, p. 76).

A call to action regarding the importance of briefing hand-in-hand with a proactive attitude on the part of the translator, and the potential risks of intermediaries, comes from legal scholarship in the form of Kennedy (2000) who, addressing both lawyers and translators, propounds:

---

[8] In fact Nord (1997, p. 30) cites 'Fraser, 1995, p. 73', but does not list Fraser in her bibliography. It would appear that Nord is referring to p. 73 of Fraser's 1996 paper 'The Translator Investigated', published in the journal *The Translator*, referenced in this book as 1996a.

> Attorneys must provide '*product specifications*', the *purpose* and role of the document to be translated. Translators *should not translate without* this information. The translator and translation service *share the blame* with their client in failing to communicate and receive this information. One way that this can be achieved is by *direct communication* between a translator and a client, rather than indirect communication via a translation service's intermediary. (2000, p. 442, emphasis added)

It is noteworthy that Kennedy evokes generally improving 'communication between the translation industry's participants and its clients' (2000, p. 443), while concluding that 'no industry, country or organization can approach the legal translation problem [*sic*] alone' (2000, p. 444).

4.2. Briefing and Outsourcing in Practice

4.2.1. BRIEFING IN RELATED AND COMPARABLE BUSINESS SECTORS

The definition of 'brief' in *The Oxford Companion to Law* reads as follows:

> a document of instructions to counsel to appear in court including also the *papers relevant to the case, copies of pleadings, proofs of the evidence* of witnesses, etc. prepared and sent by the instructing solicitor. (Walker, 1980, p. 152, emphasis added)

The process of 'instructing' a lawyer or barrister to appear in court would be unthinkable without the provision of relevant documents. The principal-client thus provides the agent-lawyer with their requirements and with information the agent will need in order to aim for a satisfactory outcome—through the intermediary of a solicitor in some countries such as the United Kingdom, Australia, or Hong Kong. Where a lawyer's client is an individual, that client has the role of lay principal (see section 1.2.5 [Chapter 1]), and the expert lawyer-agent will elicit the information and documents they require to carry out their work. If the client is a corporation, in-house counsel may be able to act as expert buyers of the lawyer's service, depending on the complexity of the legal issue involved in the case. When lawyers purchase translation, they themselves become lay principals.

Briefs are not only used in the domain of the law, however. Advertising and copywriting are both professions that exhibit knowledge asymmetry between clients (principals) and the service provider (agent). When a company decides to procure the services of an advertising agency, one of its first actions is to establish a 'creative brief'. The Australian Government, in its Communication Unit guidelines,[9] describes the brief as follows:

---

[9] Retrieved from http://www.australia.gov.au.

> A good advertising brief will explain *why you need* an advertising activity; *define* as closely as possible the *objectives* of your advertising activity; and place your advertising into the *overall framework* of your communication activities. (undated, p. 2, emphasis added)

As in the previous example of the barrister, the theme of contextual information is considered important to a successful outcome, as well as the stating of purpose/aims.

Similarly, in its guidelines for commissioning a professional copywriter, the British Council advises as follows:

- Decide what the *objectives* of the piece are, what your message or messages are and how you want to communicate this to your audience.
- Brief the copywriter on our *tone of voice* [register] guidelines. [. . .]
- Refer them to our editorial guidelines and ensure they become familiar with them, so that they follow our *house style* rulings.
- Develop a relationship with a small number of copywriters. *Over time* they will become more and more *familiar* with our brand and our house style and this will ensure greater *consistency* over your suite of materials.
- Allow enough time and budget for proofing and re-writes. The Brand Team are *happy to be involved* at the proofing stages if required.
- Your copywriter should preferably speak English as their first language to ensure copy does not become localised.[10]

These guidelines contain several points that are also relevant when commissioning translation. In common with the advertising brief, we can see that, first and foremost, the aims of the commissioned item are to be specified. Here, however, the idea of 'familiarity' and a regular principal-agent relationship is raised—the usefulness, in particular as regards consistency, of having a service provider that is familiar with the customs and specificities of the commissioner. Lastly, the commissioner offers to be *involved* once the first draft has been produced, to make amendments or offer an opinion.

The management of copywriting as a way to 'enhance corporate credibility' was studied by Petelin, who recommends that, in order to be credible, organizations consider the following:

- *savvy hiring practices*;
- enlightened training practices;
- *insightful and responsible briefing processes*;
- *collaborative* designing processes;

[10] British Council website, 'Commissioning a copywriter'. Retrieved from http://brand.britishcouncil.org/tone-of-voice/commissioning-a-copywriter/ (emphasis added).

- transparent composing processes;
- accessible archiving practices;
- supervised *collaborative* writing processes;
- empathic mentoring practices. (2002, p. 173, emphasis added)

Regarding the briefing process in particular, Petelin stresses:

> It is crucial that managers brief writers from the outset of the document production process about the *intended readership, purpose, scope and dissemination* of the document. (2002, pp. 176–177, emphasis added)

She thus recommends a collaborative approach, as do the British Council guidelines, and underlines the importance of informing the text creator of, *inter alia*, the end-user and intended purpose of the text, all based on the caveat that failure to do so is likely to undermine corporate credibility—an asset that most organizations protect fiercely. By extension we can imagine how much the credibility of a law firm, company, or organization could be affected by an unsuccessful legal translation, in a best-case scenario where it does not have more serious and far-reaching effects.

The Partnership for Public Procurement, the largest procurement association in the world with a global community of over 94,000 in over 150 countries, disseminates a Specifications Practice document,[11] which recommends in particular: 'The characteristics of specifications for the provisions of services should state the outcome that the user wishes to achieve', 'explicit information' about requirements, and 'a clear statement of intended use' (2012, pp. 1–3).

From the preceding examples, readers will be able to discern recurrent themes—identification of aims, end-users, intended purpose, and contextual information—deemed to be essential criteria for the successful production of documents intended for communicative ends in a wide range of areas.

4.2.2. MARKET INITIATIVES ON TRANSLATOR BRIEFING FROM PROFESSIONAL BODIES AND INDIVIDUALS

Certain professional bodies have issued advice on the procurement of general translation—not specifically legal—aimed at translators and their clients.[12] In 2000, the United Kingdom's Institute of Translation and Interpreting (ITI) and the American Translators Association (ATA) published a pocket-sized 28-page guide, entitled *Translation: Getting It Right*, authored by Chris

---

[11] Dated 2012, downloadable from http://www.globalpublicprocurement.org/Documents/Resources/public-procurement-practices/SOPSpecifications.pdf.

[12] This section focuses on initiatives stemming from the English-speaking world, some of which were subsequently translated into other languages. It would be most interesting to explore and compare initiatives originating in other regions.

Durban.[13] The first foreign-language adaptation, in French, was disseminated by the *Société française des traducteurs* (SFT), and had five sponsors, including PricewaterhouseCoopers and Euronext Paris, thus embracing, to some extent, client stakeholders.

In 2008, this 28-page guide was reworked to produce an 8-page leaflet entitled *Translation: Buying a Non-Commodity—How Translation Standards Can Help Buyers and Sellers*, this time written by Durban in collaboration with Alan Melby, which was endorsed and published by 10 professional bodies in nine countries.[14] It contained the following note:

> *Getting it Right* is packed with useful information for purchasers of translation services, but was never intended to be exhaustive. This brochure, *Buying a Non-Commodity*, is the next step for translation buyers and sellers (both individuals and organizations).

The two pamphlets do not contain any template for a brief, and only the second contains a rough checklist in running text. In fact the advice, although including the soundest principles, is presented in rather an unsystematic way—which may well have been intentional for a variety of reasons. For the purposes of analysing how the briefing components from the second pamphlet could, based on the aspects of theory explored, feed into a brief for legal translation, in Table 4.1 I have aligned them with theoretical points broached in this book.[15]

In addition to the preceding guide distributed under its auspices, the ATA also offers its own *Client Outreach Kit,* which is unfortunately only available to ATA members, restricting its circulation and somewhat defeating its stated goal of widespread dissemination.[16] Much of the pack is devoted to the pitfalls of not using professional translators, with examples of translation errors, and it frequently cross-refers to the guide described earlier, *Getting it Right*. The remainder mainly emphasizes the importance of planning ahead.

The European Legal Interpreters and Translators Association (EULITA) is unusual insofar as it is a professional body specifically covering the *legal* translation and interpreting field, across several countries. Unfortunately, it

---

[13] It has been revised over the years; see Durban *et al.* (2014). Currently, 11 language versions are made available by the International Federation of Translators: Brazilian Portuguese, Catalan, Dutch, English, German, Greek, Icelandic, Italian, Japanese, Russian, and Spanish, as of 26 October 2014. Downloadable from http://www.fit-ift.org/?p=26.

[14] In Germany (BDÜ), UK (ITI), Italy (AITI), France (SFT), Holland (VZV), Spain (ASETRAD), Switzerland (ASTTI), USA (ATA, ILR), and Argentina (CTBA). I will not broach the extent to which these guides were/are disseminated to the translation profession or to clients, since, despite any prominence they may have in the community of translators, I consider that (a) they are not aimed directly at legal translation, and (b) that the extent of print runs/circulation is not an accurate indicator of the impact that they may have had.

[15] I have excluded some points as being outside the scope of this book: advice on the use of pictograms, typesetting, other points not pertaining to the legal field.

[16] Moreover, it is supplied with strict terms of use.

TABLE 4.1

Analysis of Briefing Components Described in *Translation: Buying a Non-Commodity*

Terms Used in *Translation: Buying a Non-Commodity*	Theoretical Area
Audience / intended readers	End-user
Purpose of the translation	Target text purpose
Subject area and type of document/text	Genre
Source language and regional variation	Source language variant
Target language and regional variation	Target language variant
Deadline	Logistics
Price	Logistics
Format (word processing file? XML?)	Logistics
Volume (how many words, characters, etc.)	Logistics

is open only to organizations and associations and not to individual professional linguists.[17] Historically it has been more focused on legal interpreting services, but more recently, following the QUALETRA project, published its *VADEMECUM for users of legal translations*.[18],[19] The two-page document seems to have rather mixed objectives.[20] It acts as a kind of charter ('adequate' remuneration, code of ethics, qualifications, and proofreading). It makes some tentative recommendations: 'should be able to have access to the relevant material of a translation assignment'; 'documents to be translated should be provided in a format that can be edited'; users 'should fix reasonable delivery times'; it cites 'reasonable working hours'. There is a questionable recommendation to use 'straightforward language'—which is not further defined—one also wonders to what extent it is possible to put this into practice. It seeks to raise awareness that 'legal systems of EU member states [lower case, *sic*] are very different'; 'there is therefore never full concordance of legal concepts'. In addition to the rather veiled objective(s) of the document, worsened by poor

[17] Mission statement: 'EULITA aims to bring together in its membership as full members the professional associations of legal interpreters and translators in the EU member states as well as the general associations that include legal interpreters and translators among their membership.' Despite mentioning individuals and associate membership, '[a]s associate members EULITA welcomes all interested organisations, institutions and individuals that are committed to the improvement of quality in legal interpreting and translation'. Following approaches I have made, this does not in fact appear possible.

[18] Available from: http://www.eulita.eu/sites/default/files/QUALETRA-Vademecum_final.pdf.

[19] EULITA's previous VADEMECUM has been disseminated since April 2010. It is interesting to note that the title 'Guidelines for a More Effective Communication with Legal Interpreters and Translators' belies the content, which relates exclusively to interpreting (http://www.eulita.eu/sites/default/files/VADEMECUM%20-%20Guidelines%20for%20a%20more%20effective%20communication%20with%20interpreters%20and%20translators.pdf).

[20] Some terminological confusion still subsists, without further clarification—see on page 1: 'Legal translators are translators of legal texts (*also called court interpreters/interpreters . . .*)', emphasis added.

graphical presentation,[21] it is regrettable that the text was not written in a more assertive tone—it includes a number of hedges.[22] The term 'users of translations' in the title is perhaps unfortunate in view of its apparent objectives, and does nothing to enhance professional status—a focus on how properly to instruct professional translators would have been preferable.

Other translators' professional bodies have published advisory aids that place the onus for action on the translator rather than the client, such as *Questions to Ask ITI 39 Steps*.[23] In terms of proactive attitudes, including when receiving commissions, there are a number of high-profile translators, promoting translator professionalization by speaking regularly at international events and on radio broadcasts as well as via podcasts, blogs, journal columns, and books (e.g., Durban, 2010; Jenner & Jenner, 2010; McKay, 2011). Most of these initiatives seem aimed mainly at the community of translators rather than clients, and generally do not relate specifically to the legal specialism. My searches have not brought to light any lawyers' professional bodies issuing guidelines on translation procurement.[24]

4.2.3. LEGAL TRANSLATION PROCUREMENT INITIATIVES BY SERVICE PROVISION INTERMEDIARIES AND BY INSTITUTIONS, INCLUDING DIFFERENTIATION

Translation agencies sometimes produce web pages or even multi-page guides to advise clients on translation procurement. Such texts are often a combination of summary information on procurement and a sales and marketing tool. They may even be produced in the form of a 'training' webinar. Institutional and corporate procurement materials are generally less easy to obtain from 'outside', but one example, *Writing for Translation*, published by the Translation Centre for the Bodies of the European Union, although focused mainly on good drafting principles, does also state that the translator needs 'background information', defined primarily as

- technical terms used previously;
- other documents/correspondence relating to the matter;
- official document references and sources;
- contact information as a dialogue enabler. (Piehl & Vihonen, 2010, p. 15)

---

[21] As compared with the legal interpreters' *Vademecum* with clearly stated sections, available at: http://www.eulita.eu/sites/default/files/VADEMECUM%20-%20Guidelines%20for%20a%20more%20effective%20communication%20with%20interpreters%20and%20translators.pdf.

[22] 'as far as reasonable and feasible', 'wherever possible'.

[23] http://www.literatus.gr/files/39%20Golden%20Steps%20to%20Translation.pdf.

[24] On legal interpreting, there is an initiative by the Law Society of England & Wales in the form of a Practice Note, *Use of Interpreters in Criminal Cases*, retrieved from http://www.lawsociety.org.uk/support-services/advice/practice-notes/interpreters-in-criminal-cases/.

Certain service provision intermediaries offer differentiated levels of service, often with an 'advisory' tone in their presentation. Table 4.2 shows service levels offered by an arbitrary selection of translation agencies, one generalist and two specializing in legal work.[25] The examples are intended simply to give a flavour of market initiatives. Many more can be found by carrying out a simple online search.

A cursory examination shows a lack of correspondence between the service levels offered.[26] Even when we try to draw similarities, some elements differ. It is not always clear whether self-employed translators or in-house personnel will carry out the translation, and it is often ambiguous whether proofreading is performed by one and the same person or by a second person. Different nomenclature is used for similar services. No criteria are given to qualify such terms as 'expert', 'specialist' or 'highly experienced'.

4.3. Relational Aspects of Briefing

4.3.1. THE LEGAL TRANSLATION PRACTITIONER AS A HUB

Figure 4.1 emphasizes the legal translator's position as an interface between the actors associated with the source text and those associated with the target text. The translator's agency is a crucial enabler in communication between the two groups, negotiating languages, legal systems, textual genres, and purpose, whilst they act as guardians of the crux of the text.

In the light of the preceding, it is even more surprising that external legal translation practitioners seem unlikely to have direct contact with most of the actors, apart from those commissioning their work, or even know who the target text actors are.[27] Nevertheless, if the legal translator's agency is hampered and/or their output not fit for purpose, this can lead to serious consequences and at the very least high-risk situations. If legal translators were empowered and such

---

[25] Lingo24 Ltd. (UK) markets itself as a generalist: 'Whether your content is technical, legal, financial or specialist in any other way, we'll find qualified and experienced translators that are right for the job'. Retrieved 26 December 2015 from http://www.lingo24.com/services.html.

Absolute Translations (UK), state: 'As one of the main specialist legal translation companies in the UK, we currently provide over 200 solicitors and law firms with specific translators and interpreters specialising in the legal field'. Retrieved 26 December 2015 from http://www.absolutetranslations.com/en/translation_service/.

Geotext Translations (US, EU, Hong Kong) market themselves exclusively to legal professionals: 'Geotext was established to serve the legal community exclusively. Legal translation is not a subdivision of our company, but the primary focus of our business.' Retrieved 26 December 2015 from http://www.geotext.com/about-geotext.

[26] Other services offered may include, for example: For Information Purposes Only (FIPO) translation; foreign language optical character recognition; language identification; document production including formatting to mirror original files; summary translation; e-discovery support; on-site staffing; or multilingual lawyer or attorney review services.

[27] See in this regard section 5.5.2.e (Chapter 5).

TABLE 4.2

Comparison between Service Levels Offered by Service Provision Intermediaries

Service(s) Provided	Lingo24 Ltd.	Absolute Translations	Geotext Translations
Translation by a specialist then proofread by a second specialist	**Level 3: Professional translation** Translation of content by a *native, professional translator* with separate editing by *another*. Ideal when accuracy is paramount, and when you need content translated by someone with *specialist* knowledge of your sector.	**Specialist Translation and Proofreading** The translation will be carried out and proof read [*sic*] by a *professional translator*. The translation will then be proof read [*sic*] by a *second independent translator.* Our expert translator will be matched to the *specialist* subject of your document.	**Certified/Sworn Translation** Produced by a *highly experienced linguist* who is an *expert* in the language pair and subject matter. A supplemental, line-by-line review for accuracy from a *second expert linguist* before being finalized by our QA (quality assurance) team.
Translated by a specialist then proofread by a generalist		**Specialist Translation** The translation will be carried out and *proof read* [*sic*] *by a professional translator.* Our expert translator will be matched to the specialist subject of your document.	**Geotext Translation** Produced by a linguist who is an expert in both language pair and subject matter. Every Geotext translation is *copy edited* [*sic*] *and proofread* in-house by Geotext's expert QA (quality assurance) professionals.
Translated by a generalist and proofread by a generalist		**Standard Translation and Proofreading** The translation will be carried out and proof read [*sic*] by a professional translator. The translation will then be proof read by a second independent translator.	
Translated and proofread by one person only	**Level 2: Basic translation** Translation of content by a native speaker of your target language. This is ideal when human sensitivity is important, but where price trumps perfection.	**Standard Translation** The translation will be carried out and proof read [*sic*] by a professional translator.	
Machine translation (optional post-editing)	**Level 1: Machine Translation** An ultra low cost, real-time translation tool. And we think it beats Google Translate for quality, confidentiality, regular updates or large volumes of content, and when the business case doesn't justify using a professional translator.		**Machine Translation** Geotext offers machine translation (MT) with optional post-editing, which can be useful when cost is of particular concern or there is not enough time to produce a human translation. Translations intended for production, publication, and/or court or tribunal submission, however, should always be produced by human translators.

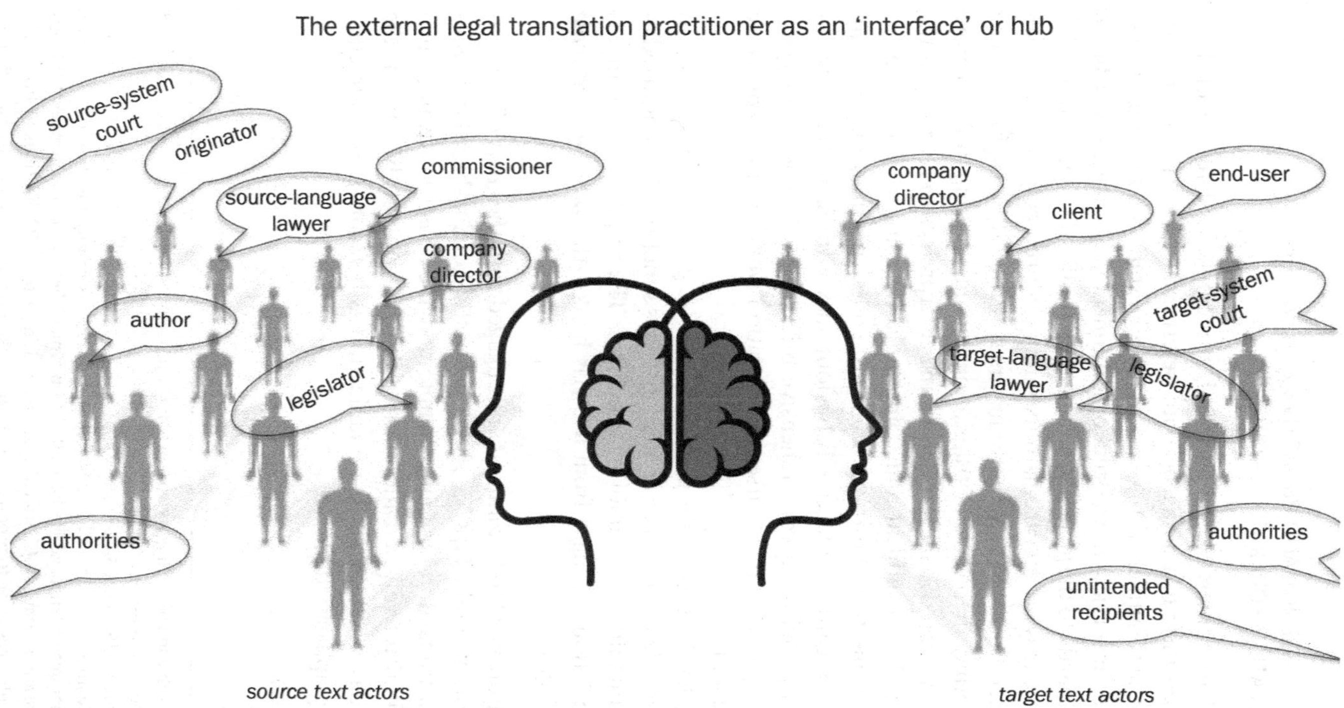

FIGURE 4.1. The external legal translation practitioner as an 'interface' or 'hub'.

a 'hub' status recognized, it would render the results of their (complex) labours far more effective.

4.3.2. RELATIONAL AGENCY AND PROACTIVE BEHAVIOUR TO STIMULATE INFORMATION FLOWS

How legal translators interface, notably with principals, and report on how they have exercised their textual agency can be crucial—for example, if there are errors and/or ambiguities in the source text. Despite the fact that translators providing their services as external practitioners may have a subordinate position—owing partly to the general status of their profession (see section 1.1.3 [Chapter 1]) and partly to precarious outsourcing contracts, professionalism surely requires them to act in a proactive manner. As noted by Inghilleri: 'The current focus on ethics in the field of translation and interpreting looks to more pro-active ways for professional translators and interpreters to respond to the complex social, political, ethical and communicative nature of their tasks' (2010, p. 192).[28] Some translators' associations' codes of ethics may contain provisions in this regard.[29] Proactive behaviour may consist in boosting information flows by eliciting a comprehensive brief from the client, querying whenever necessary during the course of translation work, and by requesting feedback (Figure 4.2).

Clearly, the level of empowerment granted or grasped—the extent to which the translator feels his or her textual agency is sanctioned or endorsed—is critical in maintaining such information flows. The importance of this is voiced by a translation manager from a Swiss bank—the *Banque Cantonale Vaudoise*—who urges,

> [...] translators need to be *aware of* and engaged with the *goals* of the content they translate and adapt. [...] [C]ollaborative, dialog-based processes can empower translators, enabling them to take the constructive, informed risks that will drive value creation in multilingual content. Because at the end of the day, multilingual communication is a *team sport*. (Jemielity, 2012, p. 49, emphasis added)

---

[28] There may be value in researching to what extent the proactive supply of services is widespread across all industries, so as to position translation.

[29] Examples from the UK: point 3.4 of the Code of Professional Conduct, Institute of Translation and Interpreting, 'Members shall draw the attention of their clients to any significant ambiguities, errors, omission or imprecise language in the material on which they work' (September 2013 version); Code of Professional Conduct, Chartered Institute of Linguists, 4.1 Obligations to Principals, 'Practitioners shall at all times strive to produce work of the highest standard, and shall ensure that the Principal is aware of any factor that may affect the standard of the work produced' (November 2007 version, as amended in 2008 and 2012).

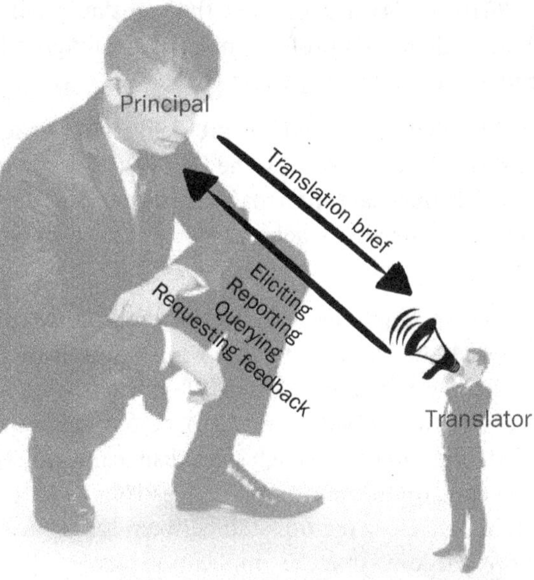

FIGURE 4.2. Information flows relating to the legal translation brief.

This principal is fully aware of the benefits offered by a collaborative relationship with translators. Equally, the translators themselves need to take ownership of relationships with their clients. The concept of 'relational agency' coined by Edwards (2005, 2010) can illuminate this aspect further,[30] in order to emphasize the legal translator's status as a skilled professional to be respected. She pinpoints the intersection of 'practice boundaries' where two or more professions are 'involved in accomplishing tasks together' (2010, p. 46). In the case of outsourced legal translation we may evoke, for instance, boundaries between sole traders and firms or organizations, boundaries between translation and legal professions, and boundaries between linguistic and legal knowledge. Although Edwards warns that these spaces can be 'uncomfortable places to be' (2010, p. 43), for various reasons, including power imbalances, she points out that engaging in collaborative working practices can have very positive outcomes. However, she notes that practitioners 'need to be able to label their own expertise' and 'demonstrate a strong sense of their own identities as practitioners whose actions can make a difference in the world' (2010, p. 1).

By not simply absorbing, in a passive and unquestioning manner, the demands made by clients, but by engaging in what Edwards calls 'purposeful

[30] Defined by Edwards thus: 'as professionals work in and between work settings and interact with other practitioners and clients to negotiate interpretations of tasks and ways of accomplishing them' (2010, p. 13).

practices' (e.g., 2010, p. 74), I posit that the translator will enter into a virtuous circle whereby their own professionalism is highlighted and more highly valued. Fraser makes the following comparison:

> [I]n most fields where professionals are delivering services – we expect to be asked a series of questions by the [. . .] doctor or other professional, designed to elicit the exact information they need if they are to meet our requirements or, indeed, to help us understand our own requirements. (2001, p. 35)

For legal translators, such a 'series of questions' could correspond to elucidating all aspects that should be contained in the translation brief. Relational agency also intersects with the previously described concepts of goal divergence and goal congruence, since it involves 'working together purposefully towards goals [. . .], and using the resources that each specialism can bring to bear' (Edwards, 2010, p. 61). She calls upon the work of Engeström to emphasize the importance of 'maintaining a close relationship between longer-term goals [. . .] and day-to-day actions', arguing that the 'implications for [. . .] professional agency are strong' (Edwards, 2010, p. 50):

> Human agency gains unusual powers when future-oriented activity-level envisioning and consequential action-level decision-making, come together in close interplay. (Engeström, 2005, p. 313)

The parallel with the 'envisioning' of the target text and the translation strategy to be selected is self-evident. As in the outsourced legal translation market, Engeström's object of study embraces complex international 'knotworking'[31] which takes place within different types of organizational units or entities, and involves various individual agents (2005).

4.3.3. LEVELS OF INTERPRETIVE AUTONOMY

In terms of how the legal translator's textual agency is perceived, and with the ultimate aims of empowerment and a more specific brief, the interdisciplinary[32] concept of 'interpretive autonomy' conceived by Ng (2014) is pertinent:

> Interpretive autonomy refers to how [the extent to which] independently translated legal material can stand on its own in the new linguistic environment of the target language [and in law] without referring back to the source language. (Ng, 2014, pp. 54–55, my insertions)

---

[31] Knotworking: 'work organization in which collaboration between the partners is of vital importance, yet takes shape without strong predetermined rules or central authority' (Engeström, 2005, p. 318).

[32] Having its basis in comparative law, sociology, and translation.

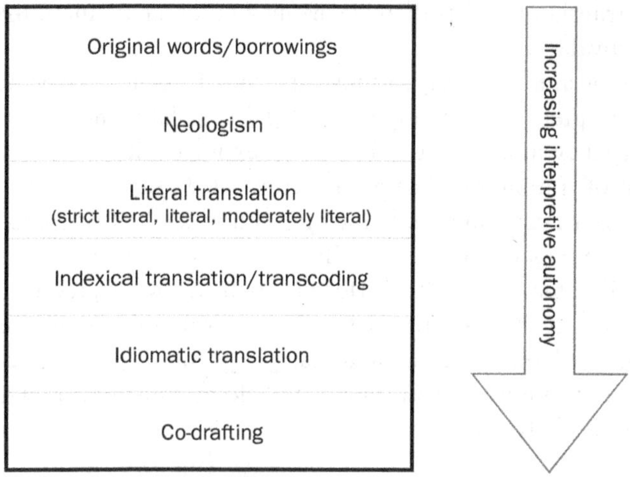

FIGURE 4.3. View of translation techniques used in legal documents.
Source: after Ng (2014, p. 55).

The term, and indeed the concept, is composed of elements which ought to speak relatively clearly to legal professionals commissioning translation, since the 'interpretation' of the law is the bedrock of their occupation. Figure 4.3 shows Ng's ordering of translation techniques according to increasing interpretive autonomy on the part of the translator.

Ng defines idiomatic legal translation as 'an act of ceding a substantial share of interpretive control [from the source language] to the target language' (Ng, 2014, p. 59, my parentheses). Insofar as Ng situates idiomatic translation between 'indexical translation',[33] and co-drafting where there is full collaboration between legal drafters and translators, 'idiomatic' legal translation may be viewed as corresponding to a great deal of outsourced work.

By the same token, we may see legal translation as a delegation of interpretive control to the legal translator. Ng claims that the 'long-standing approach of treating translation as solely textual, coupled with the concomitant ideal of equivalence, clearly fails adequately to capture what is happening on the ground' (2014, p. 63). Might we then shift our focus from the text to the translator-agent who has a given amount of power to interpret the text? If 'the notion of equivalence can be justifiably argued as a view interested in preserving the supremacy of the source language' (Ng, 2014, p. 63), then any translation work is by the same token 'downgraded'. Would it not be more productive for us to educate commissioners to decide what degree of autonomy they wish to

[33] Indexical translation: the target text does not stand alone, but points to an indexed item. If we need to refer to the original source for information or authority, the status of the translation remains

afford their translator, rather than idealizing an ultimately unattainable goal of so-called equivalence?

It is important, however, to underline that I do not advocate extending unlimited interpretive autonomy to the legal translator, but rather to render the latter's agency more effective by stating explicitly, in the translation brief, what degree of autonomy is being imparted—for example with reference to the covert–overt positioning described in section 2.4.3 (Chapter 2),[34] and depending on the target text purpose. Thus overt legal translations, such as certificates or diplomas, could be performed with a low degree of interpretive autonomy, while covert legal translations (e.g., terms and conditions to be published and to be binding in the target language) would be carried out with a higher degree of interpretive autonomy and closer consultation with the client and/or their legal advisors.[35]

4.4. Towards a Tailored Brief for the Legal Translation Context

In the light of all of the discussions set out thus far, I will now review the various theoretical components to be included in a brief for the outsourced legal translation context.[36] I must point out that the brief as described in this section relates to the technical instructions required by the translator to carry out his or her work. It does not correspond to the logistic and commercial terms usually set out in a purchase order, which might typically contain deadlines, language pair, and tariff.[37] I posit that the 'translation brief' is often confused with a purchase order, and this misconception is explored in sections 5.5.2.a, 5.5.2.i (Chapter 5), and as part of my survey findings.

From a functionalist viewpoint, Nord's 'intended text function(s)' (1997) must be judged an indispensable component of the brief (see section 2.4.1 [Chapter 2]). While speculating on the terminology that might best speak to commissioners, we may also consider merging this with Nord's 'motive' or 'reason', and borrow as an umbrella term what other authors[38] have referred to as the '*intended purpose*'. It seems unlikely that lawyers or other actors commissioning translations would possess, or need to possess, sufficient technical

accessory. In the business and judicial contexts where self-employed legal translators mainly operate, the source text is rarely available or accessible to, or usable by, those receiving translations.

[34] See also Scott (forthcoming).

[35] Future work might consist of studying which (sub)genres are suited to which degrees of interpretive autonomy, in particular non-legislative genres, since one of the key focuses of Ng's work so far (2014) is legislative.

[36] My final proposal for a legal translation briefing template is presented in Chapter 5, after the survey data and findings.

[37] These logistic and commercial terms are nevertheless included in the full template presented in Chapter 5.

[38] Cao (2007); Chromà (2008); House (2015); Pym (2010).

knowledge to stipulate the *linguistic* function required (i.e., appellative, referential, conative, etc.), so it seems judicious to dispense with that component. Additionally, in a legal translation context, Nord's 'medium' (e.g., channel, layout, brochure) may not warrant being singled out as a component as such, but could fall under the 'purpose' component if the need arose.

A second necessary component is the definition of receivership (see section 2.4.2 [Chapter 2]). Nord refers to 'target-text addressee(s)' (1997), while Mayoral Asensio finds that the latter term is 'not easily applied to official translation' and not well defined, suggesting instead the term 'recipient' (2003, p. 10). As noted earlier, Nord herself distinguished between 'addressees', understood to be provided directly with the text by the translator, and 'receivers'[39], understood as the ultimate readers of that text (1997, p. 22). However, the direct recipient/receiver of the translator's work may well be an intermediary of some kind, and/or not necessarily the person for whose use the translation is intended (see Chain of Supply, section 1.1.7 [Chapter 1]). I offer the term '*end-user*', once again as a term that might speak more clearly to the market.

There are some additional points not included by Nord (1997) that might usefully complete a legal translation brief. As already noted in this book, the *applicable law(s)* relating to the source and target texts in question is(are) an ineluctable component of a properly formulated legal translation brief. This knowledge will enable the translator to select appropriate terms and/or explicitation for legal concepts found in the text, and may even affect the text's macrostructure, or have other consequences. It is important to note in this regard that the law governing the text may correspond to the law of the country of origin of the source, the law of the country where the target text is to be performed/enacted/binding or received, or any legal system selected[40] by the parties. Equally, if the purpose of the translation is a 'pivot', for subsequent translation into another language, the legal concepts may require specific handling. Where no instruction has been given on this issue, the translator should make a chosen strategy plain, and record this, to avoid any debacle at a later date.

The genre may be self-evident from the document, but in some cases it may not. Consider, for example, financial documents, elements of tender packages, or reports. We have seen in sections 2.3 (Chapter 2) and 3.2.3 (Chapter 3) the relevance for translators of genre awareness. I therefore posit that there is value in eliciting from the commissioner or principal the '*text type*'.[41] I choose the term bearing in mind once again the need for clarity for market actors.

---

[39] Also used by Šarčević (2000).

[40] E.g., as part of 'forum shopping'.

[41] I have chosen this term, as used by Cao (2007), notwithstanding Trosborg's arguments whereby text types cut across genres (1997b, p. 12), for optimum communication with market actors, and for

As discussed in section 3.2.4 (Chapter 3) on intertextuality and interdiscursivity, *reference documents* such as case files, cross-reference material, laws, technical information, previous translations, style guides, endorsed/required glossaries, acronyms, websites, and so on, are of great importance. The *(legal) status* of the target text should also be specified (see sections 2.4.2 [Chapter 2] and 4.2.3) and it may well affect the translator profile[42] to be chosen and/or determine how language is used—in the case of translations for gist, for example. The brief should specify which *language variant* is used in the source text—it may not be immediately obvious—and which variant is to be used in the target text, which may in certain cases be enmeshed with the law applying to the text(s).

Lastly, the brief should state the extent to which a literal or target-oriented approach is preferred—in other words it should define the 'opacity' of the translation. Literal translation may suit, for example, texts destined for the study of comparative law or official certified translations, whereas a target-oriented approach may be more appropriate for texts intended for publication or signature in the target language. This point could be articulated for commissioners by using *covert-overt* positioning (see section 2.4.3 [Chapter 2]).

Nord's 'time and place of reception' (1997), is a thornier issue in the field of legal translation. Regarding spatial deixis, the same translation may be sent to shareholders in five countries, sharing the same language but not the same legal system and therefore not having the same legal cultural view. It may also be sent first to one 'recipient' and then, owing to a change in circumstances, forwarded to another. Temporal deixis is equally unstable: for example, once translated for signature, a contract may then, three years later, be the subject of a dispute, and may be used in litigation proceedings. Hence, since a legal translator and often also the commissioner are not in a position to know the 'future of the text', one solution could be to '*indelibly mark*' on the document itself the purpose for which the translation was briefed and performed, and/or its 'status'.[43] I provide three examples in Figures 4.4, 4.5 and 4.6, retrieved from the public websites of the authorities and institutions in question.[44]

---

that reason, follow Nord in treating 'genre' and 'text type' as synonymous (1991/2005, p. 15). To avoid any misinterpretation, I must also point out that there is a close link between 'genre' and 'purpose'. Trosborg, for example, asserts that genre categories are defined by communicative purpose (1997b, pp. 3–24). It is thus vital to emphasize that the discussions in this section relate to the most suitable terms for clear and effective communication with the market, and not to terms as they are used by Translation Studies scholars.

[42] This might include machine translation in some specific instances (see section 1.1.6 [Chapter 1]).

[43] See, amongst others, Samuelsson-Brown (2010, p. 111). Other information such as the date of the translation and the name of the translator might also be included.

[44] Financial Supervisory Authority of Norway: http://www.finanstilsynet.no/Global/English/Laws_and_regulations/Regulations/Regulations_Responsibility_Internal_Control.pdf; Luxembourg

KREDITTILSYNET **The Financial Supervisory Authority of Norway** Translation as of October 2004 Translated by Government Authorised Translator Peter Thomas. *This translation is for information purposes only. Legal authenticity remains with the official Norwegian version as published in Norsk Lovtidend.*

FIGURE 4.4. Indelible marking: statement of translation purpose, status, name of translator, and date, Financial Supervisory Authority of Norway.

MEMORIAL	*Unofficial English translation*
Official Journal of the Grand Duchy of Luxembourg	
Compendium of legislation	
A — Number 73 7th of June 2005	
Law of 30 May 2005	

FIGURE 4.5. Indelible marking: unofficial translation status, Luxembourg legislation, made available on the website of the national data protection authority.

33. The Framework Convention for the Protection of National Minorities and related instruments have been translated for the purposes of their implementation and better information of the society of the purposes of this Convention. The translated Convention is available at official web portals of the Ministry of Reintegration and the joint web-site of the Council on Tolerance and Civil Integration under the President Office and UN Association of Georgia[49].

FIGURE 4.6. Indelible marking: statement on translation purpose, Council of Europe Second Report (2012).

Such permanent references to the criteria according to which a translation was performed could significantly reduce the problems that arise when purposes intended at the outset change: for example, when texts translated for information purposes only are subsequently adopted as legally binding.

Hence, a skeleton structure of a brief to instruct legal translators might be based on the following list. As regards the order of the components, I suggest separating questions relating to the source text from those relating to the target text, for although translators and translation scholars focus on the 'mapping' of various aspects of the two texts, commissioners are more likely to view as discrete entities the text they currently hold and the text they wish to receive.

---

legislation: http://www.cnpd.public.lu/fr/legislation/droit-lux/doc_loi30052005_en.pdf; Council of Europe Second Report: https://www.coe.int/t/dghl/monitoring/minorities/3_fcnmdocs/PDF_2nd_SR_Georgia_en.pdf.

Preliminary list of Legal Translation Brief Components

- intended purpose of source text—why was it written;
- text type (genre) of source and target texts;
- source text status (legally binding or not, courtesy, etc.);
- reference material, particularly including intertextual/interdiscursive elements;
- the legal system(s) and law(s) governing the source and target texts;
- language variant(s) of the source and target texts;
- intended purpose of target text—why is it being translated;
- end-user of target text;
- target text status (legally binding or not, courtesy, etc.);
- (c)overtness of the target text.

Regarding terms to be used in the briefing template when communicating with commissioners/clients, I propose '*document for translation*' instead of 'source text', and '*translated text*' instead of target text—once again in order to speak clearly to market actors. The preceding list should also take into account the complex Chain of Supply (section 1.1.7 [Chapter 1]), possibly harvesting the information required from more than one actor. Indeed, it would be most useful for the brief to contain contact details whenever possible for the drafter of the source text, to enable the translator to resolve any uncertainties or queries that might arise during translation. Where the drafter is not in a position to make decisions regarding the target text, access to a decision-maker should be provided.

It should be noted that such a legal translator's brief goes no further than the minimum requirements for a lawyer's brief or for a creative agency's/copywriter's brief—which, without exception, include the papers relevant to the case/assignment, why the work is needed; listed and defined objectives; and placing the job into its overall framework. As noted throughout this book, legal translators cannot be expected to work effectively without this information.

5

A Triangulated Survey of the Outsourcing of Legal Translations to External Practitioners

> Knowledge of the audience and purpose of the
> translation could have had a major effect
> on the (usefulness of the) translation.
>
> —Participant 232T, *original parentheses*

The survey described in this chapter sought to explore the outsourcing of legal translation through two questions related to briefing: How does the briefing process work within the outsourced legal translation environment? Are legal translation principals and/or translators working as external practitioners satisfied with that process? And it considered two questions related to performance: Do the principals express any issues vis-à-vis the performance of translations received? Do such legal translation principals and/or translators have any suggestions to improve performance?

5.1. Research Paradigms and Methodology

First, it is important to underline the fact that this research has been carried out (1) by a practitioner, (2) in order to improve practice where possible, and (3) to improve the 'situation in which the practice takes place' (Robson, 2011). These three criteria place the project in the broad category of 'action research', for Robson (2011), among others. A fourth feature can be added to these in order to complete this definition of action research—'the improvement of *understanding* of practice by its practitioners' (Carr & Kemmis, 1986, p. 165, original emphasis). More specifically, the process is an example of 'practitioner research'[1] (Cochran-Smith & Donnell, 2006) or 'insider research' carried out by a researcher 'who possesses intimate knowledge of the community and its

[1] Other terms include 'participatory action research', 'practitioner-led inquiry', or 'community action research'.

members' (Drake with Heath, 2011, p. 1, citing Hellawell, 2006, p. 483). In my daily life, I inhabit two worlds, those of academia and practice, reconciling their diverse needs. Like many of my fellow professional legal translators, I am also located in the 'no-man's land' between the fields of linguistics and the law (see in this regard Goddard, 2010, and Balkin & Levinson, 2006). On the positive side, my professional network, as a legal translator of 25 years' experience, was a key enabler for data collection, as will be discussed in section 5.3.2.

The lack of 'cross-fertilization' between lawyers and translators means that the Translation Studies researcher comes up against many barriers when attempting to obtain data from the legal field. This is in addition to the obstacles generally arising when academic researchers attempt to access professional discourse practices, and which have been amply discussed in the literature.[2] Nonetheless, the positive outcomes of academic-practice partnerships are often stated beyond academia, even in the press and by governments. A practitioner-researcher (or researcher-practitioner) may thus be deemed to be privileged. In fact, they 'must take great pains in order for their research to be accepted as sufficiently robust, and may be mistrusted by both "sides"—by academia for not having a sufficiently proven "track record", and by practitioners for no longer being "one of them"'.[3] Other restraints to practitioner research have been pointed out by Maclachlan and St. Clair (2008), in particular that 'sustaining [research] with no concomitant reduction in workload is exceptionally difficult'. They postulate that this issue might be mitigated by funding and/or study leave.

Table 5.1 sets out a number of potential perils to be borne in mind when undertaking practitioner research, extracted, where pertinent, from Denscombe (2007), together with the measures that I took to address them.

Last but not least, it is important to broach the ethical issues relating to action research. I reproduce in the following the four key requirements laid down by Winter (2005), developed by Denscombe (2007, p. 129):

- The development of the work must remain visible and open to suggestions from others.
- Permission must be obtained before making observations or examining documents produced for other purposes.
- Description of others' work and points of view must be negotiated with those concerned before being published.
- The researcher must accept responsibility for maintaining confidentiality.

---

[2] E.g., Welch, Marschan-Piekkari, Penttinen, & Tahvanainen (2002); Okumus, Altinay, & Roper (2007); Kaur Johl & Renganathan (2010).

[3] Scott (2015b).

TABLE 5.1
Addressing the Perils of Practitioner Research

Disadvantages of Action/Practitioner Research as Analysed by Denscombe (2007, pp. 129–131)	Measures Taken to Address Such Disadvantages
The practitioner's involvement restricts the scope and scale of the research due to a 'worksite' bias.	This study did not take place within a specific worksite, and had a global scope.
Ownership of the research is contestable owing to a partnership relationship between practitioner and researcher.	Although certain informants were sought out by leveraging my network, actual clients formed only a negligible number. Furthermore, no funding or other assistance was provided by such sources for the research project.
Action research tends to involve an extra burden of work for practitioners.	This was a significant difficulty during the course of the project, in particular because it was self-funded.
The researcher is likely to have a vested interest in findings and cannot be 'detached' as traditionally required by scientific disciplines or by positivist paradigms.	Whilst the author has an interest in the professionalization of legal translators and improving the quality of processes, the outcomes of this project would not give rise to any personal gains.
Practitioners cannot escape the 'web of meanings' of their practice community due to their 'insider knowledge', and outsiders may have alternative perspectives.	The use of the qualitative data analysis software NVivo was deployed in order to ensure that the data were examined from as wide a range of perspectives as possible, using internal tools such as compound queries and matrices, and by using corpus-derived methods such as word frequency lists.
Findings cannot be generalized beyond a specific 'case'.	The project was conceived as a first foray into the operation of a hitherto relatively unexplored segment of the translation market in order to make some initial suggestions for the improvement of practice, to be subsequently discussed, trialled, and built upon. It does not set out to provide definitive or quantitative conclusions.

Regarding the first point, the work was always intended to be made publicly available. The second point does not relate specifically to this research, and the responses examined were provided expressly for the study. Concerning the remainder, informed consent was obtained, and the data were anonymized. Moreover, the tools involved in the data collection phase were examined in detail by a university ethics committee (see section 5.3.1).

As already mentioned, no previous research seems to have concentrated on the outsourced legal translation market and its operation. I was thus unable to take counsel from the literature regarding the most suitable methodology for this specific area. I have adopted a mixed methods approach based largely on a qualitative stance, whilst incorporating certain numerical elements. My main reasons for choosing the qualitative route comprise the following: an aim of exploration rather than measurement; the project is a first foray; my subjective position as market stakeholder. Lastly, the difficulties of accessing informants in the niche market of legal translation made probability or random sampling impracticable.

Notwithstanding the preceding, the final paradigm should be described as 'mixed methods' or 'multi-strategy design',[4] seen to offer the following potential benefits relevant to the survey: a more complete, comprehensive picture of the topic at hand; answering several research questions to address a wider range of issues than would be possible with a single-method design; the ability to deal with the complex setting of 'real world research' (Robson, 2011, p. 167).

In the introduction to this chapter, the reader will have noted that two groups were targeted as informants. With the aim of rendering the findings as robust as possible, I applied the concept of triangulation.[5] Four forms of triangulation have been established: 'data triangulation', which may entail sampling differences either relating to informants, or to time, space, social, or geographical situation; 'investigator triangulation', with more than one researcher involved in collection and/or interpretation; 'theoretical triangulation', where several theoretical positions are applied; and finally, 'methodological' triangulation, where several methods for data collection are used.[6]

In this study, data triangulation was effected by 'mirroring' the questions asked of one group (principals) by questions asked of the other (translators), and methodological triangulation was implemented to an extent by using both closed and open questions. The aim was therefore to improve the accuracy of findings, rather than providing a fuller picture (Denscombe, 2007), although the latter occurred as a by-product of the process.

5.2. Scope and Environment

Two groups formed the focus of the survey—on the one hand, those outsourcing legal translation, and on the other, those to whom it is outsourced.[7] To use language from agency theory (see Chapter 1), one group comprises 'principals',

---

[4] Robson (2011); Brannen (2005). Despite the so-called incompatibility thesis, which states that qualitative and quantitative approaches are distinct paradigms that are incompatible with each other (Howe, 2003, pp. 29–45), many theorists have supported multi-strategy designs, and this third paradigm is now thoroughly established (e.g., Creswell, 2009; Nagy Hesse-Biber, 2010).

[5] 'Triangulation refers to the use of more than one approach to the investigation of a research question in order to enhance confidence in the ensuing findings' (Bryman, 2004, pp. 1142–1143). This measure was taken following feedback expressed at a conference presentation by a Legal Translation Studies scholar, also a practicing translator, Dr G. Pontrandolfo, University of Trieste.

[6] E.g., Bryman (2004), who also cites Denzin (1970).

[7] Regarding the persons who kindly accepted to provide me with insights into their professional worlds, I have chosen the term 'participant', or in certain contexts 'informant' where the latter was more appropriate. I have followed the advice of the Association for Qualitative Research in electing not to adopt the term 'respondent': '... the research subject is no longer regarded as a passive object to be studied, being kept in the dark about the research and its objectives and simply 'responding', but as a valued partner in an exploratory process' (http://www.aqr.org.uk/glossary/respondent).

and the other 'agents'. My approach was gender-indifferent[8] for both principals and agents.

As principals, I elected to target lawyers both at law firms and those working as in-house counsel within corporations, and translation agencies operating in the legal field. I did not preselect such law firms, corporations, or agencies on the basis of size, whether by numbers of employees or by turnover.[9] Commissioners and translators working within institutions were not targeted, because of the considerable differences in procurement processes, generally leading to closer collaboration between principals and agents, and more rigorous frameworks governing translation processes. A small minority of participants worked partly within such environments, and this is stated wherever relevant.

With reference to the Chain of Supply model set out in section 1.1.7 (Chapter 1), I focused on commissioners, service provision intermediaries, and self-employed translators, and their influence on performance of the translation task. I noted many avenues open for subsequent research that might examine the roles of the other parties involved, such as procurement intermediaries, content intermediaries, proofreaders, or the police.

I decided to canvass globally, maintaining my underlying premise that this research project was to be an initial foray into the relatively unknown ground that is the outsourced legal translation market. The advent of the Internet has meant that it is now a feasible option for researchers with limited financial resources to gather valid data from a hitherto unimagined locale, as long as certain precautions are taken. These will be discussed more fully later in the data collection section.

5.3. Data Collection

5.3.1. SURVEY DESIGN

Given that the research questions explore a service provision process in a global market, and aware of the difficulties accessing informants, as noted in the literature,[10] I opted for questionnaires made available online[11] rather than structured interviews. This was done to offer participants flexibility (accessible at

[8] A considerable amount of research has been done on the *general* translation market—as opposed to the legal specialism—regarding the predominance of female workers (Sela-Sheffy & Shlesinger, 2008).

[9] Having initially attempted to include court personnel during a pilot study, I then excluded them, partly owing to difficulties gaining access to such persons, and partly because of the way in which commissioning is carried out (national rules, frameworks) and assignments are paid (set rates). In many countries, principals at courts consult official lists of approved sworn/certified translators (see in this regard Monjean-Decaudin, 2012; Vigier, Klein, & Festinger, 2013).

[10] E.g., Vandendaele, Bruyer, & Jacobs (2015).

[11] Hewson notes that 'specialist difficult-to-reach populations can be obtained fairly time and cost effectively' using web-based surveys (2015, p. 281).

any time), a user-friendly interface,[12] and expeditiousness, without any form of external pressure (options to withdraw and/or remain anonymous).

I was aware of possible issues with self-reported data (Chan, 2009, p. 110), whether online or in other contexts, but deemed that the scope and setting of the study would offer little propensity or situational pressure to give socially desirable replies (Donaldson & Grant-Vallone, 2002), and that the advantages in terms of access to the target population outweighed the risks in this regard. I also considered that one of the potential advantages of structured interviews (i.e., more interviewer control) might in this case have led to increased bias, which further reinforced my decision. A further merit of online data collection was the potential catchment area.

Wright says of online survey research that

> [a]dvantages include access to individuals in distant locations, the ability to reach difficult to contact participants, and the convenience of having automated data collection, which reduces researcher time and effort. Disadvantages of online survey research include uncertainty over the validity of the data and sampling issues, and concerns surrounding the design, implementation and evaluation of an online survey. (2006, p. 3)

Whilst data from a web platform can be exported in electronic form and processed 'automatically'[13] if a researcher so wishes, Wright's statement should be qualified: although no transcription is required, since data are entered by study participants, human error could be a factor at that stage. To address the disadvantages put forward by Wright (2006): in line with the stated aims of the study, the qualitative aspect of the project made sampling issues less relevant than in a purely quantitative approach; in terms of questionnaire design, it was piloted in the field to refine its content and presentation as much as possible; implementation was made as robust as possible through 'filtered' channels;[14] and rigour was exercised in evaluating the survey results through the use of qualitative data analysis software (see section 5.4). Lastly, I feel that weight is given to the validity of data by the fact that the vast majority of participants[15] stated their names and positions, in spite of being under no obligation to do so. I fully recognize that the online format may perforce exclude certain members of the population who are less conversant with the Internet, but I am confident

---

[12] In terms of presentation, the questionnaire offered the benefits usually associated with online platforms: relative consistency in displaying data entry forms, conditional branching of questions or 'skip logic' (Hewson, 2015, p. 281), and pop-up help windows.

[13] The term seems more readily applicable to activities such as web scraping or text mining, for example.

[14] Closed professional groups or direct professional contacts

[15] 90 per cent of principals, 91 per cent of translators.

that significantly improved access to informants outweighs this possible downside, especially in view of the profiles sought (e.g., lawyers and translators).

I chose Wufoo as the survey platform.[16] Since the study involved human participants, confidentiality and ethical considerations needed to be addressed from the outset. In terms of data security, Wufoo is fully compliant with the US-EU Safe Harbor Framework,[17] regarding the collection, use, and retention of personal information. All of the instruments used in the project were submitted for ethical review[18] and obtained a favourable opinion before data collection commenced.

A single online form was used for each target group (principals and agents), comprising an information notice, participant profile details, and the questionnaire itself.[19] Participant profile details were concentrated in the early part of the questionnaire, to ensure that the information was captured, to ease participants in gently, and to increase response rates (e.g., Teclaw, Price, & Osatuke, 2011). Potentially sensitive personal data were not requested, and no individual question reply was mandatory. In the remainder of the questionnaire, both closed and open questions were used, with the aim of striking a balance between investigating specific issues and adding richness to the data. A number of filter or contingency questions were included. Questionnaires had an easy-to-read graphical interface, using various devices such as scroll-down menus, check boxes, and radio buttons, in list form and in simple tables, and participants were also given the opportunity to express their views freely with several open prompts, with text boxes of varying sizes. Help boxes were provided for clarification purposes, appearing upon mouse hover near the relevant question.

As explained in section 5.1 regarding methodology, the principals' questionnaire was triangulated with that of the agents (translators). Thus the questions reflected or mirrored each other, as shown in Table 5.2, aiming to render the data collected more robust, and to see whether there were differences in the ways that the two groups regarded the issues involved.

Both questionnaires were piloted in order to refine their design. Two key issues arose from the initial analysis of the principals' pilot survey data, both related to the translation brief. It appeared far from systematic for legal

---

[16] Less costly than SurveyMonkey, its sister company from the same Group.

[17] I am aware of potential changes in the light of the CJEU judgement of 6 October 2015 (Case C-362–314, *Maximillian Schrems v Data Protection Commissioner* [2015] EU:C:2015:650), but, pending any national direction on the matter, I must point out that the data were collected prior to that date.

[18] To the Faculty of Humanities and Social Sciences Research Ethics Committee of the University of Portsmouth.

[19] An information notice was supplied to participants at the start of the questionnaire, with an option not to disclose their name, while stating the researcher's intention to anonymize data and ensure confidentiality, and offering an opportunity to be informed of the project's outcome. There were three versions of the questionnaire: pilot questionnaire for legal translation commissioners, main phase questionnaire for legal translation commissioners, questionnaire for freelance legal translators.

TABLE 5.2
Triangulation of Key Questions between Principals and Translators

Principals	Translators
7. Which providers do you use most for legal translation?	4. Who are your MAIN clients for legal translation (or your employer if you work in-house)?
8. How often, in practice, do you inform translators of the intended purpose of the translation when commissioning?	6. How often, in practice, are you informed of the intended purpose of the translation when you receive the order?
9. How often, in practice, do you provide the translator with the profile of the final user of the translation when commissioning?	7. How often, in practice, are you informed of the profile of the final user of the translation when you receive the order?
10. What information does your firm's translation order usually contain?	5. What information does a translation order usually contain?
11. During the translation process, how would you describe interaction with translation providers if questions arise?	9. During the translation process, how would you describe interaction with clients if questions arise?
13. After proofreading/checking, how often do you give translators feedback for their information?	11. After proofreading/checking, how often do you get feedback from the client?
14. What type of texts do you commission?	2. What sort of documents do you translate?
16. Does your organization mainly work in one specific language pair?	3. Please select below the language pair that you most commonly translate.
20. Do you find some types of document particularly troublesome? If so, please specify below.	10. Do you find some kinds of document particularly troublesome? If so, please specify below.

translators to be provided with the intended purpose of the translation or with details of the end-user. This finding was thus explored in further detail during the main survey, as will be seen later. In the light of comments received and issues noted, I made the following amendments to the principals' questionnaire for the main phase:

- the questionnaire was reorganized into a more logical structure comprising five sections;[20]
- a question was added about the purchase order;[21]
- a specific question was added, asking principals' opinions about informing the translator of the intended purpose and final user of the target text;
- a question was added concerning the genre of source texts translated;[22]
- in view of the importance of the field of comparative law and its relationship with legal translation, a question was included identifying the source and target legal systems applying to texts to be translated;

[20] 'About your organization'; 'About your legal translation providers'; 'About the types of translated texts you commission'; 'Identifying quality issues'; and 'Ways to improve legal translation'.

[21] 'What information does your firm's translation order usually contain?'

[22] 'What types of texts do you commission?'

- some demographic questions were added or amended.[23]

On the basis of the preceding, which did not fundamentally change either the aims of the survey or the data to be collected, I elected to treat both the pilot and main phase of the principals' survey as a single data set, but have made it clear in the following sections where there is a significant difference between them. The agents' questionnaire was also piloted, and taking into account feedback received, no amendments were subsequently made, apart from a technical modification of the 'country' menu.

5.3.2. ACCESS TO PARTICIPANTS

The following gives the measure of the challenge that I faced: 'one of the greatest difficulties when trying to research business and professional discourse successfully is said to be gaining access to the field' (Vandendaele, Bruyer, & Jacobs 2015, p. 105; citing Candlin & Crichton, 2013). Aware of this, I had a multi-strategy approach using various 'routes' in order to find participants.

I contacted a small number of university law schools, but unfortunately was not able to put in place any collaboration for data gathering. Whilst university–industry partnerships have been widely promoted and discussed in the last 25 years, a lack of collaboration among university departments has been less extensively documented, although Philpott *et al.* (2011) refer to a significant 'divide between disciplines'. In an era of increasingly 'interdisciplinary' research, it might be helpful to find ways of promoting inter-faculty dialogue, both for PhD students and for more established scholars, to the benefit of all involved.

I also contacted lawyers' associations and professional bodies in the United Kingdom, France, and those with European coverage, but received no replies.[24] I attempted to enlist the aid of senior figures in such bodies at legal theory lectures and international conferences. None of these efforts was successful at the data-gathering stage. Translators' professional bodies were a little more accommodating, albeit via my personal network.

In view of the lack of support forthcoming from academia and professional bodies, I then decided to leverage my own network of contacts built up over a career spanning 25 years, and by making use of my attendance at international conferences in the field. For example, in the pilot study, a conference in Geneva that I attended in person for professional reasons proved to be a good source of contacts, and led to seven commissioners participating. Direct

---

[23] 'Language pairs handled'; 'How often do you commission legal translation?'; size of organization; a workplace entitled 'Corporation'; and 'paralegal' and 'CEO' as positions.

[24] I sought their direct backing: through the insertion of an announcement of the project in a newsletter or mailshot, a presentation of the project at membership meetings, or suchlike.

personal emails sent to potential commissioner-participants produced a further nine positive replies. At the same time as direct contacts were being made, I used a technique known as 'snowballing' (Denscombe, 2007), or 'chain sampling'[25]. This further extended the number of participants.

Online recruitment was also attempted, using closed LinkedIn lawyers' groups, but was unsuccessful. An announcement through the LinkedIn Legal Translation Network Group, however, led to a large number of translators participating. A post on a well-known legal drafting blog as a result of a personal communication led to 10 replies from commissioners in the pilot study alone. Additionally, a social media strategy was launched, including a blog,[26] Twitter feed, and Scoop.it topic, and a simple project website was also created, primarily as a repository for details and links to surveys.

There were also some serendipitous encounters and enablers. A chance meeting at a European conference on translation led to a mention on the website of EUATC (the European Union of Associations of Translation Companies), aimed at translation agencies specializing in legal work, which unfortunately did not give rise to any survey responses. As the study progressed, I observed, incidentally, that lawyers having had problems with translations, or family ties with translators or interpreters, or working extensively internationally, were far readier to participate.

The consequence of the 'opportunistic' sampling approach evoked is that data were collected from participants worldwide, and the data pertain to various language pairs, rather than focusing on one particular country, language, jurisdiction, or area of law. Since the aim of the project was primarily to seek out potential evidence to support the hypothesis, grounded in my experience of the market, that there might be room for improvements in the briefing of legal translators, the strategy was considered justifiable.[27]

A 'bottom-up' approach, involving contacts at grass-roots level in the market, proved far more successful than a 'top-down' approach involving institutions. Inter-faculty dialogue, and how professional bodies could be encouraged to open doors for academic enquiry, may merit further investigation. The successful leveraging of action researchers' personal and professional networks, as well as online strategies, should not be underestimated, the essential

[25] Defined as 'when the researcher accesses informants through contact information that is provided by other informants' (Noy, 2008, p. 330).

[26] www.wordstodeeds.com. Although I curate the blog personally, its aim is to build bridges between academia and practice, and between translators and legal professionals. As such it is in no way a marketing tool for my practice (completely separate website), and I appear as the anonymous curator 'WordstoDeeds'. Information on my identity is available only on an unobtrusive internal page, should readers be concerned about the authenticity of information posted. Many translator and commissioner participants were recruited through my blog (ascertained via click-throughs).

[27] It is hoped that subsequent research will further flesh out the data, and look in particular at other language pairs, other legal systems, and court personnel.

caveat being the need for researchers to be fully trained in and informed about the pitfalls of such steps in terms of data robustness.

5.3.3. THE DATA-GATHERING STAGE

I was able to monitor the progress of data gathering in real time through the Wufoo platform, by setting up automatic alerts via email.[28] Questionnaires were accessed electronically as they arrived, were stored and backed up on the platform, where they were exportable in Microsoft Excel, .txt, or .csv format. The platform has certain spam protections in place: a Smart CAPTCHA system to exclude robots, together with coding checks during the submission process, and email address verification. Nevertheless, some manual filtering was required—a manageable and easy step effected by deleting lines in the Excel files exported.

5.4. Data-Analysis Methods

Information on how participants reached the survey was obtainable through the Wufoo 'Analytics' service, which sorts entries by continent, by country, by city, by Internet browser and operating system, and, usefully, by referrer. The platform also allows 'Reports' to be designed by the researcher and generated at any time during or after the data-gathering process. Functions include the following: selection of fields, time periods and/or entries, conditional filters, production of data grids, pie and line charts, and bar graphs. There are, however, limitations, such as on the quantities of data that can be displayed, and on the formats of reports exported—they are mainly designed to be viewed online. I therefore made only limited use of this feature, mainly in early phases of the project. At that stage I also used some graphing features on the Excel exports from Wufoo. Using these tools, a first analysis of preliminary results from the pilot study was produced, an extract of which was presented in the form of an infographic, for an academic conference (see Figure 5.1).

In order to be able to drill down into the data in a more sophisticated way, for increased methodological rigour and to acquire an array of perspectives, I decided to use the qualitative data-analysis software NVivo.[29] I felt that software would provide me with more scope than a manual approach (e.g., Jones, 2007; Lewins & Silver, 2007). Before making this choice, I also trialled an online package called *Dedoose*,[30] but found that it did not suit my requirements in terms of handling Excel files and particularly in dealing with questions with

[28] The platform also allows for alerts via text message to a mobile device.

[29] For a comprehensive scholarly discussion of NVivo, see Seidel (1998); Bazeley (2009). Versions used were NVivo 9 and subsequently NVivo 10 (QSR International Pty Ltd.).

[30] http://www.dedoose.com.

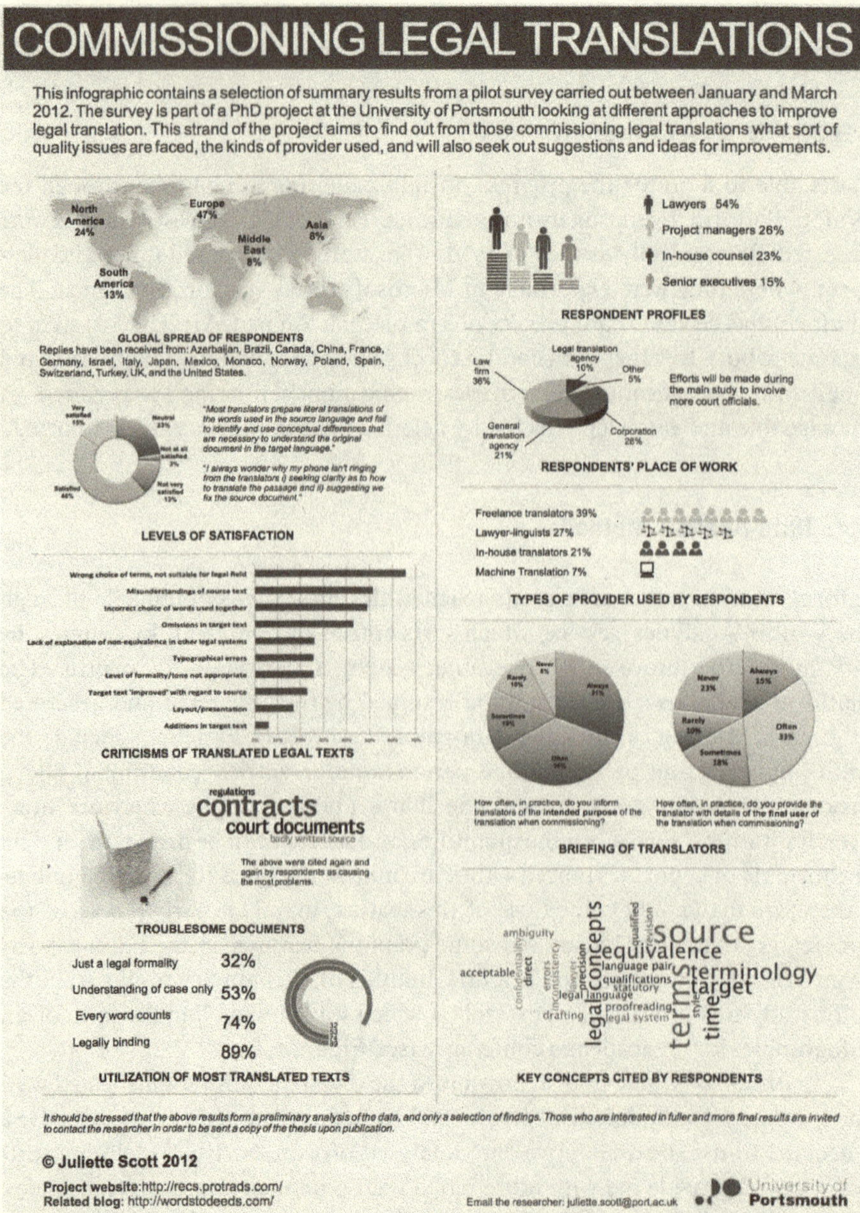

FIGURE 5.1 Infographic showing selected results from the pilot study (46 participants).

multiple answers. The availability of ongoing one-to-one NVivo training support[31] also influenced my decision.

NVivo facilitates traceability, or an 'audit trail' (Lincoln & Guba, 1985), from the very outset, notably by automatically date-stamping the user's actions.

[31] Offered by the University of Portsmouth through an external provider, QDA Training plc.

All nodes[32] created have a descriptor box where the intention behind the node creation and criteria or parameters for inclusion are noted. Besides, the evolving node structure provides further opportunities for review through the exporting of 'code books' at regular intervals. Figure 5.2 summarizes the coding steps carried out.

I began building the database by exporting Excel files containing all raw data from Wufoo, and importing them into NVivo. At this stage, a first round of attribute coding was applied automatically for demographics and closed questions. In addition, I distinguished three data sets according to the type of participant: principals involved at the pilot stage, principals involved in the main phase of the study, and translators (agents).[33]

In the second round of coding, open questions were assigned to separate nodes. The next step was to create a number of key 'theme'[34] nodes, using the overarching research questions as a basis. A further round consisted of sequentially coding the open question replies, attributing relevant statements to existing nodes, and where applicable creating new nodes. I used code book exports to restructure nodes, collapsing them or subdividing them where appropriate. New themes emerged as coding proceeded. The cycle was repeated several times, consistent with methodologies from the literature (e.g., Bazeley, 2009; Bazeley & Jackson, 2013).

Some corpus linguistics methods were applied, such as filtered and unfiltered word frequency lists, text search (KWIC[35]), and visualizations such as word trees, cluster analysis, and word clouds, to obtain further insights into the data. I carried out a final verification of coding robustness by cross-checks, random sampling, queries, data sorting, and comparison with the original data sets. I was then able to write up my findings using the coded data by running specific queries and generating output as required.

I also produced a conceptual map linking themes and sub-themes from later iterations of coding to one another, and to the research questions. I will use portions of the map, at theme level, as outlines for and to illustrate the presentation of results in section 5.5.

To sum up, I was satisfied that my initial aims in terms of methodological rigour and varied perspectives were met by using NVivo for data analysis. There are, however, a number of downsides to this particular package, including complexity/lack of user-friendliness, bugs, and some incompatibility with data in

---

[32] 'Node' is the term used within NVivo for the storage of codes, and is a reference pointing to segments of data, as discerned and assigned by the researcher-user.

[33] As noted in section 5.3.1, I have chosen to discuss the two commissioning data sets together when presenting the results, given that changes made between the pilot and the final main version were (a) easily identifiable and separable by using the software, and (b) without notable influence on core investigations.

[34] Robson (2011, pp. 474–489).

[35] Key Word In Context.

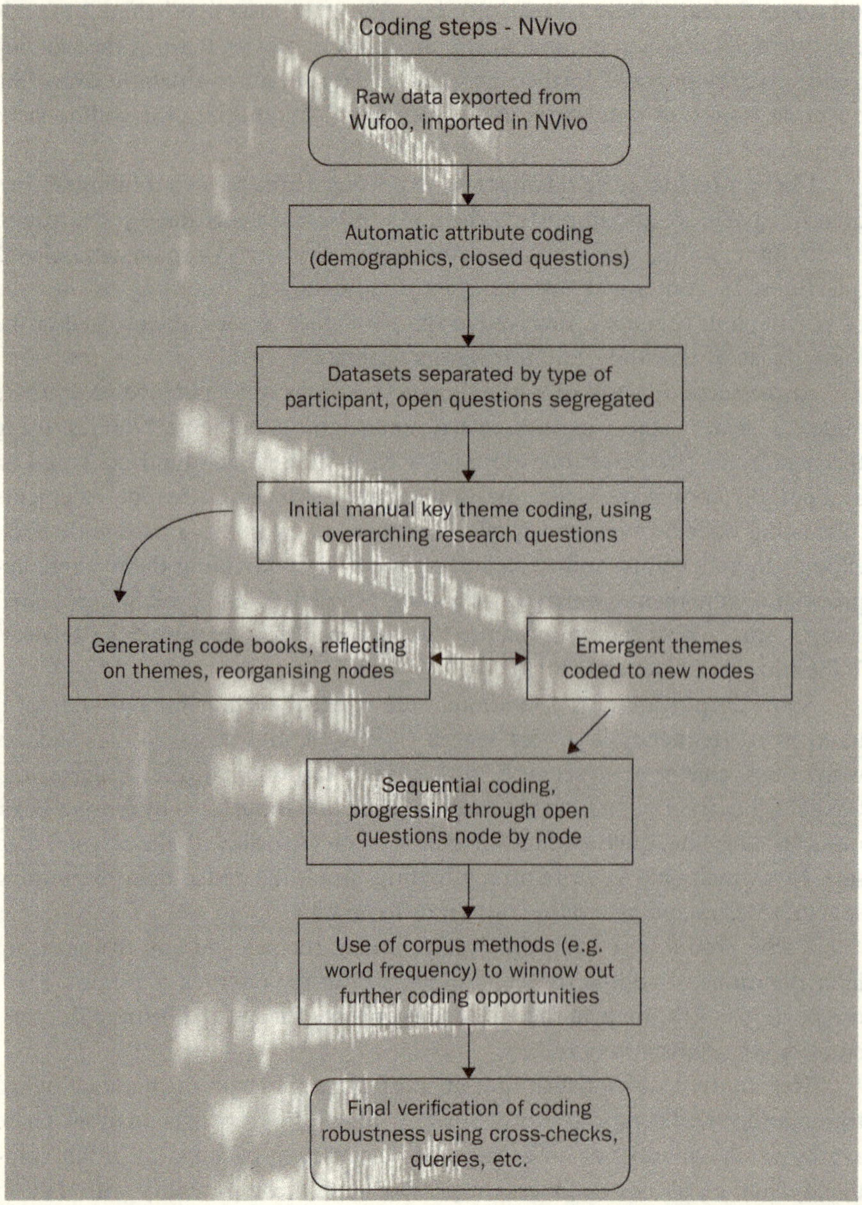

FIGURE 5.2 Coding steps.

Excel format. Such issues require the researcher to invest considerable time and energy to resolve them. Nevertheless, depth of insights and a rich array of inferences can be achieved.

5.5. Presentation of Data Collected

First, a reminder of the research questions that formed the basis for the data quest:

- How does the briefing process work within the outsourced legal translation environment?
- Are legal translation principals and/or translators working as external practitioners satisfied with that process?
- Do the principals express any issues vis-à-vis the performance of translations received?
- Do such legal translation principals and/or translators have any suggestions to improve performance?

To address the preceding, the presentation that follows is structured using themes arising out of the data, and those themes are related to the theoretical models already discussed (briefing template components in section 4.4 [Chapter 4], and tesseract of legal translators' textual agency in section 2.5 [Chapter 2]). It should be stressed, however, that the themes were not chosen lightly,[36] but were teased out following a lengthy process of reflection and refinement, and after careful consideration of the literature on qualitative data analysis, as outlined in the previous section.

Insofar as all participants were professionals, I did not consider it appropriate to make any question mandatory, although replies were, in fact, received for the vast majority.[37] Total numbers of replies may therefore differ slightly, and percentages have been calculated on the basis of the sample size for each individual question. The data provided give a general overview, and, as stated, do not fall under a quantitative paradigm.

5.5.1. DEMOGRAPHICS

I shall begin by providing an overview of survey participants,[38] using the demographic data collected.

---

[36] See, in particular, Bazeley (2009).

[37] I was not in a position to offer any incentives to participants. Moreover, scholars disagree about the merits of incentives with respect to survey validity (see Göritz, 2006).

[38] In order to verify the genuine nature of the participants, as described in section 5.3.3, the data-collection platform offers a number of protections to exclude robots and spammers. In addition, 90 per

5.5.1.a. The 'Principals' Data Set

The term 'principals' refers in this section both to 'commissioners' and 'service provision intermediaries' (for a discussion of these terms see the Introduction and section 1.1.7 [Chapter 1]). Both may act as principals in respect of the agent-translator, depending on the particular pathway wended by the Chain of Supply in the given business relationship. As already stated, this data set includes those who replied to a pilot questionnaire and those who replied to the final version of the questionnaire, since changes made following the pilot did not have any noteworthy bearing on core issues.

This data set includes a total of 84 persons holding positions at law firms, in corporations, the judiciary, and at specialized and general translation agencies. Figures 5.3 and 5.4 show, respectively, job titles as stated by participants, and their organizations.

The category 'Others' in Figures 5.3 and 5.4 includes law faculty, government, and legal support service companies. Some participants held more than one position simultaneously.

Owing in part to recruitment methods, such as the leveraging of my professional network, the 'principals' data set may be slanted towards higher-end firms.[39] It is therefore possible to speculate whether the discoveries made show a more positive situation than would be the case if the data set had included lower-end establishments. The map in Figure 5.5 illustrates the geographical spread, over 33 countries and five continents, showing participants' countries in Light gray.

As can be seen from Figure 5.5, the contribution of the online channel, together with other recruitment sources, yielded a relatively thick sample of countries, although of course the fact that the survey was drafted in English led to obvious limitations.

5.5.1.b. The 'Agents' Data Set

The 'Agents' data set includes a total of 303 participants (236 self-employed, 48 in-house, and 19 others or who did not specify) (Figure 5.6). They were thus mainly self-employed professional legal translators, acting as external practitioners (see Chapter 1). The term 'professional' was included in recruitment information, as I wished to focus on practice and exclude noise in the data from student translators.

The 'Other' category includes three academics, one person retired from a career comprising both freelance and in-house activities, a person who was

---

cent of principals and 91 per cent of translators provided their email address and asked to be sent the results of the survey. I was also able to recognize many of the names provided as being well known and respected professionals in the legal translation field.

[39] Including leading law firms and well-known international corporations, for example.

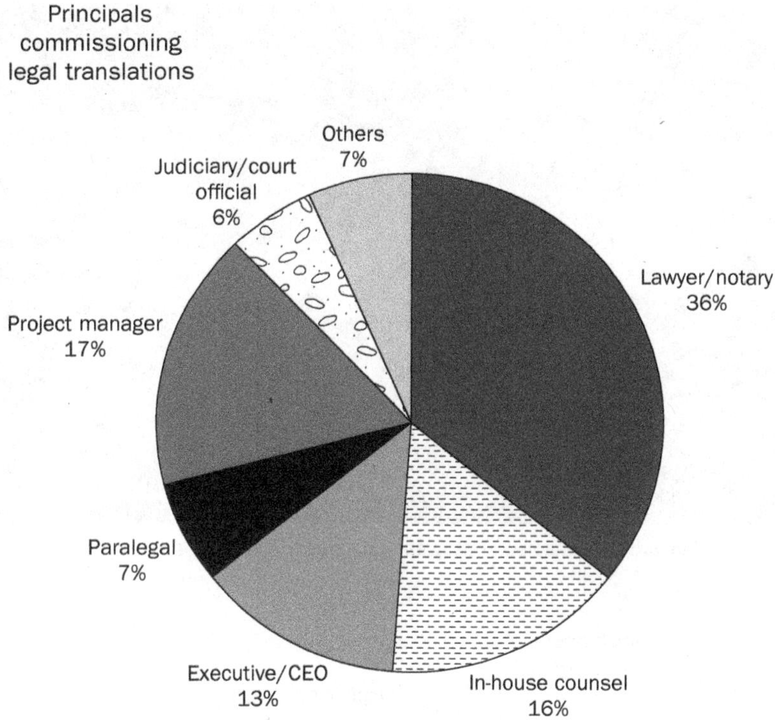

FIGURE 5.3 Breakdown of the 'Principals' data set by position held.

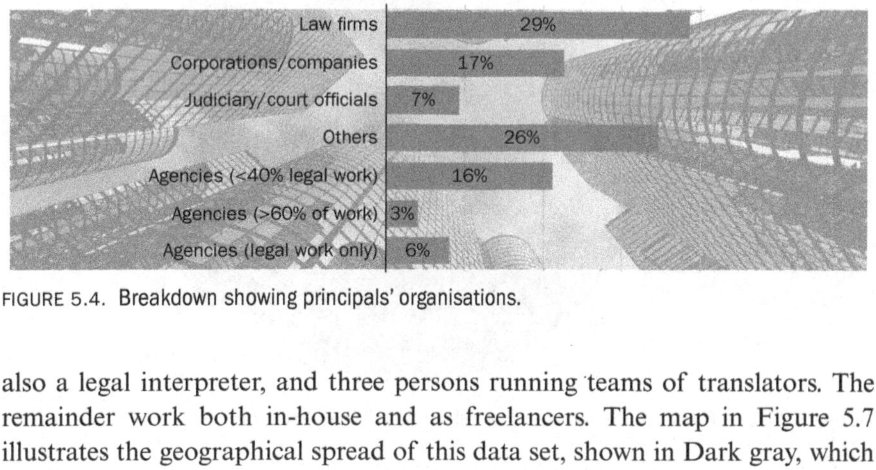

FIGURE 5.4. Breakdown showing principals' organisations.

also a legal interpreter, and three persons running teams of translators. The remainder work both in-house and as freelancers. The map in Figure 5.7 illustrates the geographical spread of this data set, shown in Dark gray, which includes persons from 41 countries[40] and six continents.

---

[40] Translators participating expressed difficulty when answering the question 'Which country are you from?' By the nature of their occupation, they may have a country of birth, of habitual residence, of current residence, and have moved countries several times.

FIGURE 5.5. Map giving an overview of geographical spread, 'Principals' data set.

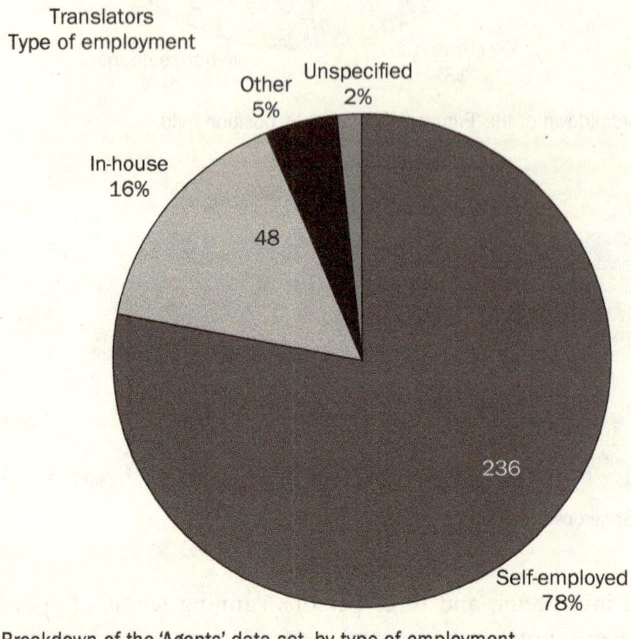

FIGURE 5.6. Breakdown of the 'Agents' data set, by type of employment.

There are references in the literature to translation being a predominantly female profession, such as the epithet 'pink-collar' (Sela-Sheffy & Shlesinger, 2008, p. 80). Of those who disclosed their gender in this data set (Figure 5.8), 69 per cent were female and 31 per cent male.

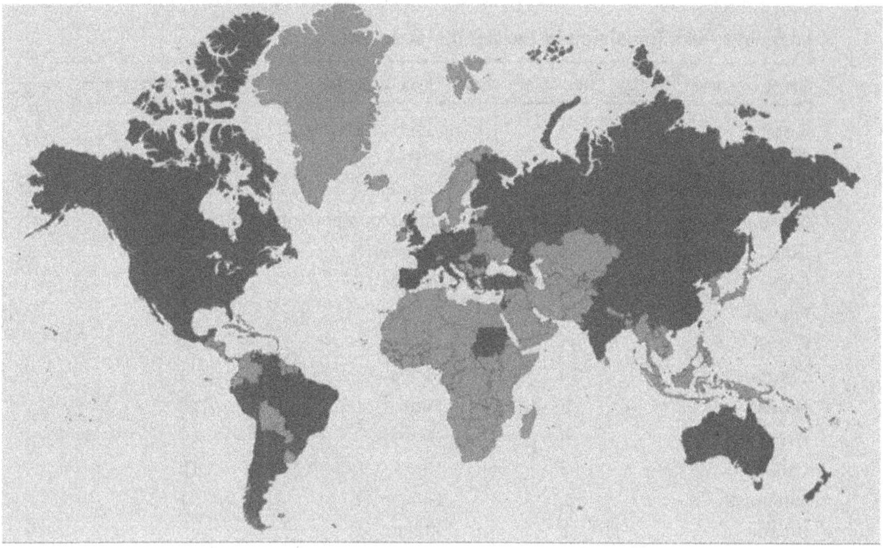

FIGURE 5.7. Map giving an overview of geographical spread, 'Agents' data set.

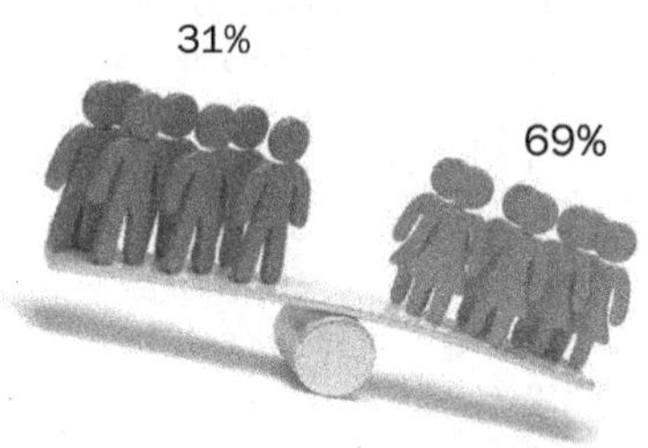

FIGURE 5.8. Gender split, 'Agents' data set.

The source and target languages of translators participating in the survey, as well as the numbers of translators for each language, are shown in Table 5.3.

In the following sections, which include citations from the data, reference numbers are internal to NVivo (i.e., distanced by one or more levels from participant codes) to preserve anonymity. Following Corden and Sainsbury (2006), who have looked extensively at the practice of using verbatim quotations to report on qualitative social research, I have illustrated my findings by interspersing my participants' 'voices' verbatim, apart from obvious small typographical errors, which have been corrected.[41] Where necessary, I have added a few words for clarification, indicated by the use of square brackets. A further

[41] It is important to remember that the survey was global in terms of geographical reach, and the majority of participants were not native speakers of English who kindly entered their responses in that language, many of whom asked to be informed once the research was published.

TABLE 5.3
Language Pairs Translated by the 'Agents' Data Set

Source Languages	Nos. of Translators	Target Languages	Nos. of Translators
Arabic	2	Albanian	1
Chinese, Cantonese	1	Arabic	2
Chinese, Mandarin	1	Catalan	1
Croatian	6	Chinese, Mandarin	1
Dutch	11	Croatian	2
English	100	Czech	2
Finnish	3	Dutch	3
French	31	English	149
German	34	Finnish	1
Greek	6	French	13
Hebrew	4	German	10
Italian	13	Greek	15
Japanese	1	Hungarian	1
Korean	1	Italian	25
Maltese	1	Latvian	1
Mongolian	1	Polish	2
Polish	5	Portuguese	11
Portuguese	15	Romanian	2
Romanian	1	Russian	1
Russian	4	Slovak	1
Slovak	1	Spanish	26
Slovene	1	Swedish	1
Spanish	30	Turkish	2
Turkish	2		
Urdu	1		
Not specified	27	Not specified	30

argument in favour of the use of verbatim material is that the end-users and readers of this book are likely to include not only academics but also legal and translation professionals, and thus the raw data may be more accessible for them. In citations I use the convention 'Participant [number]T' for translators; 'Participant [number]PP' for principals at the pilot phase of the survey; and 'Participant [number]P' for principals at the main phase of the survey.

5.5.2. BRIEFING PROCESS

This section addresses the two research questions concerning briefing.[42] After an overview of how external practitioners are currently being 'briefed', it uses

[42] How does the briefing process work within the outsourced legal translation environment? Are legal translation principals and/or translators working as external practitioners satisfied with that process?

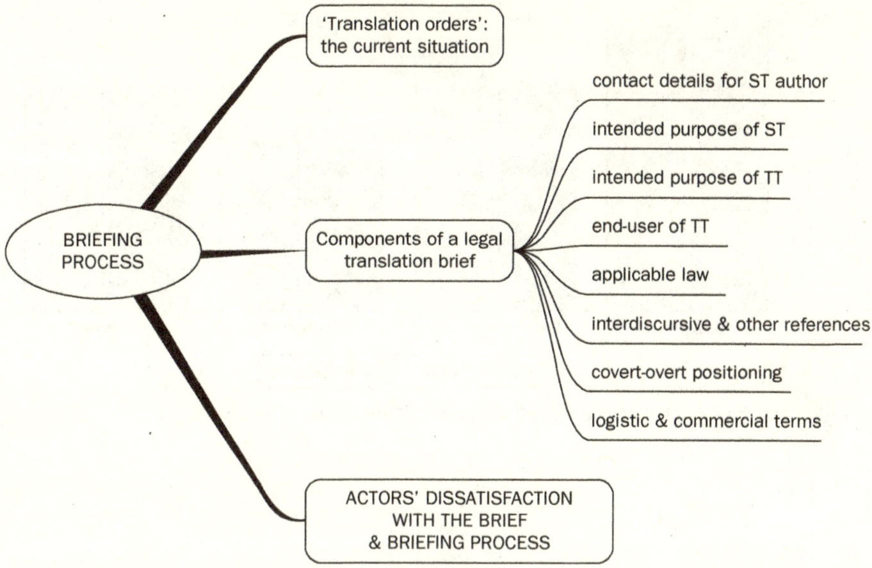

FIGURE 5.9. Briefing: research questions and themes

the components of the model legal translation brief proposed in Chapter 4 as the themes under which the data collected are organized and presented, and concludes with actors' views on briefing, as shown in Figure 5.9.

5.5.2.a. 'Translation Orders': The Current Situation

In order to engage with how, broadly speaking, survey participants were briefing [principals] and being briefed [translators], one question[43] asked, 'What information does [your firm's]/[a] translation order *usually* contain?' (emphasis added: it is important to note that the question did not ask what was *always* contained). It took the form of a table with radio buttons. An opportunity was also provided to add 'Other information' in a free text box. Participants were not required to provide replies to all questions: the response rate for this section of the survey was approximately half to two-thirds of the total and ranged from 39 to 42 principals, and 267 to 296 translators, depending on the question. Owing to the difference in the size of the data sets, I have converted the numbers of principals and translators who provided replies into percentages for comparison purposes.

Figure 5.10 shows that deadline, language pair, file format, and tariff were reported to be 'usually' included in the translation order by a *majority* of participants. I have called these 'logistic' constraints (see discussion in section 3.4 [Chapter 3]).

[43] Qu. 10, principals (main phase only); Qu. 5, translators.

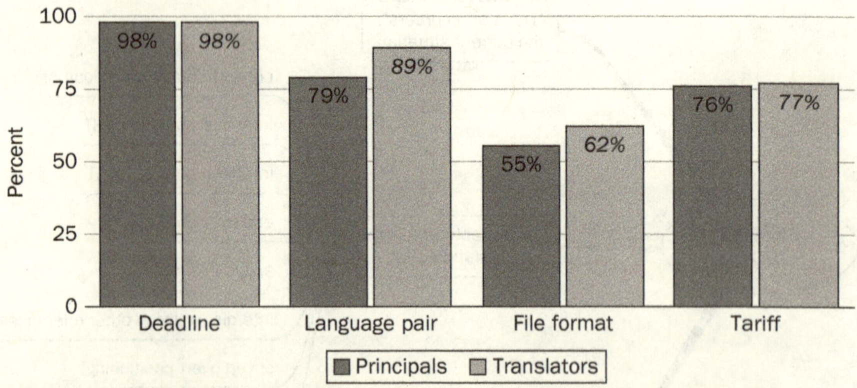

FIGURE 5.10. Elements usually included in the translation order.

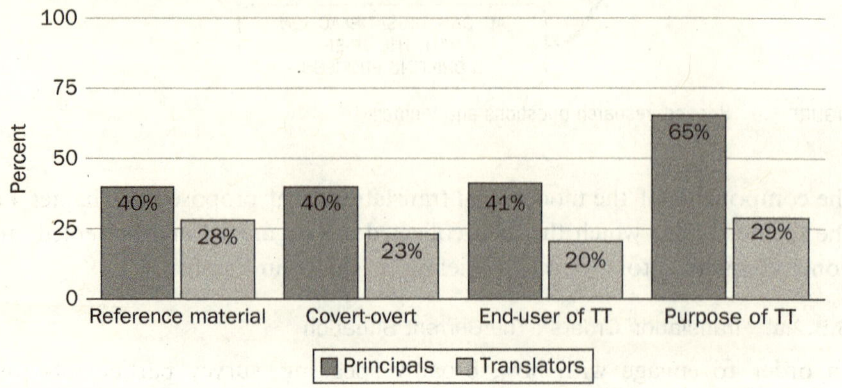

FIGURE 5.11. Elements not usually included in the translation order.

On the other hand, Figure 5.11 shows that reference material, covert–overt positioning, end-user, and intended purpose were reported to be 'usually' included in the translation order by a *minority*[44] of participants.

In the second group of items, the principals and the translators differ in their reporting considerably more than in the first group. A broad-brush reading of the preceding data would seem to indicate that principals feel that they are briefing translators slightly more fully than is in fact the case, which is even more marked for the point relating to target text purpose. However, as has been stated several times, numerical data can, within the scope of this study, only be used as conjecture, to be further elucidated in part by the textual comment collected, and conceivably by further research. Additionally, this may reflect the slant towards higher-end principals, as noted in section 5.5.1.a on the

[44] With the exception of the TT purpose for the principals.

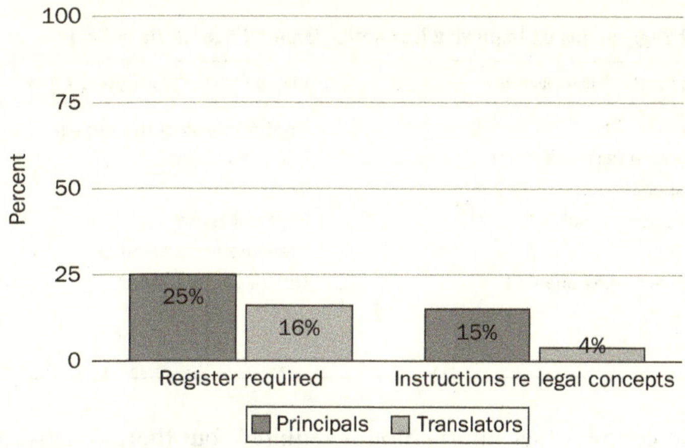

FIGURE 5.12. Elements rarely included in the translation order.

demographics of the data set—that is, the principals in my survey may actually brief their translators more fully than the 'average' legal translation principal.

This portrayal of the situation will be further examined, in the light of the free text data collected, in the following sections. Nevertheless, if we bear in mind translation scholars' arguments described in section 3.2.5 and Chapter 4, even the higher figures whereby between 40 per cent and 65 per cent of principals state that they *usually* supply the information is not an optimum situation.

Both data sets reported that the remaining two elements, the register required and instructions on how to handle legal concepts, were included the least in their translation orders, as shown in Figure 5.12.

Only four principals took the opportunity to add other items that they include with their translation orders:

- Contact person/recipient of translation (Participant 36P);
- Exact length (signs [characters]) (Participant 41P);
- Customer-based translation memory export, which ensures coherence of translations regarding terminology and style (Participant 42P);
- If the translation is to be certified/notarised; method of delivery (email, secure post, etc.) (Participant 49P).

The translators, on the other hand, provided a wealth of additions, amounting to 2,500 words. I have distilled them for brevity into two sets: those likely to assist in performance of the translation task (left-hand column in Table 5.4), and other issues, relating mainly to contractual requirements and logistics (right-hand column in Table 5.4).

In the light of the data described in the foregoing section, I posit that the 'translation brief' is often merely a purchase order. This is perhaps understandable on the part of 'lay principals' (see section 1.2.5 [Chapter 1]) who are not

TABLE 5.4

Overview of Suggestions on Improving Translation Orders ('Agents' Data Set)

Points Likely to Assist with Translation Task	Other Contractual and Logistical Points
House style	Confidentiality of the project
Guidance about a particular term	Level of urgency
Language variant	Word count
Certified/notarized or not	Payment terms
Draft/final	Pressure to lower rates
Expectations regarding quality	Use of CAT tool/TEnT
Layout	
Contact person	

aware that certain other information is required, but there is a risk that such inadequate information may also be accepted as the status quo by some translators. That possibility will be further elucidated in my findings and conclusions.

The following subsections examine the data by using themes relating to the components of a legal translation briefing template, sketched out in section 4.4 (Chapter 4).

5.5.2.b. Access to Source Text Drafters

As already discussed in Chapter 1, and in particular section 1.1.7 on the Chain of Supply, it is more frequent for translators to have access to the source text drafter(s) when they work in-house—at institutions or law firms, for example. The desirability of such access in the legal translation context has been demonstrated, for example, by Strandvik (2014) in the context of institutions. One principal answered the question 'How could the translated legal documents you receive be improved' as follows:

> Through consultation with the sender of the document and, possibly, by contacting the author of the document. (Participant 36P)

A minority of survey participants stated that they work in-house. One such person commented:

> I usually get the name of the author(s) of the text and have the luxury of consulting with them directly if I have any questions or if there are any problems in the [t]ext. (Participant 258T).

The use of the word 'luxury' seems to indicate that this participant is aware that this is not the norm. It appears, from survey participants' replies, to be very unusual for external translation practitioners to be provided with contact details for drafters. A sample of translators' comments regarding such access follows:

> I rarely have any way to contact the author to check. (Participant 84T)
>
> Not in the position to tell the author. (Participant 113T)

Sometimes, translators' access has to be brokered by intermediaries:

> My client could not get our queries answered by the author of the contract. (Participant 160T)
>
> Working via an agency makes it next to impossible to reach the author. (Participant 34T)

Such lack of dialogue has clear negative implications if the source text is ambiguous and/or contains errors (see section 3.2.1 [Chapter 3]), and is discussed further in section 5.5.3.a.

5.5.2.c. Intended Purpose of Source Text

Although the survey did not specifically seek to investigate this aspect, some participants made passing references, such as,

> Authors are not aware that they are producing the source text for translation, i.e., that final user will see the translation, not the original. (Participant 109T)

In this instance the translator makes the interesting point that some texts are actually drafted expressly to be translated, and not to be used 'as is'. It would be clearly be of great value to inform the translator in such cases. This might feasibly apply to pleadings, for example, whereas the translation of texts created previously and later used in evidence is highly unlikely to be foreseeable. Equally, of course, many source texts do stand alone, and their purpose may or may not be reflected in that of the target text.

5.5.2.d. Intended Purpose of Target Text

As we saw in Chapter 4, knowledge of the intended purpose of the target text has been widely put forward in the literature as one *sine qua non* for producing a successful legal translation. I asked both groups whether this information was communicated,[45] and Figure 5.13 shows the answers triangulated across the two data sets, which is conspicuously different from the recommendations made by translation scholars. Only 34 per cent of principals systematically inform their translators of the intended purpose of the target text, and only 9 per cent of translators receive this essential information from their principals.[46]

---

[45] The questions were: 'How often, in practice, do you inform translators of the intended purpose of the translation when commissioning?' (principals) and 'How often, in practice, are you informed of the intended purpose of the translation when you receive the order?' (translators).

I should make the reader aware at this point that in several of the open questions, participants grouped together issues relating to the intended purpose of the target text and to the end-user. The two questions were situated next to each other in both questionnaires (principals and translators); it is therefore difficult to speculate whether this positioning was responsible for the preceding trend or whether in fact actors see these issues as entwined, although it is worth noting that the literature also tends to link the target text's intended purpose and end-user (see section 3.2.5 [Chapter 3]).

[46] As already noted, the difference in these figures could well be due to the 'high-end' nature of the 'Principals' data set, whose procedures may be more rigorous than those commonly practised. Hence the situation across the board in the outsourced legal translation market may be even more alarming

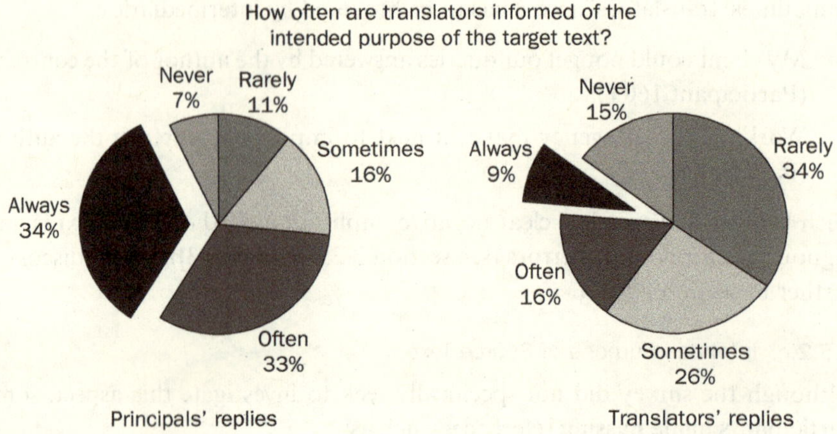

FIGURE 5.13. How often translators are informed of the intended purpose of the target text.

These data were further supported by the fact that, in open questions, many translators and principals in the survey expressed regret that the intended purpose of the target text was not always specified at the briefing stage. The following narrative below is a vivid illustration of how this materializes in practice.

> Circumstances: Minutes of a professional association conducting a disciplinary hearing. Tight deadline and no time for consultation. Issue: Extremely badly-written source text with paragraph-long, rambling, very vague sentences. Very difficult to work out the intention of the source text. Even more difficult to reproduce this in the target language as this involved reproducing vague, difficult-to-understand text – using a very authoritative-sounding and formal tone of voice. *Knowledge of the audience and purpose of the translation could have had a major effect on the (usefulness of the) translation.* (Participant 232T, emphasis added)

Another translator explained that, for her, not knowing the intended purpose made documents troublesome:

> Not being provided with a reason for the translation in order to focus your efforts on what is truly important and what is not. (Participant 51T)

Several principals nevertheless made it clear that they understood the importance of this aspect of the brief, as well as of making the translator aware of the end-user profile,[47] while another included 'Better understanding of the purpose' (Participant 28PP) in their suggestions to improve performance.

---

than my findings here. Notwithstanding, the 'bottom line' remains the same—that translators are not systematically provided with this key information.

[47] [Translators] 'also need to consider the purpose of the translation and the target group' (Participant 42P), and 'The translator should be more careful at [*sic*] the intended purpose of the paper' (Participant 59P).

In contrast to the body of opinion making the case for the intended purpose to be known, one translator, a lone voice, held that it was not desirable for the legal translator to be given further contextual background:

> I would consider it unethical as a legal translator to be told the purpose of the translation. [...] I think a legal translator should, in the interests of remaining objective, not know too much about the background to the case. (Participant 49T)

Two points come to mind here: (i) a source-oriented approach to legal translation,[48] and (ii) the dangers of focusing too closely on purpose, as explored by Pym (1996). In view of the functionalist position discussed in section 2.4.1 (Chapter 2), I will not make further comment.

Having asked whether the intended purpose was communicated or not, the survey then investigated, if not already the case, whether principals would consider it a good idea to do so.[49] As can be seen from Figure 5.14, the majority was in favour. None of the participants returned the answer 'No, it's a bad idea' to this question, and none selected the reply 'We don't know what the purpose will be'.

5.5.2.d.1. Deducing Purpose from the Source Text

If the purpose of the target text is not provided, an alternative might be to 'deduce' or 'infer' it from the source text (see section 4.1.1 [Chapter 4]). A few translators held that it was possible, to an extent, to guess purpose (and, for that matter, end-user or other information) from the text itself:

> Texts usually speak for themselves – litigation – the parties, what are they arguing about, what is the purpose of the text, final user etc. (Participant 273T)
>
> Often the context and purpose are clear enough to me, though the client does not indicate this. If I feel there is a need to know in a particular instance, I ask, and perhaps 3/4 of the time I get an adequate answer. (Participant 283T)
>
> Profile of the end user and purpose are usually clear from the content. (Participant 38T)

---

[48] Baaij carries this idea to the extreme, and pares legal translation down to 'linguistic' translation only when performed for the purposes of comparative legal research, which, he holds, the translator may 'contaminate' (2014).

[49] 'Do you think that informing the translator of the intended purpose of the translated text would be useful? (Question 24P).

A 'help' box was provided as follows: 'Intended purpose here means what is done with the translation, for example: to help a lawyer understand the case; to reply to the adverse party; to be sent to a court in another country; for discussion/negotiation & signature (e.g., contracts); to be held on file due to official requirements, etc.'.

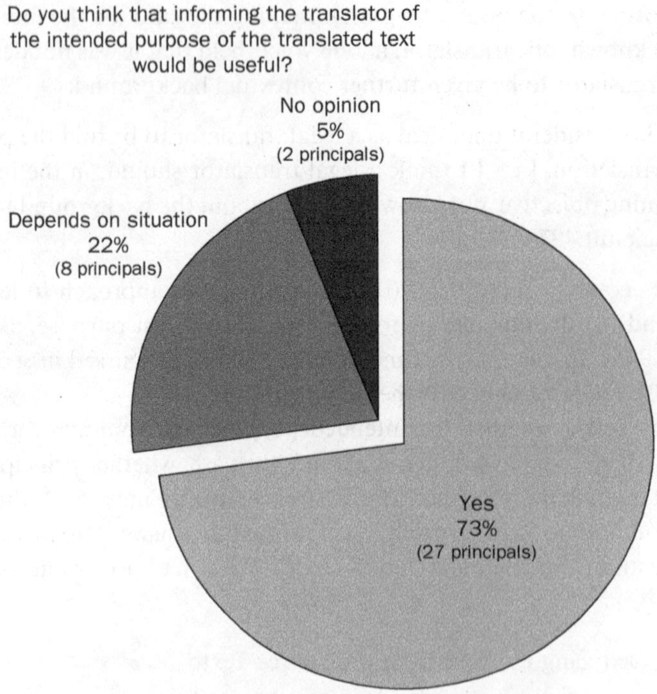

FIGURE 5.14. Principals' opinions of informing translators of target text purpose.

Another translator stressed the fact that this ability was made possible by the length of their relationship with the client (an agency):

> Although the information [reference material, covert-overt positioning, register, handling of legal concepts, end-user, TT purpose] is rarely contained in the order, I know what is expected in the light of our long-established relationship. (Participant 144T)

One principal described how translators at their company acquired, over a long period of time, the ability to guess purpose:

> Usually, after a few years, the translators at our firm 'get' what is necessary in a given case, but junior translators (even qualified lawyers) don't. (Participant 28P).

5.5.2.d.2. Differentiating Target Text Status

As discussed section 2.4.2, the differentiation of service levels, and prices, according to target text status is already being practised by certain translation agencies, including those specializing in legal work. A briefing template could offer predetermined status categories, and I therefore polled principals on this

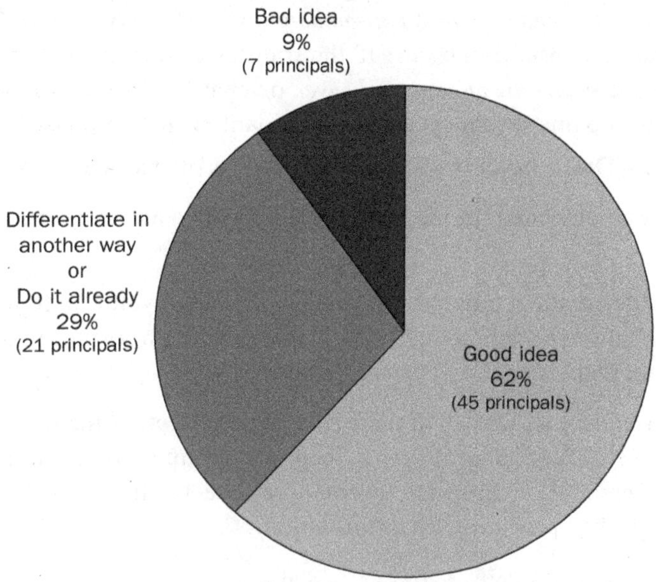

FIGURE 5.15. Principals' opinions of differentiating target text status.

point.[50] As Figure 5.15 shows, a majority of principals, 62 per cent (45 persons), were favourable.

Among those who differentiated in a different way are the following:

> '*[A]nnotated translations' for internal use* of the lawyers, before final version is agreed. (Participant MP, my emphasis)

> We differentiate only between translations intended 'only for *internal use* and understanding' and *all other translations*, regardless of whether binding or non-binding. (Participant 14PP, my emphasis)

> '*[S]ummarized translations*' to concentrate on what is essential, as instructed by the lawyer in charge of the case. (Participant 15PP, my emphasis)

> (a) [F]or reference and discussion purpose only; or (b) for execution (signed by the parties). (Participant 36P)

> [D]epending on the *ultimate/end user* and of course, on whether the translated document is going to be *binding* or have any official purpose. (Participant 60P, my emphasis)

---

[50] Adapted after E. Wagner (Chesterman & E. Wagner, 2002), the survey question read: What is your opinion of differentiating levels of quality—for example into these three levels: (a) Translation for gist to find out which case documents need translation; (b) translation intended to be a non-binding text; (c) translation intended to be a legally binding text. This was followed by the open question, 'If you differentiate in another way or think this is a bad idea, could you give more details?'

> *Translation intended to be a non-binding text is the only way we believe you can translate legal documents.* If the translated document is to be legally binding it needs an *in-country lawyer* or civil law notary to amend it to bring it into line with local laws. (Participant 3P, my emphasis)
>
> Level I – Draft, Level II - Fully-edited and certifiable (Participant 6PP)

One agency commended the idea, but denied they had any responsibility in this regard:

> Good idea in theory, but as an agency it is generally not up to us to decide this. We always assume that high quality is very important unless specifically advised otherwise. (Participant 2PP)

It seems from the preceding that there is scope to educate principals on making quality levels explicit, and also that there are grounds for creating a standardized differentiation in order to compare 'like for like' (see section 4.2.3 [Chapter 4]) when procuring legal translation.

5.5.2.d.3. The Status of Translated Legal Texts

As an extension of the discussions in the previous sections, Figure 5.16 shows the survey data on target text status in ascending levels of sensitivity.

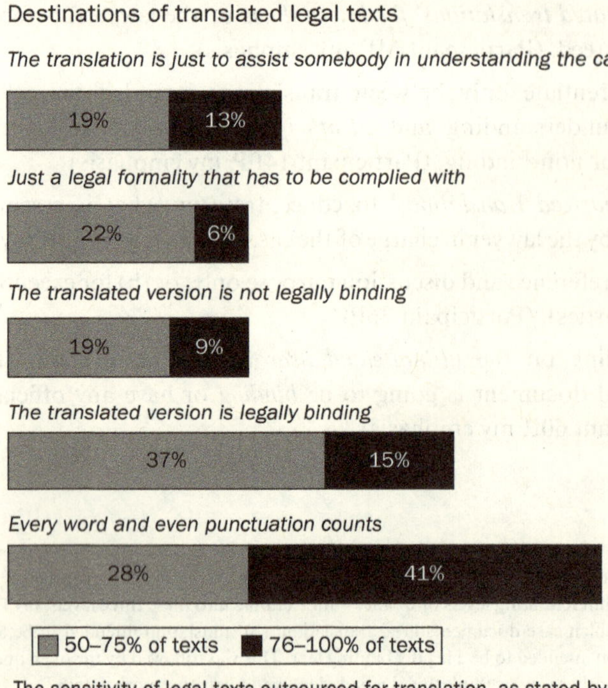

FIGURE 5.16. The sensitivity of legal texts outsourced for translation, as stated by principals.

The first level corresponds to what is referred to by some service provision intermediaries as 'FIPO' (For Information Purposes Only). The second level might include, for example, documents filed for the public record (though the idea of 'just a formality' may lead to many issues later on if there is an error, especially and even if not immediately obvious). The third and fourth levels relate to whether the text is legally binding, and in the fifth every component of the text is crucial—such as is the case with legislation, or high-value contracts, or in many other contexts, depending, of course, on the viewpoint of the commissioner. Overall, it is important to note the preponderance of sensitive texts among those outsourced.

5.5.2.e. End-User of Target Text

As argued in Chapters 2–4, knowledge of the profile or identity[51] of the end-user[52] is deemed valuable in order for successful legal translation to take place. The survey asked whether this information was provided,[53] and Figure 5.17 illustrates that the results are quite different from theoretical prescriptions, in a similar fashion to those on intended purpose (see section 5.5.2.d). Only in a minority of cases (6 per cent) did the translators say that they were always informed of the end-user's profile,[54] while 19 per cent of principals reported providing it.[55]

As in the previous section, having asked whether the end-user was communicated or not, the survey then investigated whether principals would deem it a good idea to do so, if it were not already the case.[56] Their answers are shown in Figure 5.18.

The majority of principals were in favour; while one-fifth found that it would depend on the situation, one person chose the answer 'We don't know who the end-user will be', and no participant selected the reply 'No, it's a bad idea'.

---

[51] For confidentiality purposes, it may be desirable to provide a profile rather than specific details.

[52] I.e., those readers for whom the text is intended, as opposed to those into whose hands the text may subsequently fall.

[53] 'How often, in practice, do you provide the translator with the profile of the final user of the translation when commissioning?' (principals). 'How often, in practice, are you informed of the profile of the final user of the translation when you receive the order?' (translators).

[54] It is also very important to note that the question used the word 'profile' and not 'contact details'—i.e., any concerns about confidentiality should have been set aside. This was further emphasized in the questionnaire by using a floating information box, the text of which read: 'By details, I don't mean name or address, but just the general profile of the user—e.g., lawyer, judge, general public, etc.'.

[55] As noted in the second footnote to section 5.5.2.d with regard to intended purpose, the difference in these figures could well be due to the 'high-end' nature of the 'Principals' data set. Either figure is, once again, far below the recommendations made by translation scholars.

[56] Do you think that informing the translator of the type of end-user of the translated text would be useful (e.g., lawyer, general public, official authority, etc.)?

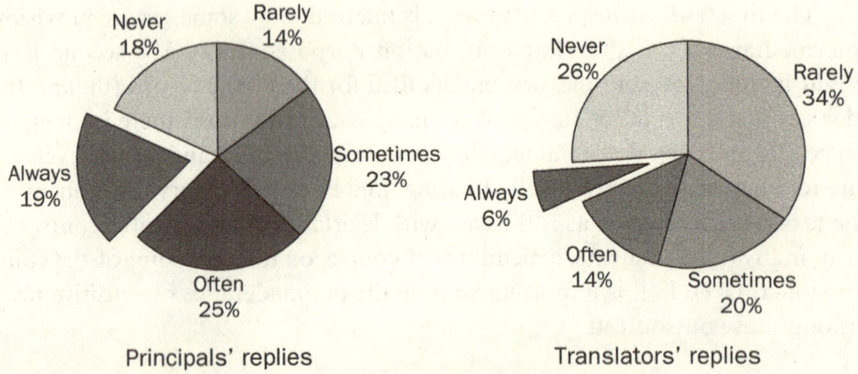

FIGURE 5.17. How often translators are made aware of end-users' profiles.

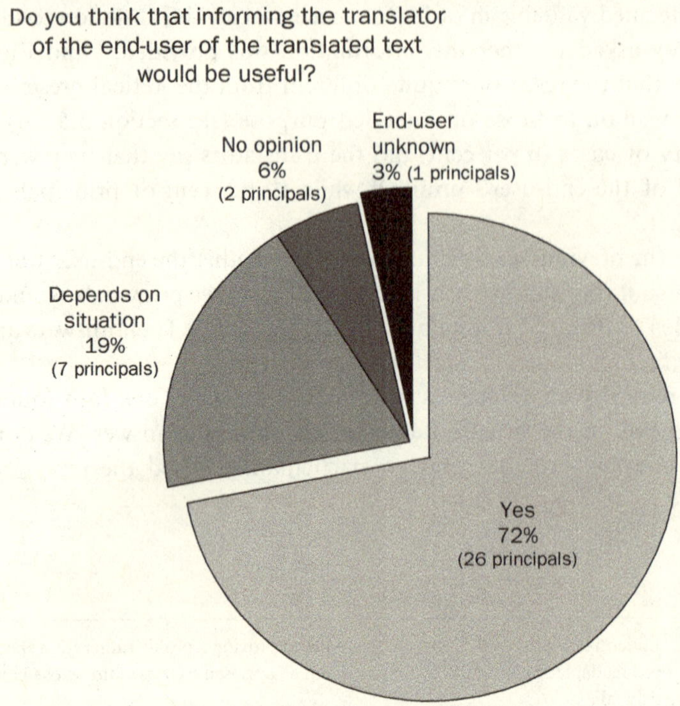

FIGURE 5.18. Principals' opinions of informing translators of end-user(s).

Several of the examples provided by principals and translators in replies to open questions and relating to the issue of specifying the end-user have already been included in the foregoing section on intended purpose—as noted, the two items were often discussed together by participants. The following translator's comment, however, is specific to this section:

> The end-client is almost never made known. Which is a shame, because knowing helps a translator to take into consideration the end-reader.

> *[. . .] But never a clue about who the translation is intended for – lawyers? Lay readers? Frustrating.* (Participant 231T)

This stance is echoed by the many regrets expressed by translators about the length, inefficiency, and indirect nature of the chain of supply (see also section 5.5.2.j). One translator, a lone voice, thought that it was preferable for the final client to have only one point of contact:

> [...] as most of my work is through agencies, I can contact the agency which then contacts the end-customer about my questions. I would not even expect to be able to contact the end-customer directly. The end-customer should ideally have only one interlocutor. (Participant 102T)

The preceding participant appears to have a very different relationship with their agency from that of other translators replying to the survey. Unlike the vast majority, Participant 102T feels able to obtain all information needed from the agency, and is confident that queries are being passed on to the final client-commissioner.

5.5.2.f. Applicable Law

The law applying to the source text and the target text may be the same, or it may differ. As demonstrated in Chapter 4, the translator needs to be made aware of this information. It appears from the data, however, that they are not systematically informed. The following example from the data is not an exception.

> Sometimes, the country of origin is mentioned, e.g., Canada, UK, US, French Territories etc. but not always. As a translator, I have to keep reminding the client to provide me with this information. It is important when translating into my mother tongue to make sure that the correct legal system and reference documents is [*sic*] researched/consulted and even more important for reverse translations. However, *I did find myself translating court documents for a case that involved 3 different jurisdictions, without being clear where each document was to be submitted or if the materials were being translated for information purposes etc.* On that occasion, I felt that they were concerned about confidentiality and therefore had provided minimum background information. (Participant 139T, my emphasis)

The preceding translator alludes to the issue of language variants, and to the relevant legal systems governing the source and target texts,[57] giving an example of a case where they were translating: 'without being clear where [to which

---

[57] This participant notes that research under the governing legal system is '*even more important for reverse translations*', which I have understood to mean translations performed out of the translator's native language and into a non-native target language—also referred to as 'inverse' (Biel, 2011, p. 165).

court] each document was to be submitted'. In addition, target text status was not differentiated. Overall, the translator stresses the fact that clients do not provide this information systematically, that it has to be elicited, and that in this case the principal may have deliberately restricted the contextual information supplied, for reasons of confidentiality (see section 3.1.3 [Chapter 3]). The likelihood of the preceding target text having been unfit-for-purpose is extremely high given the number of parameters not supplied in the brief—to recap: language variant(s); legal system(s) governing the source and target texts; intended purpose; end-user; and even its status—possibly FIPO,[58] possibly legally binding.

5.5.2.g. Interdiscursive and Other Reference Material

As we saw in section 5.5.2.a concerning the translation order, reference material does not seem systematically to form part of the brief either. Several participants lamented the provision of bad quality reference material and/or translation memories:

> Sometimes the translation agency provides a translation memory containing existing translations that are not very high quality – then I am torn between being consistent with the previous translations or using a different translation. (Participant 20T)
>
> I was supplied a glossary and background documents on the subject and a very extensive TM but when I researched it in internet [*sic*], I found that the terminology the client used was a bad and incorrect translation and yet I felt obliged to use it. What I would have translated properly (at least I think so) had to conform to the client's standard. That was frustrating and it meant that I had to do hours and hours of checking minutely to ensure that my proper translation was then 'downgraded' to reflect the client's style and incorrect terminology. (Participant 107T)

It is worth underlining the extra work entailed in this instance to comply with what was in effect the client's inferior quality standard. The next translator stresses the heightened need for reference material when dealing with litigation documents:

> In litigation matters if I'm not aware of the background or any documents relating to the litigation or previous briefs, it is very difficult to know exactly what has been going on. (Participant 156T)

The relevance of the case file as a prerequisite to carrying out work ought nevertheless to be self-evident for litigators. Another translator cited missing reference material as her worst translation experience: 'It was a patent not

[58] For Information Purposes Only.

identified as such with no number. I got faulted for not matching the 'official abstract"' (Participant 4T). Some comments on lacking contextual information were sadly obvious: 'Replies to letters or emails without sight of the originals'[59] (Participant 144T). And lastly, one translator reported: 'Even if we insist on background information we quite often do not get [it]' (Participant 89T).

5.5.2.h. Covert–Overt Positioning

I argue in section 2.4.3 (Chapter 2) that the expression of expectations concerning the covertness or overtness of a legal translation forms a key part of the translation brief. If there is no instruction regarding the extent to which a target text is to be a word-for-word translation, or the extent to which the text should read as an original from the target culture, there is a strong likelihood of the translator's product being rejected or criticized. Accounts from the survey of this occurring at the translation performance stage can be found in section 5.5.3.h.

Some commissioners demand literal translation, as noted by this translator:

> Some court/police persons require 'word-by-word' translations, and I have to explain the difference between the meaning of the translation when the translator must express the idea into another language. (Participant 46T)

To clarify the preceding: by 'meaning of the translation' this participant refers to how he feels the translation should be performed—that is, by conveying meaning and ideas and not simply transposing words. An overt translation is preferred by Participant 60P, a principal, and is included in their definition of fit-for-purpose: 'in format substantially identical or as close as possible to the original source text'. Other principals require the opposite, such as the following, who describes how translated documents they receive could be improved: 'Less literal translations, more translations of meaning' (Participant 72P).

On occasion, clients may attempt to deploy the covertness or overtness of the translation for their own reasons:

> I have encountered cases where the customer wanted me to 'upgrade' his/her academic grade by using a literal – and wrong – translation into Finnish. Now I solve the problem by leaving the actual foreign title in the original form, a practice encouraged by the authority responsible for the recognition of foreign credentials. (Participant 42T)

Such dilemmas should be regulated by legal translation practitioners' codes of ethics. The point made by the participant raises once again the issue of the

---

[59] 'Originals' refers here not to source texts, but to previous emails or letters to which the replies in question pertain.

potential for translation to be used for adversarial (or unscrupulous) purposes (see section 3.2 [Chapter 3]).

5.5.2.i. Logistical and Commercial Terms

As we saw in section 5.5.2.a, both data sets reported that translation orders for legal texts focused on logistic and commercial terms rather than specifications relating to the technical performance of translation work. In view of my research objectives, which sought to explore whether the briefing process was operating optimally with a particular view to performance, I have focused in the foregoing sections on such technical aspects. Now, however, I will briefly discuss the more material aspects of the brief.

The deadline was cited by almost all participants (98 per cent) as being included in the translation order. In open questions, time was seen overall as a constraint, and will be discussed later in relation to translation performance. Specifically concerning the brief, however, some comments illustrate the fact that good logistics and good communication could make a considerable difference to time pressures. For example,

> An in-house lawyer was pressured by a client and promised to deliver a 40 page translation the same day BEFORE contacting me on my capacity. After saying it wasn't feasible, I was told that it didn't matter, today was the ultimate deadline, they simply needed the translation, no buts. I promised a maximum of 20 pages at most, translated at break-neck speed and delivered the same day. First thing the next morning I received a phone call from the same lawyer demanding the rest of the translation.... (Participant 145T)

Clearly, in the legal world, the production of documents and, by extension, translated documents, is often difficult to plan. In the preceding example, despite a non-negotiable deadline at the end of a day, it emerged that further time was in fact available. We also have a glimpse of the effects of the many intermediaries in the Chain of Supply—the time pressure comes in this instance indirectly, from the lawyer's client.

Tight deadlines cropped up frequently in the data. In the following case the participant underscores the fact that there are periods where she is left without any means of contacting the client—in this case an agency:

> Not the worst, but common: the 'Friday afternoon' syndrome, where great pressure is exerted by an agency to complete a long and urgent job, usually for a court case starting in the US on the Monday, and then the agency being out of contact over the weekend so that difficulties, such as missing pages, can't be reported. (Participant 144T)

As in the previous example, better logistics might have resolved this issue. The importance of dialogue and uninterrupted information flows is also at the forefront.

Since my research questions focus on briefing and performance, I did not attempt to collect data on pricing levels (a major research project in itself).

The survey simply asked whether or not a price was included in the translation order. Here I will limit myself to touching upon the terms used by participants in open questions, insofar as the terms used may reveal, and indeed affect, translator status: 'rate'[60] was used three times as much as 'fee'[61] by translators when discussing price in free text boxes of the questionnaire relating to other issues. Since many participants were not native speakers of English, this is not reliable data, but may merit further research.[62]

Given the nature of legal translation, ensuring confidentiality before work starts is clearly a key issue. On the one hand, professional translators are bound by codes of ethics, and on the other, principals may wish to lay down their own terms—either in an overall contract relating to the outsourcing relationship, in a long-term or job-specific non-disclosure agreement (NDA), or with the translation brief. In any case, it would be reasonable to suppose that such requirements ought to be stated or agreed prior to performance. Interestingly, it was in fact a translator, and not a principal, who raised the issue:

> The worst part of doing legal work is the (1) disregard for confidentiality on the part of the translation buyers (I am the one reminding them of NDAs, for example). (Participant 203T)

In this case it would be interesting to know whether the 'buyers' are intermediaries,[63] and what role they fulfil within their organization.

5.5.2.j. Actors' (Dis)satisfaction with the Brief and Briefing Process

Although a number of expressions of satisfaction and dissatisfaction have formed part and parcel of the foregoing points, I now include an overview relating directly to satisfaction with the briefing process itself. I provide cross-references to salient examples from the data appearing earlier in this chapter.

In order to poll translators' opinions of briefing, Question 8 of the survey asked: 'Are you satisfied with the amount of information you are given by those placing the translation order?'

Figure 5.19 shows their levels of satisfaction in percentage terms, with the numbers of translators shown in white inside the diagram: the majority, two-thirds, ranged from taking a neutral position to being 'not very satisfied' or 'not

[60] Commonly used when referring to hotels, energy, currency, for example. 'Low' was the second most common collocate according to corpus analysis output from the Sketch Engine using enTenTen (retrieved on 1 June 2018).

[61] Commonly used when referring to lawyers, investments, private schools, for example. 'Pay' is the second most common collocate according to corpus analysis output from the Sketch Engine using enTenTen (retrieved on 1 June 2018).

[62] The word 'rate' was used once in the questionnaire, which could then have primed translators to use the same vocabulary. See also section 1.1.3 (Chapter 1) on status signals and terminology.

[63] A well-known translation blog notes, in 2010, the 'common practice' whereby some agencies attach sensitive documents in 'a blanket e-mail [sent] to numerous translators' (retrieved from http://translationmusings.com/2010/02/09/confidentiality-in-the-translation-industry/).

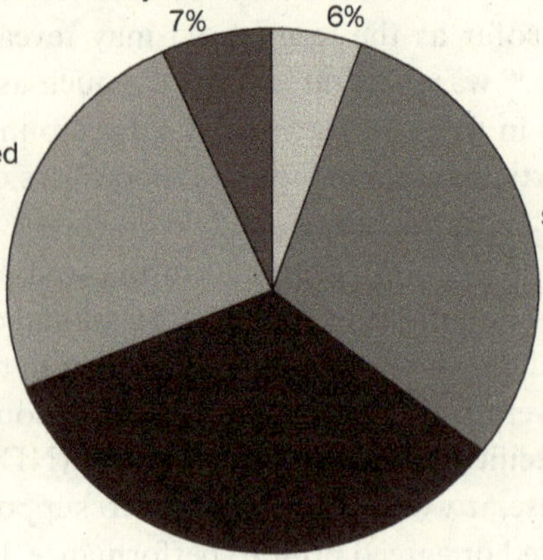

FIGURE 5.19. Translators' satisfaction with briefing.

BOX 5.1

Comments on the Informality of 'Translation Orders'

There is never any info I can use in terms of readers, users or context. It is usually guesswork, unless, as with court cases, it can be seen online. [. . .] my work also comes directly from law offices. (Participant 1T)

Only very basic things are specified in the order – the rest is entirely up to the translator. (Participant 17T)

The translator is simply left to get on with the job as s/he sees fit. (Participant 49T)

I have been translating for my law firms for years and have never had an 'order' as such – just emails, of an increasingly informal nature, attaching the document and giving a deadline (usually 'as soon as possible'). (Participant 108T)

Usually there is no formal order. I work regularly with a number of law firms, and they simply send the texts by email (occasionally by post), and the rates and other terms of reference are generally 'as usual'. (Participant 286T)

Sometimes requests to send portions progressively. Insistence that the best quality must be delivered is not uncommon. Inquiries about discounts and unpaid urgency are common. (Participant 177T)

I usually get just a deadline and nothing else. (Participant 92T)

at all satisfied' with the amount of information supplied to them. The selection of comments in Box 5.1 offers further insights into recurring issues.

These segments illustrate the range of translators' prime complaints: reference material not supplied; very limited specifications given, sometimes comprising solely a deadline; and the informality of orders. They also lament ongoing price pressure, including requests for rush deliveries at standard tariffs.

The majority of translators in the sample were unsatisfied with briefs they received. The principals, on the other hand, did not directly express any satisfaction or dissatisfaction, and we might suppose that this results from a lack of knowledge of the consequences. It is worth considering the extent of the translator's responsibility to elicit a comprehensive brief from the principal, potentially also educating them (see section 4.3.2 [Chapter 4]). This and the following subsections provide examples from the data exploring what happens when translators ask questions. First, it is interesting to report on what is *not* to be found in the data—that is, no principal complained about any translators' queries. Indeed, one person expressed concern about a lack of proactive behaviour on the part of the translators they deal with, as summarized here:

> I always wonder why my phone isn't ringing from the translators i) seeking clarity as to how to translate the passage and ii) suggesting we fix the source document. (Participant PP34)

As well as concern regarding a lack of interaction, the preceding participant acknowledges in passing the likelihood of source text quality issues, and, interestingly refers to 'seeking clarity as to how to translate', which might well relate to an underlying awareness of the lack of a comprehensive brief.

The translators expressed much dissatisfaction regarding the extent to which requesting more ample information upstream was seriously affected by the intervention and/or non-intervention of service provision intermediaries, mainly referred to by them as 'translation agencies'. In view of the number of concerns expressed by the translators about these intermediaries, I have examined them under a number of subheadings on the pages that follow. I have not repeated general concerns on insufficient briefing, given their inclusion in other sections of this chapter.

5.5.2.j.1. Translators' Comments on Service Provision Intermediaries

(i) No direct access to drafters/clients to ask for clarification (see also section 5.5.2.b)

> I work for agencies and as a rule they don't allow a translator to contact their client for questions (the one I am translating for). For instance: I have a question on a very specific term, invented by the lawyer who wrote the text. The agency does not understand the question, has not read the text, is not familiar with legal texts, does not contact the lawyer, asks the whole world for advice (still without understanding the problem) BUT does NOT ask the author of the text (afraid to look ignorant?, afraid to lose his client to me when I talk to him directly?). Very annoying. (Participant 273T)

There are several issues expressed in the preceding extract: impeded direct contact with the drafter of the source text; the fact that this agency does not relay queries, either for fear of losing face, or because they are afraid of being by-passed in their commercial relationship with their client.

(ii) Agencies acting simply as passive mail carriers

Translators in the survey found that agencies often did not examine texts before subcontracting the work: to take an example from Participant 273T in the preceding, the agency 'has not read the text'. It seems that translators often have to point out that the text is in a language that they do not translate, or that pages are missing, for instance.

(iii) *Lack of specialist knowledge* on the part of the agency

Several translators reported, as in the foregoing extract, that agencies are often 'not familiar with legal texts' (Participant 273T). Although some service provision intermediaries are specialized in legal translation, legal documents are often also handled by agencies that cover many different fields (see section 4.2.3 [Chapter 4]).

(iv) Inexperienced agency staff

Criticisms of limited experience often concerned project managers, the habitual point of contact for translators:

> There are agencies with clueless, inexperienced project managers, those with no linguistic background or project management skills. I try to stay a mile away from those, after being burned a few times early in my career. (Participant 231T)

In some cases, their comments related to sales staff:

> In other words, agencies – especially the 'accountant-run' multinationals – depend on sales people to secure jobs, and they make unrealistic promises that are very hard for both the project manager and the translator to meet. (Participant 144T)

A common bone of contention was no first-hand translation experience on the part of project managers or sales personnel—that is, that they could not understand the complexities of the translation task.[64]

(v) Unrealistic timescales

In addition to 'impossible deadlines' cited by several participants throughout the data (see also sections 5.5.2.i and 5.5.3.d), when participants specifically

[64] The role of project managers and their 'balancing act' in attempting to achieve trust from commissioners and translators has been researched by Olohan and Davitti (2015), though not in a specific context of legal translation.

discussed intermediaries their comments included references to periods when translators are left without any means of contacting the agency:

> The timing was such that I had to complete the assignment in the evening, when it was already night in Europe, for delivery the next morning. It was therefore impossible for me to contact the agency before the assignment was due [in order to inform them of bad quality text requiring more work than initially agreed]. (Participant 164T)

(vi) Insufficient or bad-quality reference material

One example of an agency providing substandard reference materials can be found in section 5.5.2.g. In the following case the translator feels that she is able to *ask* for what she needs, but at the same time adds that (as she sees it) the agency is unable to *obtain* it from the final client anyway:

> [I] can ask for references and similar material (but the agency is often unable to obtain this from its own client). (Participant 144T)

(vii) *Confidentiality issues* involving agencies

Confidentiality may be a hindrance at the briefing stage due to redacting of source texts (see also section 5.5.3.d). Texts may also be sent out by agencies without due regard for confidentiality (see section 5.5.2.i).

(viii) A *general unwillingness* on the part of agencies *to interact or engage with the end-client regarding technical issues* that need resolving before translation can go ahead: some project managers are 'reluctant to query their clients' (Participant 190T).

To summarize, it seems from the points in this section that an overall picture of lack of dialogue and passive behaviour on the part of service provision intermediaries is being painted by translators. Further research in this area may be worth undertaking.

5.5.3. PERFORMANCE OF OUTSOURCED LEGAL TRANSLATION

In the following section I address the two research questions looking at performance.[65] As illustrated in Figure 5.20, I open with insights from the data into source text quality, considerations on the legal translator's profile, and views on tools, as well as a number of points relating to logistic constraints and dysfunctions, and then use the components of my model—the tesseract of the legal

[65] Whether principals express any issues vis-à-vis the performance of translations received, and whether legal translation principals and/or translators have any suggestions to improve performance.

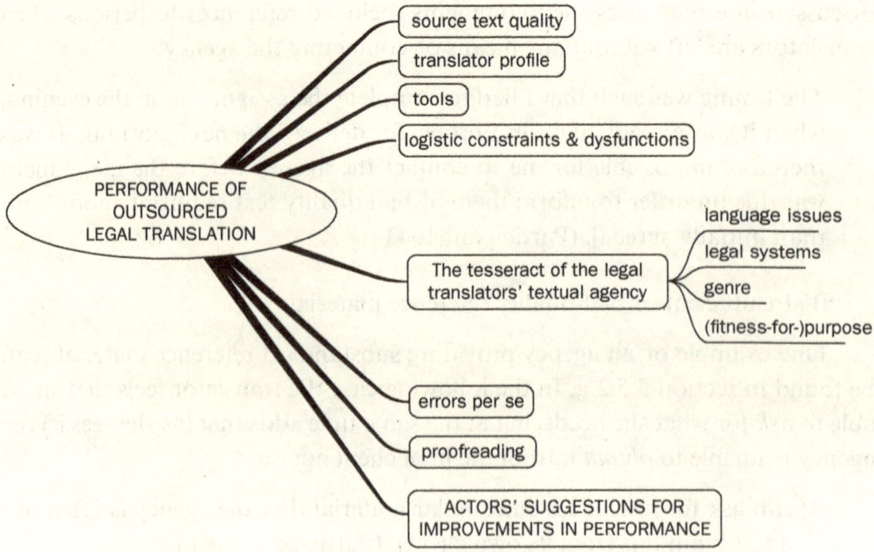

FIGURE 5.20. Performance of outsourced legal translation: research questions and themes.

translator's textual agency (see section 2.5 [Chapter 2])—as the themes under which the data collected are organized and presented. Issues relating to errors and proofreading are then discussed, and finally, principals' and translators' suggestions for improvements in performance.

5.5.3.a. Source Text Quality

Before discussing whether, how, and to what extent a legal translation is performed, an important factor emerging from the data that needs to be taken into account is the quality of raw material—the source text provided by the principal. The issue of inferior source text quality was raised by 14 principals and 94 translators in open questions—thus by one-sixth of those commissioning and one-third of the agents.

One interesting aspect of source text quality, which repeatedly came to light, concerns the translation of legal documents drafted by non-native speakers of the source language.

> Documents are increasingly written in 'bad' English or English-non-English as source text, as a result of [. . .] globalization. (Participant 2T)

Other languages than English are also used by non-natives for legal drafting, such as French in this example:

> Recently translated documents prepared in 'French' in West Africa. The deadline was strict. It was extremely difficult to work out the niceties of the argument. (Participant 6T)

The language quality may lead to ambiguity in such cases, as well as additional work for translators. Several source text quality issues are evoked in the following segment:

> Sometimes contracts seem to be, or definitely are, bad English translations (English being my source language) from another language, or have been written in English by a [non-native] but the (agency) client just gets this from their clients with the brief 'to translate from English' and I believe many end clients if they are companies are not even aware of the bad quality of the English texts. (Participant 179T)

The first point made concerns pivot translation—that is, the English version has already been translated from an unknown previous language. Second, there seems to be a lack of assiduity on the part of the agency in question: either not checking the source text and realizing that it was a translation rather than an original text, and/or not passing this information on to the translator (see also the previous section). The third point concerns educating final clients on source text quality.

The next segment, as well as further attesting to the prevalence of source texts drafted by non-native speakers, relates more specifically to the handling of legal concepts across cultures:

> Since my source texts are in English many contracts are written by non-native speakers in less than perfect English. Quite often I encounter an expression which the author believes corresponds to a legal term in his/her mother tongue – but makes no sense to anyone outside the jurisdiction of origin – or anyone other than the author in fact. Translating into a third language is guesswork in such a case. (Participant 34T)

It seems that this drafter has transferred a legal concept into their source text using a calque,[66] which any translator would then have to handle extremely carefully when producing the target text.

On occasion, pivot translations result from the crossing of more than one family of legal systems[67] (in the following case, civil law, common law, and the Far East) and/or language family (here Romance, Germanic, and Sino-Tibetan, depending on classifications):

> A document written in English which was a result of two translations: an original [Romance language B] notary form for a lengthy power of attorney was translated into [Asian language C], and then the [Asian language C] was translated into English for signature (and then sent to me for

---

[66] A 'loan word' or 'borrowing' (Vinay & & Darbelnet, 1958/2000, p. 85) might be a safer path to choose—see section 2.4.3 (Chapter 2).

[67] With reference to Hertel (2009), and Zweigert & Kötz (2011).

> translation into [variant of Romance language B]). The English was almost impossible to understand.[68] (Participant 235T)

In other instances, problems may have less to do with legal systems and arise at a linguistic level:

> Another frequently arising problem is the fact that many [of] the contracts that have to be translated from English into Greek are not written by natural English-speaking writers creating many problems with the terminology and the vouloir-dire. (Participant 147T)

Very often, translators are expected to right these wrongs, and sometimes expected to go beyond their remit:

> Translation into Italian of a legal document written in a language 'similar to English' by an Italian lawyer and sent to the client in the United States for comments. The register of the source language needs not to be described. The final result was a 'sounding normal' document in the target language which was not accepted by the law firm as such: they expected the translator not to translate the original document starting from the source language (and in the same register) but 'to write' a 'new' final legal document in the target language as [if] the translator were a lawyer and not a translator.... (Participant 2T)

Equally, however, translators can be criticized for going beyond their remit:

> Translations often tend to be only as good as [...] the source text is; if otherwise, then the translator has done too much extra work. (Participant 162T)

Even official texts may sometimes be drafted by non-native speakers:

> [N]ot all legal documents (e.g., surveys of [an international organization] concerning [...] judicial systems) I translate have been written by native speakers of the source language. (Participant 135T)

This may be particularly common in multilingual legal contexts, such as the bodies of the European Union or international organizations.

Many translators and principals complained of bad drafting in general, whether in terms of style, syntax, long sentences, consistency or otherwise. Box 5.2 shows just a few examples.

As well as poor language skills of those drafting, a failure to proofread source texts was also deplored by principals, and not only by translators. One principal found that '[s]ource texts (e.g., insurance conditions) are not properly revised before sending to translation' (Participant 8PP). Another principal

---

[68] I have anonymized the languages involved.

BOX 5.2

A Limited Selection of Survey Participants' Comments on Source Text Quality

> Pleadings. Often hastily prepared, it is often difficult to understand what the point of the argument is. (Participant 6T)
>
> At times the source text, especially in contracts, is not quite clear: The sentences are too long and writing style confusing. (Participant 8T)
>
> [S]ometimes the texts are erroneous ... written in haste ... lots of tautology. (Participant 47T)
>
> [C]onvoluted and wordy. (Participant 145T)
>
> [A]mbiguous/inconsistent terms. (Participant 267T)
>
> Extremely badly-written source text with paragraph-long, rambling, very vague sentences. (Participant 232T)
>
> The originators of legal documents sometimes amend texts without regard to coherence and consistent use of terms. (Participant 36P)
>
> [T]he biggest trouble is in poorly-drafted source documents. (Participant 36PP)

made this suggestion when asked how legal translations they receive could be improved:

> By being always reviewed by legal counsel who *review both the source and target (not just the target)*. (Participant 92P, my emphasis)

This translator distinguishes between factual errors and grammatical errors:

> Factual errors in the source (such as citing a Convention and year which do not match). Grammatical errors in the source (which are *shockingly frequent*) or generally sloppy use of Greek which makes the text nonsense or ambiguous. (Participant 84T, my emphasis)

Factual errors were in fact evoked by several translators, such as '[m]istakes in the source texts (wrong names, places etc.)' (Participant 76T). This pithy comment using a metaphor from information technology sums up the problem:

> Garbage in garbage out. (Participant 171T)

A well-reported feature of legal drafting is the use of 'boilerplate'[69]. Copy-pasting was criticized several times by survey participants, notably in the genre of contracts.

> It was a contract from Greek to English. The lawyer who drew it up probably copied-pasted various texts from various contracts, the language was very conservative, there weren't any commas or full stops. The text was really hard to understand and follow. (Participant 125T)

[69] 'Language which is used commonly in documents having a definite meaning in the same context without variation; used to describe standard language in a legal document that is identical in instruments of a like nature' *Blacks Law Dictionary* (Garner, 2009).

> [C]ontracts or agreements (often copied and pasted from other contracts/documents, inconsistent, grammatically incorrect or words missing). (Participant 160T)

New developments in drafting style were also broached:

> It often appears that the writers of documents are reluctant to improve their style of writing and rather prefer the old way of doing things. They simply ignore the fact that even the 'legal language' is developing and changing and that this should also be reflected in the texts. (Participant 142T)

Baldly speaking,

> Often the [source] text seems to be the result of a bad job of copy and paste. (Participant 107T)

I have already touched upon ambiguity, and in particular its potential as an adversarial tool in legal texts (see section 3.2.1 [Chapter 3]). The issue was raised by a number of participants, such as this relatively proactive translator:

> Also if the drafter has been too 'wordy' or unclear in documents, I usually highlight the ambiguity to the client especially for litigation documents, *in contracts I assume the ambiguity is there for a purpose*, however if it could lead to misinterpretation I usually point this out. (Participant 156T, my emphasis)

Whilst the translator brings ambiguity to the attention of their client in one genre, they do not in another. Such assumptions could hold potential risks, which could be reduced by the provision of a full brief including intended purpose.

Ambiguity may also cause issues downstream, as in this case:

> A one page document with one word that could have had one of two opposite meanings depending on the context. The only way to resolve it was to look at the law itself. The law was the opposite of US law (my legal system). It turned out to be the key and the client was very upset because the opposing counsel used the error against them. (Participant 253T)

Ambiguity can also result from the use of acronyms, tracking down the meaning of which can be especially time-consuming—'the excessive use of acronyms resulting in extra time for research' (Participant 175T)—and they may be mistranslated, particularly where no reference material has been provided.

The (il)legibility of source texts was referred to by several translators, and one principal:

> The actual print can often be very poor quality in Arabic texts especially for court-related documents. (Participant 68T)

> Deportation document that had numerous illegible parts, broken formats for forms. (Participant 86T)
>
> Sworn translations with handwritten text that cannot be decipher[ed] and are needed to be presented as evidence at court. (Participant 154T)

Apart from the preceding examples, other participants cited handwriting, line-spacing, poor scanning or copying, faxes, old documents, lined court paper, and seals as posing problems of legibility.

External constraints can also affect source text quality, and certain business sectors are particularly subject to time constraints. The financial market is one such:

> When under pressure to rush a press release to press (after close of market or before opening of trading the next day) when the source text itself is not logical but they have not had time to edit it properly, so the translator is the first careful proofreader, in fact. And if it goes to press in a way that is misleading (in English, but also in the other languages) there can be terrible consequences. Granted this only happens once in a very rare while, when there is some very market-sensitive news that has to be published at a very particular time and there was not enough advance warning for the authors to think through what they wanted to publish. (Participant 258T)

The preceding comment brings to the fore a point made quite frequently by translators working in the corporate field—that they may be the only person conducting a close reading of the source text.

The corporate world in general is also a fast-moving one, but this participant is resigned to the situation:

> But in general, it often happens that contracts are changed substantially at short notice or that large chunks are added/deleted.... This is one of the drawbacks of commercial law translations one has to put up with. (Participant 250T)

Efficient logistics and open channels for dialogue could nevertheless make a difference in such cases.

The data relating to source text quality bring to light a number of points: the fact that in our globalized world those drafting legal texts may not be native speakers of the language in question; source texts may be pivots or relays into other languages; and expectations or assumptions that translators will 'repair' shortcomings in the source text. Whilst sloppy drafting could and must be addressed by those commissioning translations, ambiguity may in many instances be an intrinsic part of the communicative function of the text, hence the need for open channels for dialogue so that the translator can call attention to serious underlying risks.

5.5.3.b. Translator Profile

Principals were questioned about the skills and qualifications that they considered important for those performing legal translation.

Figure 5.21 shows that principals in the survey saw translation experience and then translation qualifications as most important, together with legal drafting skills, closely followed by a legal qualification in the target language. Seen as slightly less important were a legal qualification in the source language and being a native speaker[70] of the target language. Having practised law was seen as the least important of the items polled. This result could be worth exploring in further research, particularly as regards the planning of legal translation curricula. In free comments, the principals mainly cited legal training, and notably training in comparative law. There were some particularly constructive suggestions by principals regarding collaboration:

> Have translators take a course specifically designed for legal translation given by a bilingual lawyer. (Participant 15PP)
>
> I did not interpret the word 'legal qualification' as 'being qualified to practice law'. Rather, what I think important is the knowledge and understanding

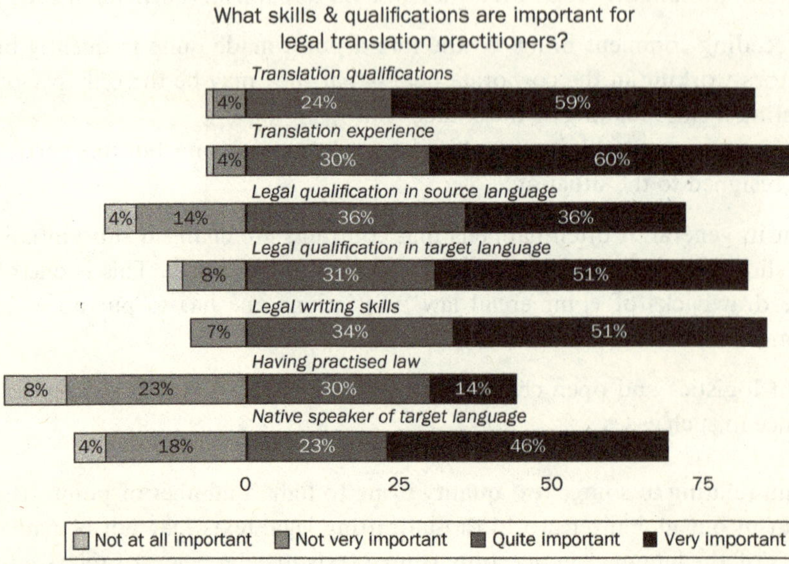

FIGURE 5.21. Skills and qualifications seen by principals as important for legal translation practitioners.

[70] In view of the demographics of the survey, we must take into account the fact that participants also came from countries where legal translation is commonly performed by non-native speakers.

of legal terminology and concepts, and differences/overlapping of legal terms and concepts between the source language and the target language. (Participant 36PP)

Interestingly, apart from three translators citing translation into a target language that is not their mother tongue as being the worst legal translation situation they had encountered, most comments on being a native speaker did not relate to the translator themselves but to source text drafting (see section 5.6.3.a).

One principal bemoaned the fact that translators do not always ensure that their profile fits the job at hand:

> It would be nice if every translator would be honest about their level of proficiency. I've received good test files that were followed by terrible translations, obviously not the work of the same person. There are blue boards for translation agencies but none that I know of to review the quality and reliability of individual translators. It would be great if someone would create an eBay-style database for translator feedback. (Participant 73P)

A European legal translator register might go some way to addressing this issue.[71] Further, its use might be beneficial in reducing non-professional legal translation—there were several comments on that subject: 'client asked wife to look at document', 'client's granny spoke German and they thought she could do the translation', 'bad DIY translations by in-house staff [at a corporation]'.

5.5.3.c. Tools

From afar, the unseasoned spectator of the legal translation market might imagine that machine translation (MT) is not yet (at the time of writing) at a level whereby it could be used for such sensitive texts, except under specific limiting conditions, such as the first stages in a voluminous discovery/disclosure process. However, one frustrated principal described how an unscrupulous service provider had behaved:

> Someone tried to deliver an unedited machine translation and pass it off as a genuine human, proofread translation. Needless to say we caught it and had to have it completely redone, putting us past deadline on an important project. (Participant 73P)

On the other hand, in relation to documents that are troublesome to translate and bad source quality, one translator referred to 'smuggled-in machine translation' (Participant 117T)—that is, a source text that was translated by machine

---

[71] Proposals have been made in this regard as part of the LIT Search pilot project, to explore the 'modalities and practical features' of an EU Database of Legal Interpreters and Translators (LIT Search, 2015). See also Chapter 1, note 19.

as a pivot and then passed on to a human translator to be translated into the final target language.

Six principals in the pilot study (out of 46) confirmed that they used machine translation.[72] Despite sensitivity and confidentiality issues, one principal freely admitted that

> [w]hen we need to use foreign websites (for trademark work, sometimes), we just use Google Translate. (Participant 23PP)

No reference was made by participants in my survey to MT systems purpose-built for legal translation, although, as already mentioned in section 1.1.6 (Chapter 1), proprietary software is in place at some larger service intermediaries and institutions.

Only a sprinkling of participants mentioned translation memories (TMs): half of these comments related to the provision by agencies of bad quality TMs for use in the translation (see section 5.5.2.g), and the remainder concerned technical incompatibilities. However, one might hypothesize that the lack of comment on this subject, which is nevertheless usually a central one for translators, might be due to the stated focus of the survey.[73]

5.5.3.d. Logistical Constraints and Dysfunctions

A number of logistic constraints affecting the performance of legal translations were reported. Time was regularly cited as a constraint by all participants, using words such as '(extremely) tight', 'unreasonable deadline', 'short deadline', and 'impossible deadlines'. Unsocial hours were mentioned, for example, 'overnight', 'all-nighter', and 'weekend turnaround'. Some shortcuts in the process were referred to, such as 'no time for editing', and 'no time for consultation'. One translator regretted that '[t]he amount of time is often insufficient to do proper research + translation' (Participant 51T).

Three translators explained that 'short notice' made their work troublesome. Giving the service provider notice of a forthcoming job is rarely considered by translation principals—work tends to arrive on desks (or in inboxes) unannounced. This might be a potential avenue for logistic improvement—although *all* translations of legal documents cannot be planned for, a considerable proportion *could* be, allowing for research to be initiated, as well as allowing practitioners to organize themselves and their other work accordingly.

---

[72] The question was subsequently dropped in the main phase in order to include other issues deemed more fruitful avenues in the light of the research questions.

[73] As a reminder—the questionnaire titles were, for the Agents data set, 'Legal translators—How are you briefed?' and for Principals, 'Commissioning legal translation' (main phase) and 'Survey of receivers of legal translations' (pilot phase).

Changing deadlines was not even considered as an option by the overwhelming majority of translators. There was, however, one example cited by a lone voice:

> [...] the court (the lawyer company) needed a translation with a very short deadline: a highly technical document. I proposed to summarize the text, translating was impossible, I was not going to do it. Finally, they did get the court session postponed. (Participant 35T)

Logistics may also have been responsible in the following case—a major international criminal trial—but a parallel theme that it brings to the fore, for possible future research, concerns the levels of stress to which legal translators are often subjected:

> They decided to have some court documents translated 3 days before the [major] trial began in [country X]. (Having had 30+ years to get ready for this trial!) They called me repeatedly from [country X] during the night, deleted pages to be translated after I had already translated them, repeatedly called and asked me to send whatever I had done so far.... The stress was incredible.[74]

From the body of survey responses, many 'worst' situations reported in connection with time issues seemed to involve service provision intermediaries, in particular citing communication breakdowns (see also section 5.5.2.j regarding pre-translation issues and agencies).

Finally, as a cautionary tale regarding the serious consequences of time pressure and effects on legal translation performance:

> As a certified translator, I once affixed my translation to some agreements – [...] mortgage or transfer documents I cannot recollect now. It was a large number of documents, and had to be done in a great hurry as the lawyers pressed to make the filing with a real estate register in another city on the same date. A lot of pressure resulted in me making a couple of mistakes, including 'missing out' a number from the size of a land plot – and making it only 387m^2 large in my binding translation – on which the authorities usually rely when registering rights in the register – rather than 3,387m^2. Quite a difference – was spotted by authority and a reason why they rejected the filing, so the translation had to be corrected, and new filing had to be made, which resulted in extension of client deadlines. At the end no one was happy. This taught me well to be very cautious to extreme client pressures, and really think twice before I agree to do a big job in a short

[74] I have anonymized this extract, which relates to a major international trial involving crimes against humanity.

> time – and on a short notice. PS: The numbers are not exact – but correctly represent the amount of my 'mistake'. (Participant 58T)

On occasion, texts to be translated are divided or 'split' among a number of translators. This is generally carried out for reasons of time pressure or volume, or both. The dangers of this in terms of the text relate, in the main, to consistency. The latter issue can be heightened exponentially by imperfect processes for communicating any specific house style or glossary, and worsened still further if a service provision intermediary is involved. The following is an example:

> Lots of translators on a rush job of a large piece of legislation broken down between them. Absolutely no guidance from the agency. Then, after delivery, they write and ask everyone to alter their translations in accordance with a glossary that they have produced, after the job was completed. This involved a second proofread [on the part of the translators], which was time consuming and reduced the profitability of the job. (Participant 174T)

One translator described split translation as the 'worst legal translation situation' they had encountered (Question 12, T), particularly drawing attention to the issue of consistency in terminology: 'Generally speaking—a situation where several translators are working on one text because of time restraints and there is no common glossary' (Participant 161T).

Having in mind one of the criticisms made by translators of service provision intermediaries, that is, a lack of dialogue, I will now discuss interactions during the translation process between principals and translators. Principals were asked, 'How would you describe interaction with translation providers if questions arise?' Clearly this question is a sensitive one, since it potentially involves critical analysis of principals' own processes, and as such we might expect them to report a more positive picture than is actually the case. However, despite this, they reported giving translators access to drafters only 9 per cent of the time, and translators' queries were only encouraged by 65 per cent of principals, as can be seen from Figure 5.22. The same questions were mirrored and asked of translators, and their replies are shown alongside those of the principals.

The two main observations that I would make regarding these results are that translators do not seem to have easy access to source text drafters, and that principals' expressed encouragements of translator contact do not seem to be fully perceived by the agents. However, as noted earlier, the principals and translators are two separate data sets, so this must be interpreted as a general trend only.[75] Notwithstanding, it does not seem that the two groups are working together optimally.

---

[75] Moreover, we must bear in mind, as noted elsewhere, the qualitative nature of the study and the potentially 'high' quality of principals sampled.

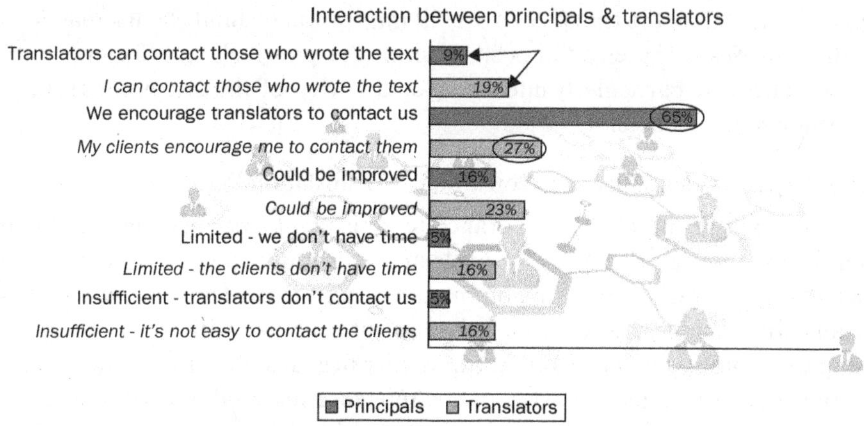

FIGURE 5.22. Interactions during the translation process between principals and agents.

Many translators lament not only a lack of dialogue *per se*, but the frequently negative impact on legal translation performance of the involvement of service provision intermediaries. In the same way as at the briefing stage (see section 5.5.2.j), translators take issue with communication channels being subverted by the agencies, and a lack of specialist knowledge on the latter's part. A particularly sore point is the issue of certain agencies' reluctance to engage with the end-client regarding technical issues. This participant sums up a commonly evoked situation:

> [. . .] the following scenario occurs with relative frequency [. . .] where an agency client is unable to answer my queries in relation to a particular legal text and lacks the confidence to pass them on to their client for fear of appearing 'unprofessional'. (Participant 118T)

One translator has put in place their own query management process:

> The feedback process with the remote-located agency in question was sketchy, despite my very well-rehearsed query management process, with my own standard forms for different types of assignment. It would have been difficult in any case to query points with [a High Court registry]: they are overworked. I generally find that my agency clients approve my query management approach, and are happy for me to use my own forms. Similarly, the end clients are usually responsive, so that I find a certain transparency in query handling. My impression is that the approach I use fosters confidence in the end client. (Participant 276T)

In the preceding segment the issue of 'sketchy' communication and feedback from agencies is raised, as it is elsewhere. This translator has put in place a 'process' and 'forms' to obtain information. The translator assumes that it would be difficult to send queries to the Court in question—presumably the final client.

On the other hand, the translator's overall impression of final clients' reactions to their queries is expressed in positive terms: 'responsive', and 'fosters confidence'. These are particularly interesting data in view of the discussions set out in section 4.3.2 (Chapter 4).

5.5.3.d.1. Confidentiality as a Constraint to Translation Performance

Confidentiality can act as a hindrance to satisfactory performance and can hamper the translator's agency.[76] Clients may redact documents before sending them for translation by blacking out names of parties or items involved in litigation, for example, by replacing sensitive information with symbols, or by using word processing macros that can render files unstable. In addition to redacting, access to interdiscursive and/or reference material may be restricted. This extract comes from a quotation included in the section on briefing and applicable law:

> On that occasion, I felt that they were concerned about confidentiality and therefore had provided minimum background information. (Participant 139T, my emphasis)

One principal included the following in the questionnaire section 'troublesome documents':

> patent applications, requiring extensive technical knowledge that is normally kept strictly confidential by the party filing the application. (Participant 14PP)

As noted in section 3.2.4, such information is crucial for the translator. Gawn refers to withheld reference materials in the following terms: 'short of a miracle, it is unlikely that a [...] version produced in such circumstances can measure up to the quality of the [...] original. It would indeed be unreasonable to expect it to do so' (1988, p. 457).

5.5.3.d.2. Document Formatting

To conclude this selection of logistic constraints to translation performance, it is worth noting that eight principals and 51 translators—almost one-fifth of the total number of participants—cited document formatting as a source of difficulty.

The following problem is a common one, which might be remedied by improved logistics and/or tasking a secretary with applying formatting either before or after translation:

> The client was very strict when it came to deadlines (which were also tight for confidentiality issues) but his documents required endless hours of

[76] See also section 4.1.1.b (Chapter 4) on ethical norms and information asymmetry.

formatting to apply changes and making the translation resemble the original. It was a daunting task. (Participant 69)

5.5.3.e. Language Issues

As already noted in the section on source text quality (section 5.5.2.a), careless drafting in terms of grammar, style, and syntax was reported by participants to have a marked effect on translation performance, making the translator's task more difficult, and, on several occasions, affecting output. There were also some criticisms relating to the nature of legal language,[77] referring to source texts and relating to: archaisms—'arcane and opaque', or 'outmoded', 'conservative' language; legal jargon; and long sentences with 'many subordinate clauses'. Others complained of ambiguity: for example, 'obscure' and 'abstruse'. Regarding target texts, one principal noted legal translation insufficiencies and errors due to a 'lack of collocational competence' (Participant 4PP). Apart from a small number of references to typographical errors, and false cognates, none of the participants discussed any further language issues regarding the target text.

Within the following subsections I highlight data provided in reply to open questions on legal translation performance relating to language variants, language pair–specific issues particular to certain source and target languages, and technical language; language-related 'errors' will be discussed in sections 5.5.3.h and 5.5.3.i.

5.5.3.e.1. Language Variants

Language variants may give rise either to difficulties in understanding the source text or in producing a compliant target text. On some occasions, translators may be less familiar with the variant, and on others the quality of the language may be inferior. A selection of examples cited includes: ''French' in West Africa', 'Mexican Spanish', 'Spanglish', 'Hong Kong Chinese', and 'Austrian German', as well as English variants: 'terminology in English language countries varies'; and Portuguese from Brazil, Portugal, or Portuguese-speaking Africa.

5.5.3.e.2. Language Pair–Specific Issues

Some participants' comments concerned certain language pairs in particular:

> There was also the issue of transliteration-transcription of Cyrillic characters. (Participant 148T)
>
> It is nearly impossible to translate e.g., from English using th[e] original style a Greek judge might use. (Participant 139T)

---

[77] See section 2.1.2 (Chapter 2).

Difficulties sometimes related to the extent to which a language is spoken, and Icelandic and Finnish were cited, as well as the following:

> English, Amharic and Oromigna (the latter two are local Ethiopian languages). (Participant 77P)

Comments were also made about the lack of resources in certain language pairs:

> Lack of specific dictionaries in Italian and Croatian. (Participant 100T)
>
> Terms and conditions for Switzerland, because an official English language terminology does not exist yet. (Participant 10PP)

There were also several comments involving lack of correspondence between Western European and Chinese language pairs.

5.5.3.e.3. Technical Language Issues

Several translators referred to the difficulties of genre mixing (Bhatia, e.g., 2014):

> When a 'legal' document ends up having a lot of technical vocabulary, i.e., when I have done translations for companies working in the energy sector. (Participant 88T)

Patents were brought up by eight translators as being particularly difficult, and by one principal. Regarding discourse communities, several participants reported difficulties with 'jargon', 'firm-specific expressions', or even 'in-house documents, with unexplained abbreviations and terms familiar only to the people involved' (Participant 144T). The following problematic 'technical' sectors and areas were cited, although no overall trend was detectable: oil and gas, dairy, airlines, banking, finance, construction, internal marketing, and distribution arrangements.

5.5.3.f. Legal Systems

Differences between legal systems give rise to some of the thorniest issues that need to be negotiated—those of (non-)equivalence (see section 2.2.2 [Chapter 2]). Figure 5.23 shows the legal systems governing the majority of participants' source and target texts, in percentage terms.

Many participants referred to lack of equivalence between the common law system and code-based, 'civil law', or 'continental' systems, and more generally to the non-equivalence of concepts. Two specific examples given were differences in levels of courts' jurisdictions, and in governmental and institutional structures. Clear instruction on the laws applying to the source and target texts, as we have already seen, is essential, as can be seen from the following story:

> The legal department manager of the agency insisted I should change the translation into Italian of 'summons' from the German legal text (which made a great difference according to the Italian law and in respect of the procedure described therein). (Participant 240T)

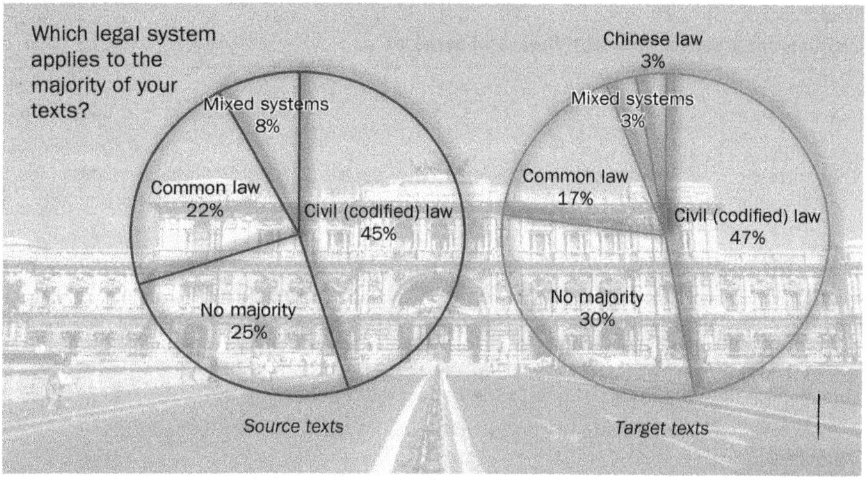

FIGURE 5.23. Legal systems governing participants' source texts and target texts.

In the next situation, however, it was not a question of the legal system applying to the text itself, but the explicitation of legal concepts existing within various legal systems that were referred to in that text:

> The text had several specific references to French, German, and English Law, which sometimes were stated in Spanish, sometimes in the original language, and sometimes with the concept explained. The problem is that the same term appeared written differently, and the Spanish at times was not too good. I researched the original concepts and noticed the inconsistencies in the original. This was an opinion that had already been published, so in English the mistakes [...] would be very noticeable. The problem was really the way the document was written, more than the terminology or content itself. (Participant 91T)

Here, whether calques or borrowings were used or not in the source text and the consistency with which such approaches were adopted gave rise to potentially very serious issues. The translator was also confronted with the difficulty of pointing out errors in the source text—which seems in this case to have been a sensitive 'political' choice.

On the other hand, the translator in the following was faced with bad source text quality via a pivot text and the transliteration of a different alphabet, in addition to very different legal systems with alien concepts, not to mention rulings from now-defunct courts. Their use of the word 'nightmare' does not seem exaggerated:

> When I had to translate a series of Court decisions from [Country A]. I had to work with an English translation, which wasn't very good to begin with. There was also the issue of transliteration-transcription of [...]

BOX 5.3

Selection of Survey Participants' Views on Footnotes

Discrepancies between the legal systems usually *require explanations in footnotes*. (Participant 87T)

Footnoting of problem areas in translation for the purpose of identifying areas that might require rewording in the source language *would be of great benefit*. (Participant 27PP, my emphasis)

Once when the figures in a claim to be submitted to court did not add up and on informing the solicitors I was told to reproduce them as given and sign the translation as true and faithful since the figures would be corrected AFTER I had submitted the job and before being sent off to the court. Needless to say I refused to do so and *sent the translation with a footnote. A rude call followed* but I stood my ground and was shortly afterwards sent the documents with the correct figures. (Participant 55T, my emphasis)

Never use translator footnotes that would be *too intrusive*. (Participant 65T, my emphasis)

Translation of documents into English for use at the courts in [Country A] and the [Country B] *court was simply unwilling to understand, why commentaries and original* [Country B] *terms were added to a translated wording*, as the legal concept would otherwise be unclear. In the end, they apologised and they accepted my original version as the [Country A] courts refused to accept the version the court had sent off. I even refused to certify the version they then sent off before they came back to me for my original translation. I refuse to work for this special court since then. (Participant 173T)

> characters. There was the usual problem of different judicial systems (e.g., in [Country A], arbitration takes place in Courts) and of concepts alien to the [Country B] jurisdiction, such as the 'Supervisory review […]' procedure. To make things worse, the case involved several decisions from authorities of [a former State, no longer exists], making terminology research very difficult. All in all, it was a translator's nightmare! I had to consult with several lawyers and fellow translators in order to present a decent translation. (Participant 148T, anonymized)

A specific technical point mentioned on several occasions was the issue of footnotes.[78] The comments in Box 5.3 give the measure of the problem. On the one hand, a large body of translators,[79] and certain principals, are in favour of using footnotes, or other means of adding translators' notes,[80] notably to explain legal concepts, names of official bodies and courts, or indeed to highlight ambiguities or errors in the source text, and on the other, there is forceful

[78] This section discusses footnotes as a means to annotate the target text. However, one translator participating in the survey pointed out that numerous footnotes in a source text can lead to a great deal of extra work—for example, if they are legal references, in terms of checking and/or finding an appropriate translation, and can also give rise to technology-related issues with certain CAT tools.

[79] Some practice guides also make this recommendation (e.g., Samuelsson-Brown, 2010).

[80] Such as square brackets surrounding an explanation inserted in running text.

opposition to this practice from both groups, either on grounds of intrusiveness or of it being 'unnecessary'.

There were some comments concerning particular 'locales',[81] and one translator made an interesting point concerning 'old' and 'new' legal systems:

> Documents in a language (French would be an example) that has a long legal tradition are more difficult than those in a language (e.g., Romanian) with a relatively short tradition. (Participant 42T).

Along the same lines, and to end this subsection on a positive note, this translator talked of recent progress in legal language in their country:

> On the other hand, the language in Turkish statutes and statutory instruments, especially those framed in the past twenty years or so, even if complex, is almost always correct, logical and consistent. (Participant 49T)

5.5.3.g. Genre and Subgenre

In this subsection I provide examples from the data on the subject of legal (sub)genres and the difficulties inherent in translation performance in order to achieve generic compliance, and begin with an overview of the proportions of genres being outsourced. Principals were asked what types of legal texts they usually commissioned, and translators were asked which types they translated. As elsewhere in this book, the figures are expressed as a percentage of those answering each question, allowing for slight variations in response rates, and allowing for the very different sizes of the data sets. Most interestingly, the results are extremely comparable, as can be seen from Figure 5.24.

Corporate documents such as contracts, terms and conditions, calls for tender, and Articles of Association were the most common genres outsourced. The next most frequently commissioned were court-related documents such as pleadings, judgments, orders, notices of appeal, and so forth. The slightly higher figure for agents might be accounted for by the fact that such translations may be commissioned directly by the court, and, as stated, the judiciary represented a minority of those replying to this survey. Two-thirds of principals stated that they commissioned notarial documents, for example, deeds, wills, and powers of attorney, together with certificates. The higher figure quoted by translators might, once again, be accounted for by direct commissioning, in this instance by the general public.

Surprisingly, legislation seems to be commissioned with a relatively high frequency. It is often assumed that legislation is translated only within institutions, whereas in fact, lawyers often request translations of certain legislative

---

[81] E.g., 'The conceptual gaps between Japanese and German law are considerable' (Participant 89T); 'The Greek legal system is different to the Anglo-Saxon one, with elements from the Roman, Byzantine and German systems' (Participant 139T).

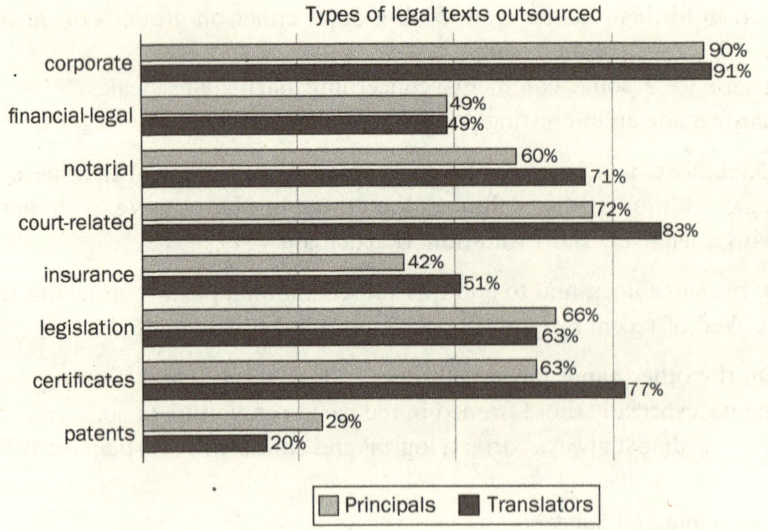

FIGURE 5.24. Proportions of legal text types outsourced by principals and translated by agents.

instruments for the specific purposes of their case. One principal noted that this can also take place within corporations:

> Multi-national corporations routinely deal with foreign laws and regulations and another survey that looks at these translations would be helpful. (Participant 32PP)

Financial-legal and insurance documents were less frequently outsourced. Nevertheless, they represent a substantial figure. The least commonly translated were patents. In view of their technical nature, their outsourcing and translation may be handled by specialists, or, hypothesizing at the other end of the quality spectrum, lawyers may now be availing themselves of the European Patent Office–Google initiative[82] and the general Google Patents engine.[83]

Other documents cited by principals were official documents such as planning permission, due diligence reports, medical charts for use in lawsuits, policy documents, and letters of request for mutual legal assistance addressed to other states. To this list translators added the following: legal opinions; police records; human rights petitions; immigration and deportation documents; exhibits; legal documents in the pharmaceutical, oil and gas, and banking sectors; correspondence; and academic legal texts.

---

[82] 'Patent Translate' now covers 32 languages (as of August 2015).

[83] Covering patents from United States Patent and Trademark Office (USPTO), European Patent Office (EPO), World Intellectual Property Organization (WIPO), *Deutsches Patent und Markenamt* (DPMA), Canadian Intellectual Property Office (CIPO), and China's State Intellectual Property Office (SIPO).

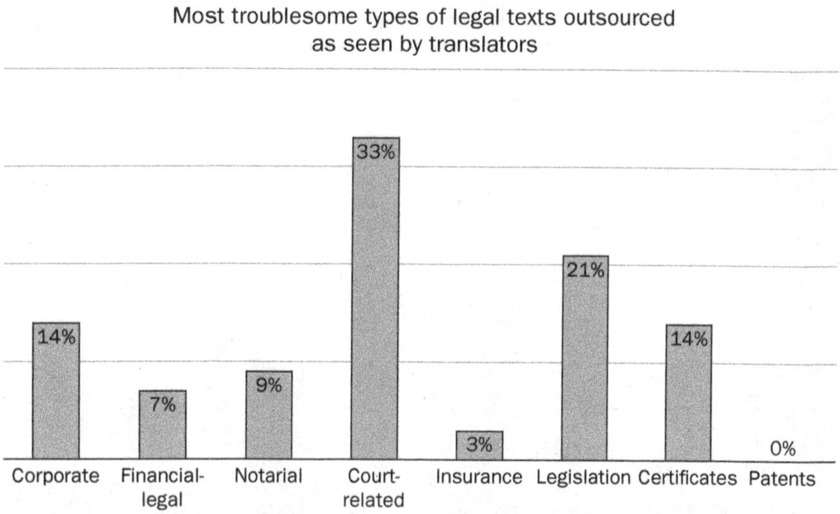

FIGURE 5.25. Text types considered to be most troublesome by translators.

Participants were then asked which they found to be the most troublesome text types. The opinions expressed by translators are shown in Figure 5.25.

For translators, court-related texts and legislation are seen to be those causing the most difficulty. It would be interesting, in further research, to drill down into the reasons for this. They are followed by corporate documents and certificates. Notarial, financial-legal and insurance documents were cited the least often, and patents were not mentioned. The latter results might, however, correspond to the smaller volumes being outsourced in this particular sample.

Figure 5.26 shows the same results triangulated with the views of principals, to provide a comparison between the two data sets.

In this instance, the question format and categories differed considerably between the pilot data set and the main phase, and I have therefore excluded pilot data for this graph. If we take a broad-brush approach, court-related documents and legislation are cited as being troublesome with largely similar frequency by principals and translators. Corporate documents were probably cited more often by principals owing to the composition of that data set (law firms and corporations), whereas the translators, who represented a broader sample of the market, deal with a wider range of subgenres. Similarly, certificates and notarial documents are far less likely to be outsourced by the principals' data set—requests for such documents are more likely to come from individuals. The following were cited as troublesome by single participants: public tenders, academic papers, patents, and legal opinions.

5.5.3.h. Fitness-for-Purpose of Target Texts

In the foregoing sections, I have presented data on legal translation performance under the themes of language (section 5.5.3.e), legal systems (section 5.5.3.f),

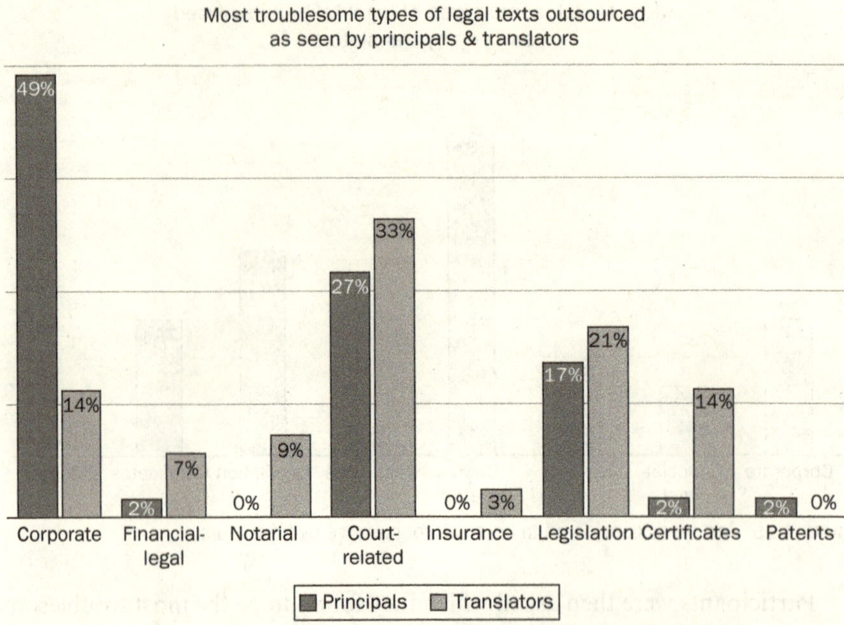

FIGURE 5.26. Troublesome subgenres triangulated between translators and principals.

and genre (section 5.5.3.g). I now examine data relating to the purpose(s) of the source and target texts, and in particular the fitness-for-purpose of the translation (see also section 3.3.1 [Chapter 3]).

5.5.3.h.1. Participants' Definitions of Fitness-for-Purpose

The questionnaire invited principals to define 'fit-for-purpose'. Wide-ranging replies were collected—from the text of a European standard[84] to far more personal and subjective contributions. One principal gave this insightful definition:

> A translation that meets the goal it is intended for (provided that translators are aware of such goal, which is not always the same goal [as that] of the source). (Participant 4PP)

This particular principal seems fully aware of the need to brief translators with the intended purpose both of the ST and of the TT, underscoring the fact that these two elements are not always identical, and hence acknowledging that some adaptation may be required from the translator. Another principal produced this demanding version:

> Accurate representation of the source (linguistically and legally), consistent terminology, free of typographic errors, sounding natural and 'native', in

[84] EN 15038, *Translation Services – Service requirements.*

format substantially identical or as close as possible to the original source text. (Participant 100P)

One might challenge whether the translator's remit involves the *legal* 'representation' of the source, and a tension may also arise between 'sounding natural' and 'close as possible' to the ST—furthermore it is not clear whether 'format' refers to layout or textual content. Nonetheless, this definition encapsulates the challenges comprising the tesseract of the legal translator's textual agency (see section 2.5 [Chapter 2]).

A lone voice, worthy of note, gave the definition 'Gist translation.' Their interpretation of fit-for-purpose was thus a *minimum* level of quality. The remaining definitions of fitness-for-purpose given by principals can be summarized in Box 5.4.

There were thus a wide variety of definitions, as already intimated in section 3.3 (Chapter 3) in relation to the market as a whole.

5.5.3.h.2. Fitness-for-Purpose as It Relates to Quality Appraisals

I have discussed fitness-for-purpose as a potential benchmark for quality (see section 3.3.1 [Chapter 3]), as adopted, for example, by the European Commission. In parallel, a lack of fitness-for-purpose may be perceived as an 'error'. I should first like to draw a distinction between errors that are inaccuracies in absolute terms, such as typos, omissions and similar, and issues that, although sometimes referred to as errors by participants in my survey, may well relate in fact to incompatibility with the purpose of the translated text—that is, suitability of terminology, register, covert–overt positioning, 'improvements', or additions. Here I will discuss the latter group, and the former will be discussed in section 5.5.3.i, under the heading 'Errors *per se*'. Figure 5.27 shows fitness-for-purpose incompatibilities drawn from principals' answers to the question, 'What are the most frequent criticisms of translated legal documents that you handle?'.

BOX 5.4

Definitions of Fitness-for-Purpose ('Principals' Data Set)

A synonym for translation quality

Usable in the appropriate context

Good enough for the circumstances

Usable as it stands without any alterations/review

Takes into account/depends on intended purpose

Takes into account end-user

Meets the intended goals

Same impact/consequences as the original text

No errors that could lead to legal problems

No errors that could lead to misinterpretation or to misunderstanding

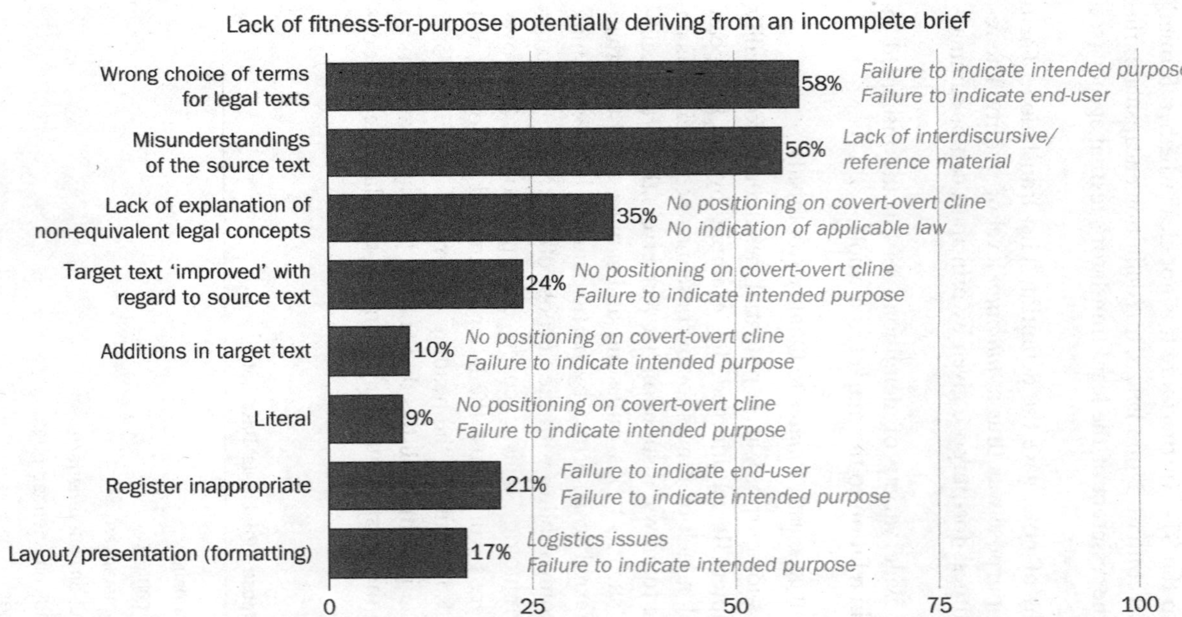

FIGURE 5.27. Principals' criticisms of translated legal documents aligned with potential briefing failures.

The criticism cited most frequently was 'wrong choice of terms, not suitable for the legal field'. Although this might be an error *per se*,[85] it could also be the result of a failure to provide the intended purpose in the brief, such as whether the document was to be legally binding or for information purposes, or indeed a failure to specify the end-user, for example, whether the general public or a specialized audience. If we assume that a translator is competent, misunderstandings of the source text could well be related to the absence of contextual background materials and references.

The next four most commonly cited criticisms were the following: lack of explanation of non-equivalence in foreign legal systems; target text 'improved'; additions made; and literal translation. These relate squarely to a failure to express the covertness or overtness required from the translation (covert–overt positioning), and, for the latter three, potentially also to unknown target text purpose, while the first may also be due to a failure to state the law applicable to the text. Inappropriate register could be the result of failure to indicate the end-user of the target text and/or a failure to state the intended purpose.

Lastly, layout and formatting issues may be the result of source text quality (see section 5.5.3.a), where PDFs, handwritten texts, or faxes are provided; and the logistics of conversion into a word-processed format; but they may also be derived from a failure to communicate intended purpose—for example, where translations are certified translation for official authorities and page layout has to be recreated manually,[86] or FIPO where layout does not need to be reproduced.

In the light of all of the preceding, I posit that a highly interesting avenue for further research is the extent to which briefing failures may affect fitness-for-purpose.

5.5.3.h.3. Expert Appraisals of Contested Translations Deemed Unfit-for-Purpose

Translations held to be deficient or unfit-for-purpose may be the subject of expert appraisal, contested and adduced in litigation, where each party may subsequently apply to the Court for a direction to instruct and rely on their own expert, and/or a fresh translation may be ordered by a judge.[87] Where contested for valid reasons,[88] such examinations should be taken very seriously, calling upon translation practitioners to prepare expert witness reports with adequate

[85] Such as collocational errors, polysemic terms, and/or unsuitability for the (sub)genre.

[86] See, for example, AUSIT Best Practices for the translation of official and legal documents (2014).

[87] It seems that there is very little literature on this subject, apart from some instances under French law cited by Monjean-Decaudin (2012).

[88] The contesting of translated documents by lawyers for adversarial purposes is an interesting avenue of research that I hope to pursue.

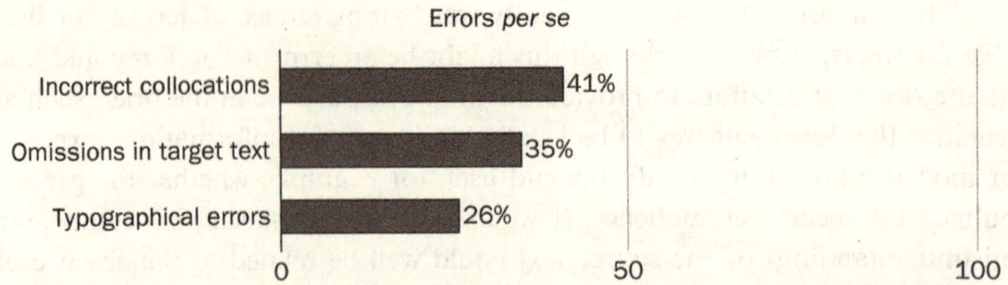

FIGURE 5.28. Principals' criticisms of translated legal documents categorized as errors *per se*.

notice.[89] One translator gave an example of an expert appraisal requested within a very short period, going completely against such prescriptions:

> Expert opinion on a series of errors in a certified third party translation of a contract from English to French – commissioned at 6 p.m. and to be drafted overnight. Client (German law firm) did not specify the language required for this expertise – it might indeed have been needed as evidence to be submitted to a French Court or to a German Court. (Participant 41T)

It is also worthy of note that the language of the report was not specified, which constitutes yet another example of failure to specify intended purpose.

5.5.3.i. Errors *per se*

As a continuation of the foregoing subsection, Figure 5.28 shows the remainder of principals' criticisms of the translated legal documents they handle. I have elected to categorize these as 'errors *per se*', as they would appear to oversights on the part of the translator and unrelated to briefing issues.

The first group is most interesting, and confirms legal translation scholars' postulates concerning the difficulty of legal collocations for translators who may not be trained in the law, or indeed for less experienced lawyers, and the need for legal collocation resources (see in this regard, among others, Biel, 2010a, 2010b, 2012; Scott 2012; and discussions in section 2.1.3 [Chapter 2]).

It is surprising to note, despite the wide availability of automatic spellchecks in word processing software, that typographical errors nevertheless represent 26 per cent of the criticisms reported. We may speculate that omissions in the target text are, like typos, due to negligent proofreading.

[89] See in this regard the UK Ministry of Justice, Practice Direction 25B—The duties of an expert, the expert's report [. . .]: 'Preliminary enquiries which the expert should expect to receive (6.1) In good time for the information requested to be available for—(a) the court hearing [. . .]; or (b) the advocates' meeting or discussion'.

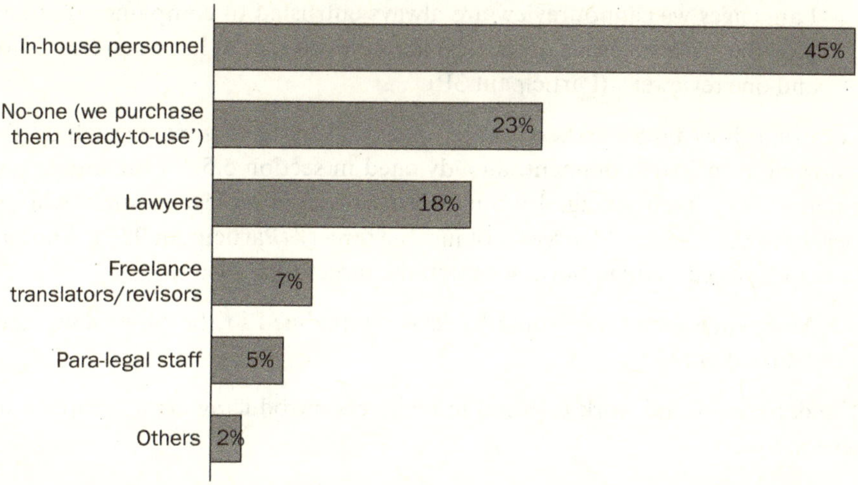

FIGURE 5.29. Proofreaders of outsourced translated legal texts as stated by the 'Principals' data set.

5.5.3.j. Proofreading

Although this book is focused on outsourced legal *translation*, proofreading is, of course, a fundamental part of the process. Professional translators proofread their own work thoroughly, and, depending on the intended purpose of the target text, there may be one or more discrete proofreading stages. I report here survey participants' comments on the proofreading[90] of outsourced translations, while references to the revision of source texts have been included in section 5.5.3.a. Figure 5.29 shows principals' answers to the question, 'Who proofreads/revises/checks translated legal documents you receive?'

It seems that, within the organizations represented in this data set, proofreading is mainly carried out in-house, although a noteworthy percentage of texts are purchased 'ready-to-use'. Lawyers proofread one-fifth of the documents—it would be interesting to ascertain on what basis such texts are selected.[91] In an open question, one principal explained how they organize the proofreading of languages they are unable to check:[92]

---

[90] Also referred to as 'revision' or 'review'. These terms may be treated as synonymous or not by different organizations and in translation standards.

[91] As already noted, it is likely that the principals data set leans towards the higher end of the market.

[92] The criteria by which principals' deem themselves 'able' to check translations would be worth examining. This may, for instance, involve in-house staff who speak the language in question (with varying levels of proficiency), but have no experience in translating.

> Languages we cannot review are always entrusted to companies that employ the same stringent review rounds as we do (use at least one translator and one reviewer). (Participant 3P)

Regarding how target texts could be improved by further proofreading, the following principal's comment, already cited in section 5.5.3.a on source text quality, is worth reiterating: 'By being always reviewed by legal counsel who review both the source and target (not just the target)' (Participant 92P). Another principal placed more importance upon the target legal system:

> More time for proofreading by lawyers qualified in the target language. (Participant 8PP)

The dangers of and work involved in reviewers introducing errors cropped up several times:

> arbitrary changes by an unknown 'proofreader' described as 'errors' – e.g., 'purchaser' instead of 'buyer', giving rise to time-consuming justification of my choice of vocabulary. (Participant 12T)
>
> I assess the chance of a proofreader not injecting errors into a legal text as very slim. (Participant 117T)

Faith may be placed in the judgement of proofreaders outside the profession as in the following example, or in other instances that of (inexpert) clients or their colleagues, and in particular non-native speakers.

> I'm a certified translator; I translated a document and had it proofread by another certified translator. Delivered final product to client whose wife spoke the languages involved. Client asked wife to look at document, and she proceeded to tear it apart erroneously. Client then refused to pay me. When I asked to see document to see what 'errors' had been found, the client refused, saying his wife was perfectly bilingual, and he trusted her more than he could trust someone he didn't live with (I swear this happened!). (Participant 80T)

As was the case in section 5.5.2.j on briefing, the issue of agencies with inadequately qualified staff was evoked:

> Despite the fact that they sell themselves as specializing in 'legal' work, agencies rarely have checkers with specific legal training or sufficient legal translation experience. (Participant 118T)
>
> 'Meddling' by agency in-house revisors who have little or no knowledge of legal terminology and style. (Participant 24T)

A very commonly expressed issue for translators when they are asked to proofread translations produced by others, that is, to provide a proofreading service as opposed to a translation service, was the dilemma between 'repairing' a bad quality target text and retranslating.

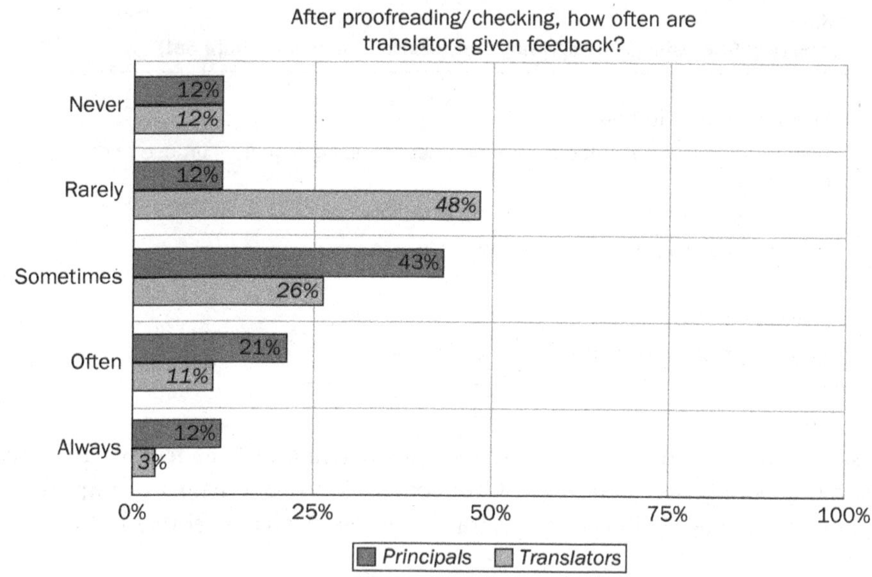

FIGURE 5.30. How often translators are given feedback after proofreading/checking.

> . . . the previous translation [was] so poorly written, that I decided to restart the translation process. (Participant 178)
>
> Worst situations were the revisions of bad translations within a very constrained timeframe, i.e., to 'save what could be saved' while the texts were full of serious errors in the legal terminology used. The bad experience was enhanced by having to convince the client the fact that more time was needed to 'fix' the texts to an acceptable level. (Participant 179T)

Where a bad target text is outsourced for proofreading, the extent of work involved may thus be difficult for the service provider to explain or prove to their client—having ramifications on price, time required, and so on.

Once proofreading has been completed, feedback may or may not be given to the translator—for training purposes, to acquaint them with house style for a long-term client, in order for them to express agreement or disagreement, or for other reasons. Figure 5.30 shows participants' replies to a question aimed at ascertaining how much feedback is given to external translators after the proofreading stage.

As readers will note from the preceding,[93] it seems that proofreading feedback is not consistently given to external translation practitioners by their principals, as reported by both groups—and is in fact given, broadly speaking, much

[93] As on other occasions in this book, figures have been presented as percentages to allow for comparison between the two data sets, which were of unequal size.

BOX 5.5

Summary of Suggestions on Improving Performance ('Principals' Data Set)

- Improving source text quality
- Sharing information with the service provider, including intended purpose and end-users
- Consulting with instructed counsel and/or drafters
- More proofreading, including by lawyers
- Using professional translators
- Translator training
- Allocating more time for the translation process

less than half of the time. This is not a positive finding,[94] as feedback in this field is generally accepted (e.g., Strandvik, 2015) to be a means of improving quality in the mid- to long-term, as translators learn what is required of them.[95]

5.5.3.k. Principals' Suggestions for Improvements in Performance

The questionnaire specifically asked principals, 'How could the translated legal documents you receive be improved?' It is worth noting that rather than focusing on errors, or criticizing translators, as one might have expected, the principals offered many productive suggestions on how improvements could be made, which are grouped and summarized in Box 5.5. Several of them relate to the principals' own processes.

I now include some pithy appreciations that were contributed. The first focuses on sharing interdiscursive reference materials:

> It is easier if you can share some rules and policies of the company with the service provider. It will help him to provide you with better documents. Whenever possible, share specific documents, contract or clauses you want him to follow. (Participant 27P)

The second is by one among several principals who stipulated knowledge by the translator of the target text's intended purpose and/or end-user as a way to improve performance. It is worth reflecting whether their awareness was provoked by the inclusion in the survey of questions on those specific points, or whether they were aware of them prior to the survey.

> By specifically knowing their final destination and use. (Participant 11P)

[94] The finding is, however, consistent with Drugan—she notes regarding feedback that it 'is rare for many freelance translators, who see little client feedback' (2013, p. 30).

[95] It is interesting to note that the principals report giving feedback to translators considerably more than translators report receiving it. This trend comes to light in other areas of this survey; however, as reiterated several times, no conclusions could thereby be drawn, owing to the qualitative nature of the study and to the potentially 'high' quality of principals sampled.

A smaller number of principals focused on proofreading as a way to make improvements: 'Proofreading. More proofreading.' (Participant 37PP). Several others cited 'review' (which may or may not equate to actual proofreading in their minds) by lawyers. The following participant, importantly, specifies review of the source text as well as the target.

> By being always reviewed by legal counsel who review *both the source and target (not just the target)*. (Participant 92P, my emphasis)

Many other comments related to heightened collaboration and interaction between actors involved, and were offered both by principals in answer to the preceding question, and volunteered by translators at various free text opportunities in their questionnaire.

5.6. Summary of Survey Findings

Before discussing the detailed findings, it is worth mentioning the interest that the survey as a whole seemed to provoke in participants: my offer of access to the final findings was taken up with alacrity, as 90 per cent of principals and 91 per cent of translators asked to be sent the results.

According to triangulated results from survey participants, legal translation briefs often constitute merely a purchase order. They contain almost systematically a deadline, the language pair and price, and to a lesser extent, file format. Far less often, they may contain reference material, a specification of the end-user and/or intended purpose, or a covert-overt positioning (section 2.4.3 [Chapter 2]). Information on the legal system(s) applying to the source and target texts and preferred handling of any non-equivalence in legal concepts is very seldom provided. From the data we may therefore surmise that legal translators are being instructed on the basis of logistic and commercial terms, as opposed to being given a comprehensive *technical* brief. The consequences for quality are considerable, especially if we take a functionalist stance whereby the translator needs to be in possession of such a brief in order to perform effectively his or her task.

Only one-third of the translators polled were satisfied with the way they were briefed. In order to remedy this situation, one might suggest that they adopt a proactive attitude and request missing information. This does not seem impossible—on the contrary, no principal criticized translators for raising queries, and in fact one principal expressed concern about why translators were not more proactive in this respect (see section 5.5.2.j). Furthermore, a majority of principals (around two-thirds) responded favourably to informing translators of the intended purpose of the target text, differentiating its status, and informing translators of the end-user profile.

The principals reported that many of the translations they outsource have sensitive status: they are either legally binding, or texts where 'every word and even punctuation counts', whilst translations for gist or those that are not legally binding were in a minority. This finding merits further investigation, particularly if combined with additional research on overall volumes outsourced, as it could suggest (i) that outsourced legal translations may be an area of potentially high (legal) risk; (ii) that far more care should be taken when outsourcing the translation of legal texts; and (iii) that informing external translation practitioners of the intended purpose or destination and status of the text could be even more relevant.

The textual genres outsourced were wide-ranging, though corporate and court-related documents and legislation figured highly and appeared to be the most troublesome. From the data, it seems that we must not assume that legislation is always translated in-house at institutions or with the commensurate resources and support. There may be interesting implications for translator training programs, that they should take into account volumes of genres actually translated in practice.

The role of service provision intermediaries in briefing and translation performance was heavily criticized by translators. Such findings are in line with those of Fraser (1997), whose respondents described translation agencies as 'merely "document shifters"', and the more recent findings of Suojanen, Koskinen, and Tuominen (2015) (see section 3.2.6 [Chapter 3]). Issues include the following: translators report great difficulties in having contact with source text drafters and/or commissioners to discuss their technical queries; intermediaries' inexperienced staff and lack of specialist knowledge; passive behaviour in their intermediary role and a general unwillingness to interact or engage regarding technical issues; insufficient briefing in general; unrealistic timescales; and insufficient or bad quality reference material. In sum, information 'atrophy' is highly likely to have an adverse affect on the target text.

Both translators and principals provided a wealth of comment on unsatisfactory source text quality—worsened by a failure to proofread and/or revise texts before sending them to the translator. Problems also ensue from the ambiguity inherent in the macrogenre. Such source text issues tend to be exacerbated when intermediaries are involved, underlining the need for open communication channels. In addition, translators stated that principals often expected them to make up for shortcomings in the source text. It is important to note that on several occasions drafters of legal texts were reported as not being native speakers of the languages employed, possibly as a result of the increasing globalization of commercial and legal interactions. The risks involved are manifold. Similarly, where source texts act as pivots or relays into another language there is a danger of content distortion during that process, both from a linguistic and a legal point of view.

On the subject of unsatisfactory translation performance, from the translator's side many criticisms and suggestions relate unspecified parameters for their task. Apart from those comments, language issues were mainly limited to usual and well-known features of legal discourse, such as its archaic nature. There were recommendations that language variants should be specified, and some observations on translation complexities present in mixed genres and arising from corporate jargon. The explication of legal concepts, for example by means of footnotes, appeared to be a key area of concern with potential for progress to be made in client education in order to address the challenges involved in negotiating source and target legal systems. Among non-technical or logistic constraints, translators foregrounded the dangers of split translations for reasons of consistency; and any redacting by principals for confidentiality reasons was also singled out as a source of risk, as it could obscure meaning.

Fitness-for-purpose, a notion offered for discussion in the survey, was interpreted variously by principals: as an expression of quality; with different criteria ranging from 'good enough' or 'usable' to 'error-free' from both a linguistic and legal point of view. Some participants added that the term 'fitness-for-purpose' signified that translations were usable without further review. It was also defined as meeting intended goals, or taking into account intended purpose and end-user.

I was able to map principals' criticisms of unsatisfactory translation performance, or lack of fitness-for-purpose, onto the briefing components postulated in section 4.4 (Chapter 4): hence 'misunderstood source texts' may stem partly from a lack of interdiscursive and/or reference material; 'lack of explanation of non-equivalent legal concepts', 'improvements or additions to target texts', and 'literal translation' may stem from a failure to specify the (c)overtness of the target text and/or to indicate intended purpose; and 'inappropriate register' may be the result of a failure to state end-user profiles. Such mapping is clearly at a very early stage, and needs to be tested and developed further. Regarding errors *per se*, whilst closer proofreading seems required on occasion in respect of omissions in target texts and typographical errors, there are interesting potential avenues for improvement in relation to incorrect collocations. It is also worth noting that it was far from systematic for translators to be provided with feedback after the proofreading stage.

When discussing the profile required of legal translation practitioners, principals added legal writing skills and training in comparative law to the customary translation experience and qualifications; a lower priority was given to legal qualifications in the target culture, and even less in the source culture; while having practised law was seen as a far less important criterion. Being a native speaker of the target language was seen as relatively important. A small minority of principals had contact with machine translation: as pivot source text material, where problems akin to those engendered by poor drafting could arise; and second as a tool for gist understanding in their legal practice. In the second case, client education should ensure that principals are fully cognizant with the potential risks and temper their expectations to the realities of the tool. There were comments from both data sets about non-professional translation, and one principal suggested an 'eBay-style database for translator feedback'—this echoes the moves currently being made at institutional level towards an EU database of legal translators as part of the *LIT Search* project.

I refer in Chapter 4 to relational agency, and boundaries where professions interact (or should interact) in performance of a given task, and even a private bank where translation is seen to be a team effort (section 4.3.2). It is, then, perhaps reassuring in the light of the serious flaws that came to light in my survey of the outsourced legal translation market, to conclude that overall, collaboration between lawyers and linguists, consultation, information-sharing, and better information flows were cited by participants on many occasions as avenues for improvement.

5.7. A Briefing Template for Practitioners

In the light of the foregoing data, the theoretical discussions presented in section 4.4 (Chapter 4), and market initiatives studied (section 4.2.2), I present here a briefing template for use by commissioners of legal translation, whether lawyers, translation agencies, court personnel, or corporations. The template is also targeted at adoption by legal translation practitioners, to assist them in taking a proactive stance to obtain the information they need to perform their work (see section 4.3.2 [Chapter 4]).

The template covers two pages (Figures 5.31 and 5.32), which could potentially form recto/verso if printed, although in view of current practice, electronic completion is far more likely.[96] The first page comprises a technical brief, and the second contains 'logistic' elements.[97] The layout takes into account client feedback from exploratory enquiries predating this doctoral project,[98] which suggested that 'tick-boxes' were more likely to elicit a response than areas for free text, and that for maximum uptake the document should be as succinct as possible. Similarly, the language used has been adapted for the target audience.[99] An area has been left blank at the top left for commissioners or translation practitioners to insert their own logo and/or contact details should they wish to do so. As part of the delivery instructions on the second page,

---

[96] Translations are invariably commissioned via email at this time.

[97] The reasoning behind this was to further underline the separation and the need for a 'technical' brief not limited to logistic requirements.

[98] In 2011, I carried out some limited field testing of a draft briefing template with eight translation agencies with whom I had professional contacts (unpublished paper).

[99] E.g., 'document for translation' rather than 'source text'; 'translated text' rather than 'target text'; 'word-for-word' translation rather than 'linguistic equivalence' or even 'literal translation'; 'translation should read like an original document' rather than 'dynamic equivalence' (e.g., Bassnett, 2002, pp. 32–38). The wording in the template shown in Figures 5.31 and 5.32 is aimed at use by translation practitioners and would need slight adapting for use by commissioners.

[Logo] LOREM	TECHNICAL BRIEF
DOCUMENT FOR TRANSLATION	
Purpose of document for translation (Why was it written/created?)	Please specify: __________ (e.g. to agree distribution, to inform our customers, submission to/issued by Court...)
Type of document for translation	Please specify: __________ (e.g. contract, correspondence, legislation...
Status of document for translation	☐ legally binding, ☐ not legally binding ☐ draft ☐ other, please specify __________
Language & country of document for translation	__________(e.g. Luxembourg French)
Law(s) governing document for translation	☐ country/State __________ ☐ Federal/EU __________ ☐ specific Act/law __________ ☐ other - please specify: __________
TRANSLATED TEXT	
Purpose (Why is it being translated?)	☐ litigation ☐ evidence in court ☐ discovery/disclosure ☐ research (of foreign law) ☐ service of proces ☐ to inform our clients/employees.................. ☐ to be filed with an authority __________ ☐ other __________
Type of translated text	Please specify: __________ (e.g. contract, correspondence, legislation...
Should the translation be 'covert' or 'overt'?	☐ Translation should read like an original document ☐ Please add footnotes for explanations of foreign legal concepts/terms ☐ Please add explanations in running text in [brackets] ☐ Please inform us of errors and ambiguities in the document to be translated ☐ Please add a note to translation if there is an error or ambiguity in the document to be translated ☐ word-for-word translation (Why? __________)
Translated text status	☐ legally binding ☐ not legally binding ☐ FIPO (for information purposes only) ☐ draft ☐ other - please specify: __________
End-user	☐ lawyer ☐ authorities ☐ general public ☐ other - please specify: __________
Translated text language & country	__________ (e.g. British English/American English)
Law(s) governing translated text	☐ country/State __________ ☐ Federal/EU __________ ☐ specific Act/law __________ ☐ other - please specify: __________
REFERENCES & PREFERENCES	
Reference materials or preferences enclosed	☐ legislation ☐ case law ☐ court rulings ☐ case documents ☐ glossary, preferred terms ☐ house style ☐ previous translations ☐ other items __________

FIGURE 5.31. Briefing template, technical section.

I have included alternative wordings to be indelibly marked (see section 4.4 [Chapter 4]), to encourage commissioners to adopt this practice.

The template is intended for widespread dissemination, and I have already initiated discussions with certain authorities to garner support, because the backing of well-known names and/or their branding could be a significant

[Logo] LOREM	LOGISTICS
Contact details for decision-maker who can deal with queries and provide feedback	
Source text file format	
Number of words	
Translated text: formatting required?	☐ Please provide text only ☐ Please recreate format of document to be translated ☐ Other - please specify: ______________________
Proofreading/Review/Revision	☐ Please provide translation proofread and ready to use ☐ We will handle proofreading ourselves ☐ Other arrangement______________________ ☐ Please liaise with our proofreader Contact details:
TERMS	
Date/time required	
Fee agreed	
DELIVERY INSTRUCTIONS	
INDELIBLE MARK	☐ Translated on [date] ☐ Translated by [name] ☐ Translation status: for information purposes/(not)legally binding/ unofficial/courtesy/for convenience... ☐ The official/binding version is [e.g. French] (link/reference)

FIGURE 5.32. Briefing template, logistics section.

factor in potential uptake in certain quarters, such as by law firms. I also intend to leverage online channels and marketing methods to boost uptake in the stakeholder community (Scott, 2015b), such as employing professional design services to optimize the visual aspect for subsequent use in the commercial world, where appearance is not a trivial matter. Translators' groups and professional bodies will also be contacted, with a view to stimulating proactive behaviour. Dissemination to translator trainers through academia and other channels is also on the agenda.

Conclusions

> The future [. . .] is full of excitement and new possibilities as long as we keep our minds open, and keep looking for more interesting and insightful answers to the questions we have been bothered about for a long time.
>
> —Vijay K. Bhatia (Bhatia & Nodoushan, 2015, pp. 127–128)

From the outset, this project has been informed and constrained by interactions—those between academia and practice, and those between legal and translation practitioners. Positioned as it is within the highly interdisciplinary field of Legal Translation Studies, it could not but be so. The following conclusions reflect that plurality. Even the very fabric of the book is apportioned between theoretical process models developed, empirical data gathered, and pragmatic findings and suggestions.

The questions that underpin my research address how outsourced performance of legal translation may be optimized, and look closely at how practitioners are supplied with their work. The term I chose to adopt for that phase was 'briefing', and its substantive form 'brief', used by scholars such as Fraser (e.g., 1996) or Nord (e.g., 1997), in creative professions such as those involving communication, and within the legal profession (section 4.2.1 [Chapter 4]). The study of the briefing and text production process also takes into consideration the environment within which legal translation is outsourced—the organization of the market—and its potential effects on the success of performance.

The theoretical notion of agency, which lies at the very heart of translation, has been a transversal one for my work, in three forms. First, the prism of corporate agency theory (section 1.2 [Chapter 1]) provides illuminating tools to explore the environment: the concepts of information asymmetry and goal divergence, the appreciation of risk, and the application of the metaphor of a contract to the two groups that were the main focus of my study (commissioners and translators), regarding them as 'principals' and 'agents'. Agency is not foreign to Translation Studies, albeit used primarily from a sociological standpoint. My second application of the concept is in the form of textual agency—the translator's mediation of the text—and its various facets. The third manifestation in this book is in the form of relational agency, as a tool to analyse market actors' behavioural interaction.

C.1. Outsourced Legal Translation *in situ*: The Chain of Supply and Its Implications

The environment in which outsourced legal translation is performed is a significant contributor to its success or failure. Clarifying how actors arrange the process, and how much or how little they interact, is helpful in order to identify hot spots for risk, and in section 1.1.7 (Chapter 1), I represent the outsourcing of legal translation as a chronological chain of stakeholder interaction. The first market dysfunction to be brought to light was the *length* of the Chain of Supply—not in itself necessarily a problem, until we note the lack of prominence of the key player actually undertaking the work—the translator. Further and related issues are a lack of troubleshooting dialogue (sections 5.5.2.b and 5.5.3.d [Chapter 5]), and also a lack of feedback (section 5.5.3.j). Once his or her allocated job is done, the translator is no longer involved, and the text, aboard its chronological 'train', speeds relentlessly onwards. This acts as fertile ground for information asymmetries and goal incongruence—or, worse still, goal ignorance and/or divergence. Such risks can, in turn, lead to serious quality issues and ultimately, to translations not being fit for purpose.

I believe that my model of the Chain of Supply can serve as a basis from which other, more refined models could be produced—specifically addressing the courts, or the corporate world, or institutions, with or without the involvement of certain intermediaries, adjusted, where necessary, for variations from country to country. In turn, such models could provide insights into potential risks and ways in which existing scenarios might be improved.

C.2. The Need for Comprehensive Briefing

The foregoing environmental model, however, relates solely to the interaction between actors as the text passes from hand to hand. The legal translation market could feasibly benefit from a more formal attitude to outsourcing upstream, together with adequate briefing. The 'translation order' appears from the data to resemble a mere purchase order, rather than specifications for a complex task (section 5.5.2.i). This has the potential for serious repercussions on target text quality, and the translation practitioners participating in my survey express deep dissatisfaction with the existing situation, whilst it seems that their clients fall very much within the 'lay principals' category, and are thus unable to assess whether briefing is operating efficiently or not. Despite that fact that full briefs are not given in many cases, principals are not reluctant to do so—on the contrary, the majority of participants thought that briefing translators more fully (e.g., intended purpose of the target text, end-user, differentiated legal status) would be useful.

In the light of information gathered during this research project, and based on the literature and market review set out in Chapter 4, I have drawn up a briefing template consisting of two pages (Figures 5.31 and 5.32 in Chapter 5), aimed at adoption by both commissioners and translators. In order to foster dissemination and uptake of the template, focus groups with lawyers, other commissioners, and translation practitioners are planned. As noted in section 4.3.2 (Chapter 4), successful implementation will require both principals and agents to instigate and take ownership of information exchange.

C.3. The Multifaceted Nature of the Legal Translator's Textual Agency

One of the frustrations expressed by the translators who participated in the fieldwork was a lack of comprehension by principals of the translation task itself. As the project progressed, I drew elements from a number of related disciplines to develop a model of the complex cognitive processes that constitute the act of legal translation, which involve negotiating between natural languages, legal systems, genres, and the purpose of the text, on both the source and target sides. The lack of linearity inherent in such cerebral activity requires a mult-dimensional model to describe it adequately, and, after rejecting several alternatives, I offer the tesseract—a mathematical polytope (section 2.5 [Chapter 2]). This model is intended to serve several purposes: to stress and enhance the interdisciplinarity at the core of the legal translation act; to convey its complexity to principals, translation trainers, and translators themselves; and, it is hoped, to encourage further theoretical reflection.

C.4. Unravelling Legal Translation Performance Constraints

The briefing inadequacies whose effects can be felt throughout the whole translation process further complicate the performance of outsourced legal translation with its multitude of constraints, and give rise to information asymmetry, goal divergence, and risk. I have drawn a tripartite distinction (Chapter 3) between groups of constraints affecting the performance process: (i) those arising upstream of performance; (ii) 'in-performance' constraints; and (iii) those coming to bear downstream.

An appreciable difference could be made to performance constraints, concomitant with briefing, by educating clients. A considerable return on investment in terms of target text quality could be reaped by extra care spent on drafting the source; while redacting by principals for misplaced confidentiality reasons could be avoided by raising awareness of translators' professional ethics codes. In-performance constraints could be alleviated by principals issuing instructions on the parameters relating to equivalence tensions, such as linguistic ambiguity; which legal system should apply to the text in question; intended purpose, end-user(s), (c)overtness; and interdiscursive reference material.

Service provision intermediaries were cited in connection with many of the dysfunctions reported by the translators in the survey, the most detrimental aspect of which was hampered information flows (sections 3.2.6, 5.5.2.j, and 5.5.3.d). The professionalism of such intermediaries was also questioned by participants on a number of occasions. Of course it is difficult to imagine a world without translation agencies: expanding needs for translation[1] mean that there is a lot of money to be made by acting as a service intermediary. However, it ought to be feasible to render client-intermediary-translator communication channels more fluid and therefore more efficient.

C.5. Fitness-for-Purpose: Meeting Expressed Requirements

Quality assessment may take many forms, but the choice of fitness-for-purpose as a benchmark for EU documents is also a good starting point for outsourced legal translation (section 3.3.1 [Chapter 3]). We should note, however, that participants' interpretations of the notion of fitness-for-purpose are wide-ranging: it seems there is scope for standardization in this regard. These various interpretations are especially important in the light of the fact that translations deemed unfit for purpose may come before the courts in some countries (e.g., France).

The implementation of fitness-for-purpose as a quality criterion hinges, however, upon the purpose of the target text being made *known* to the translator in a comprehensive brief, as already argued. I have conjectured that lack of fitness-for-purpose, seen by principals as various shortcomings in the translations they procure, might usefully be mapped to unspecified components in briefs to illustrate in a very concrete way how briefing can affect quality (section 5.5.3.h).

C.6. Professionalization and Empowerment

If we accept that the insufficient stakeholder interaction holds serious risks—and the data show what those risks may be in terms of briefing and performance—how then, specifically, can we increase the level of translator involvement? My

[1] PricewaterhouseCoopers (2012); US Bureau of Labor Statistics (2015).

suggestions fall into two overarching themes—professionalization and empowerment. The order of these two words is not trivial: in view of the perils inherent in the translation of legal documents, empowerment is highly unlikely to be granted[2] by the client community unless credibility is demonstrated by practitioners (Pym, 2015), and that credibility must be based on the highest levels of professionalism. In addition, the terminology used for and by the 'profession' could be worth investigating. It is entirely up to individual translators—through their professional bodies where possible, and even translator trainers—to revamp these signals.

A key means to lift legal translation practitioners to the status level of other stakeholders, and to move them to hub position (section 4.3.1 [Chapter 4]), would be to initiate a virtuous circle of earlier consultation and fuller instruction, enabling interaction and dialogue, thereby making their professionalism more visible, leading to further empowerment, and so forth (see also section 4.3.2). The 'indelible marking' of translated texts (section 4.4) also has the twofold aim of enhancing professionalization and increasing translator visibility.

C.7. Insights into Text Types Outsourced for Translation

Regarding types of legal texts outsourced, I suggest, according to the data triangulated across the two groups of participants in my survey, that corporate texts are widely entrusted to external practitioners, followed by court and notarial documents, texts in the financial domain, and legislation.[3] The most troublesome of these were court-related texts, legislation, and corporate documents. This finding should be further explored with respect to its implications for legal translator training.

In view of widely varying methods currently used in the market, it may advisable to put in place a standard nomenclature for the differentiation of service levels and document status (section 4.2.2 [Chapter 4]), whether elaborated by institutions, professional bodies, or academia, or better still by a partnership of actors.

Lastly, and surprisingly for those who might imagine that only less important texts are entrusted to external translation practitioners, it appears from the data that outsourced legal texts are often highly sensitive.[4] This makes the study of the ways in which they are translated all the more urgent and relevant.

---

[2] This juxtaposition is to an extent a contradiction in terms, but realistically, in a principal–agent relationship, some level of concession from the client side is inevitable.

[3] See Figure 5.24.

[4] See Figure 5.16.

C.8. Avenues for Future Research

This interdisciplinary research project has given rise to a number of avenues that could be pursued further. Indeed, we might begin with interdisciplinarity itself. As noted (section 5.3.2 [Chapter 5]), there may well be scope for enhancing inter-faculty dialogue between law schools and translation studies schools, which are often positioned within a modern languages department. This could be relevant not only at postgraduate level, but also for undergraduate courses. Early linguistic input might also widen the range of opportunities open to newly qualified lawyers who compete in a currently saturated employment market. For the purposes of training legal translators, whether initially or as continuing professional development, the opinions expressed by principals regarding the importance of legal writing skills and, to a lesser extent, comparative law merit further investigation.

As for further practice-based research into the outsourcing of legal translation, it would be interesting to drill down further into volumes performed in-house as opposed to those externalized, and in particular the sensitivity of such texts; as well as to ascertain the (c)overtness of outsourced legal translations; data on income levels in the legal translation specialism would also be welcome. The commissioning survey described in this book could usefully be developed and extended to other languages, countries, legal systems, and the judiciary.

In the area of professionalization and empowerment, psychological studies on the influence on legal translator status of terms used within the market would be most welcome, possibly drawing from marketing and branding techniques. Investigations into legal translators' stress levels would be profitable with regard to the working conditions described in the data. It will be most interesting to observe and track the development of the European legal translator register[5] and its potential to reduce non-professional legal translation,[6] or at the very least to raise client awareness of its dangers. Further research into fitness-for-purpose and its contribution to judging quality should be broadened, particularly in extra-institutional contexts.

I intend to pursue work on my theoretical process models and look forward to receiving pertinent observations from the academic community in this regard. In practical terms, avenues could comprise the following: teasing out why certain legal (sub)genres cause particular difficulty; mapping (sub)genres onto the appropriate degrees of interpretive autonomy, especially with regard to non-legislative genres; and establishing causal links between principals' criticisms of translated texts and briefing gaps. I have already begun exploring how best to disseminate the briefing template, aiming to do so in collaboration with

---

[5] LIT Search project, https://www.arts.kuleuven.be/litsearch/

[6] See section 1.1.3.

major stakeholders for maximum uptake and impact, by using innovative channels whenever appropriate.[7]

C.9. Concluding Statements

Attempting to bridge gaps between practice and academia on a day-to-day basis is not always easy, but it is a highly stimulating and rewarding task. The practitioner-researcher has to contend with an often uncomfortable position, whether from a practical point of view, juggling two careers, or in terms of credibility and acceptance by others, but has great potential to provide insights for both groups, and even to initiate fresh conversations. That role should not be underestimated by any of the stakeholders involved.

Legal texts can be a minefield of interpretation, with their complex and often ambiguous aims, as every lawyer knows. Dysfunctional working practices are currently giving rise to the most serious quality tensions when these texts are outsourced for translation. The performance of that task under such conditions will always be, whether to a smaller or larger extent, unsuccessful.

Collaboration between legal and translation professionals and better information flows are cited over and over again as avenues for improvement by those involved in my research. Establishing a long-term productive and mutually respectful relationship, within an environment of trust, working towards the joint goal of high-quality translated texts, has the potential to avoid miscarriages of justice, misunderstandings of or failures to comply with cross-border rules and obligations, failed enforcement, exposure to litigation and failed cases, distortion of legal concepts, and even to foster access to justice. Releasing the full potential of legal translation practitioners' agency will undoubtedly be beneficial for all concerned.

[7] Scott (2015b).

AFTERWORD

The unique feature of the questions that prompt practitioner research is that they emanate from neither theory nor practice alone but from critical reflection on the intersection of the two.

—Cochran-Smith and Lytle (1993, p. 15)

BIBLIOGRAPHY

Abdallah, K. (2010). Translators' agency in production networks. In T. Kinnunen & K. Koskinen (Eds.), *Translators' agency* (pp. 11–46). Tampere: Tampere University Press.

Abdallah, K. (2012). *Translators in production networks: Reflections on agency, quality and ethics*. Joensuu: University of Eastern Finland.

Abdallah, K., & Koskinen, K. (2007). Managing trust: Translating and the network economy. *Meta, 52*(4), 673–687.

Adams, J. (1996). Principals and agents, colonialists and company men: The decay of colonial control in the Dutch West Indies. *American Sociological Review, 61*(1), 12–28.

Alcaraz Varó, E., & Hughes, B. (2002). *Legal translation explained*. Manchester: St. Jerome.

Alonso, E., & Nunes Vieira, L. (2017). The translator's amanuensis 2020. *The Journal of Specialised Translation, 28*, 345–361.

Altobelli, T. (2007). *Working with barristers*. Sydney: The Law Society of New South Wales.

Angelelli, C. V., & Jacobson, H. E. (2009). Introduction. In C. V. Angelelli & H. E. Jacobson (Eds.), *Testing and assessment in translation and interpreting studies: A call for dialogue between research and practice* (pp. 1–12). Amsterdam: John Benjamins.

Artelsmair, G. (2010, November 17). *Recent developments in machine translation policy at the European Patent Office*. Retrieved from http://www.meta-net.eu/events/meta-forum-2010/slides/meta- forum2010_artelsmair.pdf.

Askehave, I., & Swales, J. M. (2001). Genre identification and communicative purpose: A problem and a possible solution. *Applied Linguistics, 22*(2), 195–212.

ASTM [American Society for Testing and Materials] International. (2006). *F2575-06 Standard guide for quality assurance in translation*. West Conshohocken, PA: ASTM International.

AUSIT [Australian Institute of Interpreters and Translators]. (2014). *Best practices for the translation of official and legal documents*. Retrieved from http://ausit.org/AUSIT/Documents/Best_Practices_2014.pdf.

Baaij, C. J. W. (2012). The significance of legal translation for legal harmonization. In C. Baaij (Ed.), *The role of legal translation in legal harmonization* (pp. 1–24). Amsterdam: Kluwer Law International.

Baaij, C. J. W. (2014). Legal translation and the 'contamination' of comparative legal research. In S. Glanert (Ed.), *Comparative law: Engaging translation* (pp. 104–122). Abingdon: Routledge.

Baker, M. (2001). *In other words*. London: Routledge.

Balkin, J. M., & Levinson, S. (2006). Law and the humanities: An uneasy relationship. *Yale Journal of Law and the Humanities, 18*, 155–188.

Bassnett, S. (2002). *Translation studies*. London: Routledge.

Bazeley, P. (2009). Analysing qualitative data: More than 'identifying themes'. *The Malaysian Journal of Qualitative Research, 2*(2), 6–22.

Bazeley, P., & Jackson, K. (2013). *Qualitative data analysis with NVivo*. London: Sage.

Bergen, M., Dutta, S., & Walker, O. C. (1992). Agency relationships in marketing: A review of the implications and applications of agency and related theories. *Journal of Marketing, 56*(3), 1–24.

Bernardini, S. (2016). Discovery learning in the language-for-translation classroom: Corpora as learning aids. *Cadernos de Tradução, 36*(1), 14–35.

Bhatia, V. K. (1983). *An applied discourse analysis of English legislative writing: A Language Studies Unit research report*. Birmingham: University of Aston.

Bhatia, V. K. (1987). Language of the law. *Language Teaching, 20*, 227–234.

Bhatia, V. K. (1993). *Analysing genre: Language use in professional settings*. London: Longman.

Bhatia, V. (1997). Translating legal genres. In A. Trosborg (Ed.), *Text typology and translation* (pp. 203–214). Amsterdam: John Benjamins.

Bhatia, V. K. (1998). Intertextuality in legal discourse. *The Language Teacher, 22*(11). Retrieved from http://www.jalt-publications.org/tlt/articles/2427-intertextuality-legal-discourse.

Bhatia, V. K. (2006). Legal genres. In K. Brown (Ed.), *Encyclopedia of language & linguistics* (Vol. 7, pp. 1–7). Boston: Elsevier.

Bhatia, V. K. (2008). Genre analysis, ESP and professional practice. *English for Specific Purposes, 27*, 161–174.

Bhatia, V. K. (2010a). Drafting legislative provisions: Challenges and opportunities. *The Loophole, 12*, 5–15.

Bhatia, V. K. (2010b). Interdiscursivity in professional communication. *Discourse & Communication, 21*(4, 1), 32–50.

Bhatia, V. K. (2014). *Worlds of written discourse: A genre-based view*. London: Bloomsbury.

Bhatia, V. K., Candlin, C. N., & Engberg, J. (2008). *Legal discourse across cultures and systems*. Hong Kong: Hong Kong University Press.

Bhatia, V. K., & Engberg, J. (2004). Introduction. *Hermes, Journal of Linguistics, 32*, 7–11.

Bhatia, V. K., & Nodoushan, M. A. S. (2015). Genre analysis: The state of the art (An online interview with Vijay Kumar Bhatia). *International Journal of Language Studies, 9*(2), 121–130.

Biel, Ł. (2008). Legal terminology in translation practice: Dictionaries, googling or discussion forums. *Skase Journal of Translation and Interpretation, 3*(1), 22–38.

Biel, Ł. (2009). Organization of background knowledge structures in legal language and related translation problems. *Comparative Legilinguistics, 1*, 176–188.

Biel, Ł. (2010a). Corpus-based studies of legal language for translation purposes: Methodological and practical potential. In C. Heine & J. Engberg (Eds.), *Reconceptualizing LSP: Online Proceedings of the XVII European LSP Symposium 2009*. Aarhus: Aarhus School of Business, Aarhus University.

Biel, Ł. (2010b). The textual fit of legal translations: Focus on collocations in translator training. In Ł. Bogucki (Ed.), *Teaching translation and interpreting: Challenges and practices* (pp. 25–39). Newcastle upon Tyne: Cambridge Scholars.

Biel, Ł. (2011). Professional realism in the legal translation classroom: Translation competence and translator competence. *Meta, 56*(1), 162–178.

Biel, Ł. (2012). Areas of similarity and difference in legal phraseology: Collocations of key terms in UK and Polish company law. In A. Pamies, J. M. Pazos Bretaña, & L. Luque Nadal (Eds.), *Phraseology and discourse: Cross-linguistic and corpus-based approaches* (pp. 225–233). Baltmannsweiler: Schneider Verlag.

Biel, Ł. (2014a). Legal translator as a communicator. [Review of the book *Legal translation in context*, by A. Borja Albi & F. Prieto Ramos (Eds.)], *International Journal for the Semiotics of Law*, *28*(1), 227–232.

Biel, Ł. (2014b). The textual fit of translated EU law: A corpus-based study of deontic modality. *The Translator*, *20*(3), 332–355.

Biel, Ł. (2017). Researching legal translation: A multi-perspective and mixed-method framework for legal translation. *Revista de Llegua i Dret (*RLD), *Journal of Language and Law*, *68*, 76–88.

Biel, Ł., & Engberg, J. (2013). Research models and methods in legal translation. *Linguistica Antverpiensia*, *12*, 1–11.

Blake, M. (2015). *Man vs. machine: Google Translate jeopardizes client confidentiality, ediscovery*. Retrieved from http://abovethelaw.com/2015/01/man-vs-machine-google-translate-jeopardizes-client-confidentiality-ediscovery.

Boaz, A., & Ashby, D. (2003). *Fit for purpose? Assessing research quality for evidence based policy and practice* (ESRC UK Centre for Evidence Based Policy and Practice: Working Paper 11). London: Queen Mary.

Bocquet, C. (1994). *Pour une méthode de traduction juridique*. Prilly: CB Service.

Bocquet, C. (2008). *La traduction juridique: Fondement et méthode*. Brussels: De Boeck.

Bogdan, M. (1994). *Comparative law*. The Hague: Kluwer Law International.

Borja, A., García Izquierdo, I., & Montalt, V. (2009). Research methodology in specialized genres for translation purposes. *The Interpreter and Translator Trainer*, *3*(1), 57–77.

Borja Albi, A., & Prieto Ramos, F. (Eds.) (2013). *Legal translation in context*. Bern: Peter Lang.

Bourn, J., Comptroller and Auditor General (2005). *Lost in translation? Responding to the challenges of European law*. London: The Stationery Office. Retrieved from http://www.nao.org.uk/report/lost-in-translation-responding-to-the-challenges-of-european-law/.

Bowker, L. (2001). Towards a methodology for a corpus-based approach to translation evaluation. *Meta*, *46*(2), 345–364.

Bowker, L., & Corpas Pastor, G. (2014). Translation technology. In R. Mitkov (Ed.), *The Oxford handbook of computational linguistics*. Oxford: Oxford University Press.

Bradford, L. R. (2009). The agency of the poets and the impact of their translations: *Sur, Poesía Buenos Aires*, and *Diario de Poesía* as aesthetic arenas for twentieth-century Argentine letters. In J. Milton & P. Bandia (Eds.), *Agents of translation* (pp. 229–256). Amsterdam: John Benjamins.

Brannen, J. (2005). *Mixed methods research: A discussion paper* (NCRM Methods Review Papers). London: ESRC National Centre for Research Methods.

British Council. (n.d.). *Commissioning a copywriter*. Retrieved 29 December 2012 from http://brand.britishcouncil.org/tone-of-voice/commissioning-a-copywriter/.

Bryman, A. (2004). Triangulation. In M. S. Lewis-Beck, A. Bryman, & T. Futing Liao (Eds.), *The SAGE encyclopedia of social science research methods* (pp. 1142–1143). London: Sage.

Bryman, A. (2006). Integrating quantitative and qualitative research: How is it done? *Qualitative Research*, *6*, 97–113.

Burling, J., & Lazarus, K. (2011). *Research handbook on international insurance law and regulation*. Cheltenham: Elgar.

Buzelin, H. (2006). Independent publisher in the networks of translation. *Meta*, *19*(1), 135–173.

Buzelin, H. (2011). Agents of translation. In Y. Gambier & L. Van Doorslaer (Eds.), *Handbook of translation studies* (Vol. 2, pp. 6–12). Amsterdam: John Benjamins.

Byers, M. (2004). Agreeing to disagree. *Global Governance*, *10*, 165–186.

Byrne, J. (2007). Caveat translator: Understanding the legal consequences of errors in professional translation. *The Journal of Specialised Translation*, *7*, 2–24. Retrieved from http://www.jostrans.org/issue07/art_byrne.pdf.

Cairns, W., & McKeon, R. (1995). *Introduction to French law*. London: Cavendish.

Calderoni, F. (2010). *Organized crime legislation in the European Union*. London: Springer.

Campos Pardillos, M. A. (2016). Increasing metaphor awareness in legal English teaching. *ESP Today*, *4*(2), 165–183.

Candlin, S., & Crichton, J. (2013). From ontology to methodology: Exploring the discursive landscape of trust. In C. N. Candlin, & J. Crichton (Eds.), *Discourses of trust* (pp. 1–18). Basingstoke: Palgrave Macmillan.

Cao, D. (2007). *Translating law*. Clevedon: Multilingual Matters.

Cao, D. (2010). Judicial interpretation of bilingual and multilingual laws: A European and Hong Kong comparison. In J. Jemielniak & P. Miklaszewicz (Eds.), *Interpretation of law in the global world: From particularism to a universal approach* (pp. 71–86). Heidelberg: Springer.

Cao, D., & Zhao, X. (2008). Translation at the United Nations as specialized translation. *The Journal of Specialised Translation*, *9*, 39–54. Retrieved from http://www.jostrans.org/issue09/art_cao.php.

Capita Translating and Interpreting. (2015). *The conundrum of quality, time and cost in the language services sector*. Retrieved from http://www.capitatranslationinterpreting.com/wp-content/uploads/2015/09/White-Paper-Quality-Cost-and-Time.pdf.

Carle, S. (2005). Theorizing agency. *American University Law Review*, *55*(2), 307–387.

Carr, W., & Kemmis, S. (1986). *Becoming critical: Education, knowledge and action research*. Lewes: Falmer.

Carvalho, L. (2008). Translating contracts and agreements. *Revista Cientifica*, *3*(1), 1–15.

Catford, J. C. (1965). *A linguistic theory of translation*. Oxford: Oxford University Press.

Chan, A. J. L. (2008). *Information economics, the translation profession and translator certification*. PhD thesis. Tarragona: Intercultural Studies Group. Retrieved from http://www.tdx.cat/bitstream/handle/10803/8772/Chan.pdf.

Chan, D. (2009). So why ask me? Are self-report data really that bad? In C. E. Lance & R. J. Vandenberg (Eds.), *Statistical and methodological myths and urban legends: Doctrine, verity, and fable in the organizational and social sciences* (pp. 309–336). New York: Routledge.

Charrow, V., Crandall, J. A., & Charrow, R. (1982). Characteristics and functions of legal language. In R. Kittredge, & J. Lehrberger (Eds.), *Sublanguage: Studies of language in restricted semantic domains* (pp. 175–190). Berlin; New York: Walter de Gruyter.

Chesterman, A. (1993). From "is" to "ought": Laws, norms and strategies in translation studies. *Target*, *5*(1), 1–20. doi: 10.1075/target.5.1.02che.

Chesterman, A. (2009). The name and nature of translator studies. *Hermes, Journal of Language and Communication Studies*, *42*, 15–22.

Chesterman, A. (2013). Models of what processes? *Translation and Interpreting Studies*, *8*(2), 155–168.

Chesterman, A., & Wagner, E. (2002). *Can theory help translators? A dialogue between the ivory tower and the wordface*. Manchester: St Jerome.

Chromà, M. (2008). Semantic and legal interpretation: Two approaches to legal translation. In V. K. Bhatia, C. N. Candlin, & P. E. Evangelisti Allori (Eds.), *Language, culture and the law* (pp. 303–316). Bern: Peter Lang.

Cochran-Smith, M., & Donnell, K. (2006). Practitioner inquiry: Blurring the boundaries of research and practice. In J. L. Green, G. Camilli, & P. Elmore (Eds.), *Handbook of complementary methods in education research* (pp. 503–518). Mahwah, NJ: Lawrence Earlbaum Associates for the American Educational Research Association.

Constantinesco, L. J. (1983). *Traité de droit comparé*. Paris: Librairie générale de droit et de jurisprudence.

Corden, A., & Sainsbury, R. (2006). *Using verbatim quotations in reporting qualitative social research: researchers' views* (Social Policy Research Unit, ESRC 2136). Retrieved from https://www.york.ac.uk/inst/spru/pubs/pdf/verbquotresearch.pdf.

Cornu, G. (1990). *Vocabulaire juridique*. Paris: Presses universitaires de France.

Corpas Pastor, G., & Duran-Munoz, I. (Eds.). (2017). *Trends in e-tools and resources for translators and interpreters*. Leiden: Brill.

Creswell, J. W. (2009). *Research design*. London: Sage.

Cronin, M. (2003). *Translation and globalisation*. Abingdon: Routledge.

Cronin, M. (2010). The translation crowd. *Revista tradumàtica, 8*. Retrieved from http://www.raco.cat/index.php/Tradumatica/article/view/225900.

Cronin, M. (2013). *Translation in the digital age*. Abingdon: Routledge.

Crump, D. (2002). Against plain English: The case for a functional approach to legal document preparation. *Rutgers Law Journal, 33*(3), 713–744.

Cunliffe, A. L., & Luhman, J. T. (2012). *Key concepts in organization theory*. London: Sage.

Dale, B. G. (2003). *Managing quality* (4th ed.). Oxford: Blackwell.

Dam, H. V., & Zethsen, K. K. (2009a). Translation studies: Focus on the translator. *Hermes, Journal of Language and Communication Studies, 42*, 7–12.

Dam, H. V., & Zethsen, K. K. (2009b). Who said low status? A study on factors affecting the perception of translator status. *The Journal of Specialised Translation, 12*, 2–36. Retrieved from http://www.jostrans.org/issue12/art_dam_zethsen.php.

Dam, H. V., & Zethsen, K. K. (2010). Translator status: Helpers and opponents in the ongoing battle of an emerging profession. *Target, 22*(2), 194–211.

Dam, H. V., & Zethsen, K. K. (2011). The status of professional business translators on the Danish market: A comparative study of company, agency and freelance translators. *Meta, 56*(4), 976–997.

Darling, D. (2004). *The universal book of mathematics: From abracadabra to Zeno's paradoxes*. Hoboken, NJ: Wiley.

Déal, E. (2004). Langue du droit et doctrine: La linguistique juridique au service de l'accessibilité internationalisée des contributions doctrinales. *Meta, 34*(2), 233–265.

De Groot, G.-R. (1987). The point of view of a comparative lawyer. *Les Cahiers de droit, 28*(4), 793–812.

De Groot, G.-R. (2006). Legal translation. In J. M. Smits (Ed.), *Elgar encyclopedia of comparative law* (pp. 423–433). Cheltenham: Edward Elgar.

Denning, A. (1991). *The family story*. London: Butterworths.

Denscombe, M. (2007). *The good research guide for small-scale social research projects*. Maidenhead: McGraw-Hill Open University Press.

Derlen, M. (2011). In defence of (limited) multilingualism: Problems and possibilities of the multilingual interpretation of European Union law in national courts. In A. L.

Kjaer & S. Adamo (Eds.), *Linguistic diversity and European democracy* (pp. 143–166). Farnham: Ashgate.

Diebold, N. F. (2014). *Non-discrimination in international trade in services: 'Likeness' in WTO/GATS*. Cambridge: Cambridge.

Donaldson, S. I., & Grant-Vallone, E. J. (2002). Understanding self-report bias in organizational behaviour research. *Journal of Business and Psychology*, *17*(2), 245–260.

Drake, P., with Heath, L. (2011). *Practitioner research at doctoral level*. London: Routledge.

Dullion, V. (1997). Lorsque traduire, c'est écrire une page d'histoire: La version française du Code civil suisse dans l'unification juridique de la Confédération. In *L'histoire et les théories de la traduction* (pp. 371–388). Bern: ASTTI.

Dullion, V. (2007). *Traduire les lois*. Louvain-la-Neuve: E.M.E.

Dullion, V. (2015). Droit comparé pour traducteurs. *International Journal for the Semiotics of Law*, *28*, 91–106.

Drugan, J. (2013). *Quality in professional translation*. London: Bloomsbury.

Durban, C. (2010). *The prosperous translator*. *Sine loco*: FA & WB Press.

Durban, C., *et al.* [un-named] (2014, May–June). Getting it right. *ITI Bulletin*, 8–10.

Edwards, A. (2005). Relational agency: Learning to be a resourceful practitioner. *International Journal of Educational Research*, *43*, 168–182.

Edwards, A. (2008). *Keynote address: Understanding boundaries in inter-professional work* (SERA conference, Perth, Scotland, 23–25 November 2008). Retrieved from http://www.ser.stir.ac.uk/pdf/301.pdf.

Edwards, A. (2010). *Being an expert professional practitioner: The relational turn in expertise*. London: Springer.

Eisenhardt, K. M. (1989). Agency theory: An assessment and review. *The Academy of Management Review*, *14*(1), 57–74.

EMT [European Masters in Translation] expert group. (2009, January). *Competences for professional translators, experts in multilingual and multimedia communication*. Brussels: Directorate-General for Translation.

Endicott, T. A. O. (2000). *Vagueness in law*. Oxford: Oxford University Press.

Engberg, J. (1999). Übersetzen von Gerichtsurteilen: Der Einfluß der Perspektive. In: P. Sandrini (Ed.), *Recht und Übersetzung: Die Übersetzung von Rechtstexten im Spannungsfeld zwischen Rechtsordnung und Sprache* (pp. 83–102). Tübingen: Narr.

Engberg, J. (2004). Statutory texts as instances of language(s): Consequences and limitations on interpretation. *Brooklyn Law Journal*, *3*, 1135–1166.

Engberg, J. (2013). Comparative law for translation: The key to successful mediation between legal systems. In A. Borja Albi & F. Prieti Ramos (Eds.), *Legal translation in context: Professional issues and prospects* (pp. 9–25). Bern: Peter Lang.

Engberg, J. (2017). Comparative law and legal translation as partners in knowledge communication: Frames as a descriptive instrument. In F. Prieto Ramos (Ed.), *Institutional translation for international governance: Enhancing quality in multilingual legal communication*. London: Bloomsbury.

Engeström, Y. (2005). Knotworking to create collaborative intentionality capital in fluid organizational fields. In M. M. Beyerlein, S. T. Beyerlein, & F. A. Kennedy (Eds.), *Collaborative capital: Creating intangible value* (pp. 307–336). Amsterdam: Elsevier.

European Commission. (2003). *Joint practical guide of the European Parliament, the Council and the Commission for persons involved in the drafting of legislation within the*

Community institutions. Luxembourg: Office for Official Publications of the European Communities.

European Commission. (2011). *What skills for a changing market? Conclusions of a symposium, 29.9.2011*. Brussels: Directorate-General for Translation. Retrieved from http://ec.europa.eu/dgs/translation/programmes/languageindustry/platform/documents/translator_profile_conclusions_en.pdf.

European Commission. (2012a). *How to write clearly*. Brussels: Directorate-General for Translation.

European Commission. (2012b). *Quantifying quality costs and the cost of poor quality in translation*. Luxembourg: Publications Office of the European Union.

Evert, S. (2008). Corpora and collocations. In A. Lüdeling & M. Kytö (Eds.), *Corpus linguistics: An international handbook* (Vol. 2, pp. 1212–1248). Berlin: De Gruyter.

Farzindar, A. (2009). *Automatic translation management system for legal texts*. Paper presented at Machine Translation Summit XII. Retrieved from http://www.mt-archive.info/MTS-2009-Farzindar.pdf.

Fernandes, L. (2006). Corpora in translation studies: Revisiting Baker's typology. *Fragmentos*, *30*, 87–95.

Ferreira-Alves, F. (2012). Translation companies in Portugal. In A. Pym & A. A. Rosa (Eds.), *New directions in translation studies: Special issue of Anglo Saxonica 3.3* (pp. 233–263). Lisbon: ULICES-CEAUL.

Février, P., Linnemer, L., & Visser, M. (2004). Life and death and real estate in France: Testing for asymmetric information in the viager market. *Risques*, *59*, 2.

Fortney, S. S. (2009). Taking empirical research seriously. *Georgetown Journal of Legal Ethics*, *22*(4), 1473–1477.

Fraser, J. (1996a). The translator investigated. *The Translator*, *2*(1), 65–79.

Fraser, J. (1996b). Mapping the process of translation. *Meta*, *41*(1), 84–96.

Fraser, J. (1997, June). Briefing? What briefing? *ITI Bulletin*, 13–16.

Fraser, J. (2000). The broader view: How freelance translators define translation competence. In C. Schäffner & B. Adab (Eds.), *Developing translation competence* (pp. 51–62). Amsterdam: John Benjamins.

Fraser, J. (2001). 'Rolls Royce quality at Lada prices': A survey of the working conditions and status of freelance translators. In L. Desblache (Ed.) *Aspects of specialised translation* (pp. 31–39). Paris: La Maison du Dictionnaire.

Freedman, A. (2007). *The party of the first part*. New York: Henry Holt.

Fry, D. (2009, November 13-14). Crisis, what crisis? Industry, what industry? In J. M. Vande Walle (Ed.), *Proceedings of the IALB-ASTTI Conference: The world in crisis—and the language industry?* Tradulux: Geneva.

Fulford, H., & Granell-Zafra, J. (2004a). The freelance translator's workstation: An empirical investigation. In *Proceedings of the 9th EAMT Workshop: Broadening horizons of machine translation and its applications* (pp. 26–27). Valetta: Foundation for International Studies, University of Malta.

Fulford, H., & Granell Zafra, J. (2004b). The uptake of online tools and web-based language resources by freelance translators: Implications for translator training, professional development, and research. In *Coling 2004: Proceedings of the Second International Workshop on Language Resources for Translation Work, Research & Training* (pp. 50–57). Geneva: University of Geneva.

Galdia, M. (2003). Comparative law and legal translation. *The European Legal Forum 1*, 1–4.

Galdia, M. (2009). *Legal linguistics*. Frankfurt: Peter Lang.

Gallego Hernández, D. (2012). *Traducción económica y corpus: Del concepto a la concordancia*. Alicante: Alicante.

Gallego Hernández, D. (2015). The use of corpora as translation resources: A study based on a survey of Spanish professional translators. *Perspectives: Studies in Translatology, 23*(3), 375–391.

Garcia, I. (2009). Beyond translation memory: Computers and the professional translator. *The Journal of Specialised Translation, 12*, 199–214.

Garcìa Izquierdo, I., & Borja Albi, A. (2008). A multidisciplinary approach to specialized writing and translation using a genre based multilingual corpus of specialized texts. *LSP and Professional Communication, 8*(1), 39–63. Retrieved from http://rauli.cbs.dk/index.php/LSP/article/viewFile/2117/2116.

Garner, B. A. (2001). *Legal writing in plain English*. Chicago: Chicago University Press.

Garner, B. A. (Ed.) (2009). *Black's Law Dictionary*. St Paul: Thomson Reuters.

Garrido Rodríguez, I. (2012). Translation in the civil service: The case of the Spanish National Traffic Authority. Analysis of the invoice as a textual genre. *Sendebar, 23*, 207–226. Retrieved from http://revistaseug.ugr.es/index.php/sendebar/article/view/36/36.

Garrido Rodríguez, I. (2015). Macroestructura de los estatutos de sociedades alemanas y españolas: Influencias legislativas y análisis contrastivo. In M. A. Recio Ariza *et al.* (Eds.), *Interacciones: Reflexiones en torno a la traducción e interpretación del/al alemán* (pp. 515–540). Frankfurt: Peter Lang.

Garzone, G. (2000). *Legal and functionalist approaches: A contradiction in terms?* Paper presented at Legal translation, history, theory/ies, and practice. Retrieved from http://www.tradulex.org/Actes2000/Garzone.pdf.

Garzone, G., & Ilie, C. (2014). Introduction. In G. Garzone & C. Ilie (Eds.), *Genres and genre theory in transition* (pp. 7–16). Boca Raton: BrownWalker.

Gawn, P. (1988). Authenticity and quality of translation. *Meta, 33*(3), 456–460.

Gémar, J.-C. (1979). La traduction juridique et son enseignement: Aspects théoriques et pratiques. *Meta, 24*(1), 35–53.

Gémar, J.-C. (1982). Fonctions de la traduction juridique en milieu bilingue et langage du droit au Canada. In J.-C. Gémar (Ed.), *Langage du droit et traduction*. Montreal: Linguatech. Retrieved from http://www.cslf.gouv.qc.ca/bibliotheque-virtuelle/publication-html/?tx_iggcpplus_pi4%5bfile%5d=publications/pubf104/f104p1ch3.html.

Gémar, J.-C. (1998, September 25). *Les enjeux de la traduction juridique: Principes et nuances*. Paper presented at Equivalences 98, ASTII seminar. Retrieved from http://www.tradulex.org/Actes1998/Gemar.pdf.

Gémar, J.-C. (2002). Le plus et le moins-disant culturel du texte juridique: Langue, culture et equivalence. *Meta, 47*(2), 163–176.

Gémar, J.-C. (2012, November 1-3). *De la traduction juridique à la jurilinguistique: La quête de l'équivalence.* Paper presented at Colloque international sur La traduction dans des contextes de plurilinguisme official, University of Moncton, Canada. Retrieved from https://www.google.com/url?sa=t&rct=j&q=&esrc=s&source=web&cd=1&ved

=0ahUKEwjfuqqAnLLbAhVFyRQKHRx0BesQFggpMAA&url=http%3A%2F%2Fwww.umoncton.ca%2Fumcm-fass-traduction%2Ffiles%2Fumcm-fass-traduction%2Fwf%2Fwf%2Fpdf%2Fgemar.ppt&usg=AOvVaw0bm7jPbEwGQd0ICzUhG1l2.

Gentzler, E. (1993) *Contemporary translation theories*. London: Routledge.

Gile, D. (2004). Translation research versus interpreting research: Kinship, differences and prospects for partnership. In C. Schäffner (Ed.), *Translation research and interpreting research: Traditions, gaps and synergies* (pp. 10–34). Clevedon: Multilingual Matters.

Gilley, K. M., and Rasheed, A. (2000) Making more by doing less: An analysis of outsourcing and its effects on firm performance. *Journal of Management*, *26*(4), 763–790.

Glanert, S. (2011). *De la traductibilité du droit*. Paris: Dalloz.

Glanert, S. (2014). Law-in-translation: An assemblage in motion. *The Translator*, *20*(3), 255–272.

Glanert, S., & Legrand, P. (2013). Foreign law in translation: If truth be told .... In M. Freeman & F. Smith (Eds.), *Current legal issues: Law and language* (pp. 513–532). Oxford: Oxford University Press.

Goddard, C. (2010). Legal linguistics as an academic and professional discipline: Identifying clients, customers, stakeholders. In C. Heine & J. Engberg (Eds.), *Reconceptualizing LSP. Online Proceedings of the XVII European LSP Symposium 2009*. Aarhus: Aarhus School of Business, Aarhus University.

Göritz, A. S. (2006). Incentives in web studies. *International Journal of Internet Science*, *1*(1), 58–70.

Gotti, M. (2012). Text and genre. In P. M. Tiersma & L. M. Solan (Eds.), *The Oxford handbook of language and the law* (pp. 52–66). Oxford: Oxford University Press.

Gouadec, D. (2007). *Translation as a profession*. Amsterdam: John Benjamins.

Goźdź-Roszkowski, S. (2004). Multi-word lexical units in legal genres: The pedagogic perspective. In B. Lewandowska-Tomaszczyk (Ed.), *Practical applications in language and computers* (pp. 401–416). Frankfurt: Peter Lang.

Goźdź-Roszkowski, S. (2006a). Frequent phraseology in contractual instruments: A corpus-based study. In M. Gotti & D. Giannoni (Eds.), *New trends in specialized discourse analysis* (pp. 147–162). Frankfurt: Peter Lang.

Goźdź-Roszkowski, S. (2006b). Recurrent word combinations in judicial argumentation: A corpus-based study. In D. Bartol, A. Duszak, H. Izdebski, & J-M. Pierrel (Eds.), *Langue, droit, société* (pp. 139–152). Nancy: Université de Nancy.

Goźdź-Roszkowski, S., & Pontrandolfo, G. (2015). Legal phraseology today: Corpus-based applications across legal languages and genres. *Fachsprache*, *3–4*, 130–138.

Graça Krieger, M. da (2002). Terminographie juridique et spécificités textuelles. *Meta*, *47*(2), 233–243.

Greenstein, R. (2009). You can't tell a book by its cover. *Asp 56*. Retrieved from http://asp.revues.org/73.

Halskov, J., Hansen, D., Braasch, A., & Olsen, S. (2010). Quality indicators of LSP texts—selection and measurements: Measuring the terminological usefulness of documents for an LSP corpus. In N. Calzolari *et al.* (Eds.), *Proceedings of the Seventh Conference on International Language Resources and Evaluation (LREC'10)* (pp. 2614–2620). Valletta: European Language Resources Association (ELRA).

Hammond, M. (1995). A new wind of quality from Europe: Implications of the court case cited by Holz-Mänttäri for the U.S. translation industry. In M. Morris (Ed.), *Translation and the law* (pp. 233–245). Amsterdam: John Benjamins.

Hanson, A. (2009). Legal process outsourcing to India: So hot right now! *SMU Law Review*, *62*, 1889–1914.

Harmon, A. R. (2008). The ethics of legal process outsourcing to India: Is the practice of law a "noble profession," or is it just another business? *Journal of Technology Law & Policy*, *13*, 41–83.

Harvey, M. (2002). What's so special about legal translation? *Meta*, *47*(2), 177–185.

Harvey, M. (2005). Incroyable mais vraie: La traduction juridique. In R. Greenstein (Ed.), *La langue, le discours et la culture en anglais du droit* (pp. 57–68). Paris: Publications de la Sorbonne.

Hendry, J. (2002). The principal's other problems: Honest incompetence and the specification of objectives. *The Academy of Management Review*, *27*(1), 98–113.

Hermans, T. (1996). Norms and the determination of translation: A theoretical framework. In R. Alvarez & M. Vidal (Eds.), *Translation, power, subversion* (pp. 25–51). Clevedon: Multilingual Matters.

Hewson, C. (2015). Research methods on the Internet. In L. Cantoni & J. A. Danowski (Eds.), *Communication and technology* (pp. 277–302). Berlin: De Gruyter Mouton.

Hertel, C. (2009). An overview of legal systems. *Notarius International*, *1*(2), 128–141.

Hertog, E. (2001). *Aequitas: Access to justice across language and culture in the EU*. Antwerp: Lessius Hogeschool, Departement Vertaler-Tolk.

Hertog, E., & Van Gucht, J. (Eds.) (2008). *Status quaestionis: Questionnaire on the provision of legal interpreting and translation in the EU*. Antwerp: Intersentia.

Heylen, K., Bond, S., De Hertog, D., Kockaert, H., Steurs F., & Vulić, I. (2014). *TermWise: Leveraging big data for terminological support in legal translation*. Terminology and Knowledge Engineering 2014, June, Berlin, Germany. Retrieved from https://hal.archives-ouvertes.fr/hal-01005842/document.

House, J. (1977). A model for assessing translation quality. *Meta*, *22*(2), 103–109.

House, J. (1997). *Translation quality assessment: A model revisted*. Tübingen: Gunter Narr Verlag Tübingen.

House, J. (2015). *Translation quality assessment: Past and present*. Abingdon: Routledge.

Howe, K. (2003). *Closing methodological divides*. Dordrecht: Kluwer.

Husa, J. (2017). Translating legal language and comparative law. *International Journal for the Semiotics of Law*, *30*(2), 261–272.

Inghilleri, M. (Ed.) (2005). Bourdieu and the sociology of translation and interpreting. [Special issue]. *The Translator*, *11*(2).

Inghilleri, M. (2010). You don't make war without knowing why. In M. Inghilleri & S-A. Harding (Eds.), Translation and violent conflict. [Special issue]. *The Translator*, *16*(2), 175–196.

International Federation of Translators, FIT Europe, Regional Centre Europe. (undated). *Code of Professional Practice*. Retrieved from http://www.fit-europe.org/vault/deont/European_Code_%20Professional_Practice.pdf.

Jakobson, R. (1960). Closing statement: Linguistics and poetics. In T. A. Sebeok (Ed.), *Style in language* (pp. 350–377). Cambridge, MA: MIT Press.

Jakobson, R. (1959/2003). On linguistic aspects of translation. In L. Venuti (Ed.), *The translation studies reader* (pp. 113–118). London: Routledge.

Jayme, E. (1995). La langue: Risque linguistique et droit international privé. In *Recueil des cours: Collected courses of The Hague Academy of International Law* (pp. 189–194). The Hague: Kluwer Law.

Jemielity, D. (2012). *Managing multilingual communications processes*. Liechtenstein: BSL Banking.

Jenner, J. A., & Jenner, D. V. (2010). *The Entrepreneurial linguist: The business-school approach to freelance translation. Sine loco*: EL Press/Lulu.

Jensen, M. C., & Meckling, W. H. (1976). Theory of the firm: Managerial behavior, agency costs and ownership structure. *Journal of Financial Economics, 3*(4), 305–360.

Jones, A., & McCracken, S. (2007). Teaching the discourse of legal risk to finance professionals: Foundations for a linguistically scaffolded curriculum. In R. Wilkinson, & V. Zegers (Eds.), *Researching content and language integration in higher education* (pp. 122–136). Maastricht: Valkhof Pers & Maastricht University.

Jones, M. L. (2007). Using software to analyse qualitative data. *Malaysian Journal of Qualitative Research, 1*(1), 2007, 64–76. Retrieved from http://ro.uow.edu.au/commpapers/429.

Joseph, J. (1995). Indeterminacy, translation and the law. In M. Morris (Ed.), *Translation and the law* (pp. 13–36). Amsterdam: John Benjamins.

Kasirer, N. (2001). François Gény's libre recherche scientifique as a guide for legal translation. *Louisiana Law Review, 61*(2), 331–352.

Katan, D. (2009). Translation theory and professional practice: A global survey of the great divide. *Hermes, 42*, 111–153.

Katan, D. (2011). Occupation or profession: A survey of the translator's world. In R. Sela-Sheffy & M. Shlesinger (Eds.), *Identity and status in the translational professions* (pp. 11–30). Amsterdam: Benjamins.

Kaur Johl, S., & Renganathan, S. (2010). Strategies for gaining access in doing fieldwork: Reflection of two researchers. *The Electronic Journal of Business Research Methods, 8*(1): 42–50.

Kedia, B. L., & Lahiri, S. (2007). International outsourcing of services: A partnership model. *Journal of International Management, 13*, 22–37.

Kelsen, H. (1991). *General theory of norms* (M. Hartney, Trans.). Oxford: Oxford University Press.

Kennedy, R. (2000). Much ado about noting: Problems in the legal translation industry. *Temple International and Comparative Law Journal, 14*, 423–444.

Khurana, R., Nohria, N., & Penrice, D. (2005). Management as a profession. In J. W. Lorsch, L. Berlowitz, & A. Zelleke (Eds.), *Restoring trust in American business* (pp. 43–62). Cambridge, MA: MIT Press.

Kinnunen, T. (2010). Agency, activity and court interpreting. In T. Kinnunen & K. Koskinen (Eds.), *Translators' agency* (pp. 126–164). Tampere: Tampere University Press.

Kinnunen, T. (2011). Expertise sharing in the field of court translating and interpreting. *Apples: Journal of Applied Language Studies, 5*(1), 92–108.

Kinnunen, T., & Koskinen, K. (2010). Introduction. In T. Kinnunen & K. Koskinen (Eds.), *Translators' agency* (pp. 4–10). Tampere: Tampere University Press.

Kischel, U. (2009). Legal cultures: Legal languages. In F. Olsen, A. Lorz, & D. Stein (Eds.), *Translation issues in language and law* (pp. 7–17). Basingstoke: Palgrave Macmillan.

Kit, C., & Wong, T. M. (2008). Comparative evaluation of online machine translation systems with legal texts. *Law Library Journal, 100*(2), 299–321.

Kittredge, R., & Lehrberger, J. (Eds.). (1982). *Sublanguage: Studies of language in restricted semantic domains*. Berlin; New York: Walter de Gruyter.

Kjær, A. L. (1994). Zur kontrastiven Analyse von Nominationsstereotypen der Rechtssprache deutsch – dänisch. In B. Sandig (Ed.), *Tendenzen der Phraseologieforschung* (pp. 317–348). Bochum: Universitätsverlag Brockmeyer.

Kjaer, A. L. (2007). Phrasemes in legal texts. In H. Burger, D. Dobrovol'skij, P. Kühn, & N. R. Norrick (Eds.), *Phraseologie/Phraseology: Ein internationales Hand-buch der zeitgenössischen Forschung/An international handbook of contemporary research* (Vol. 1, pp. 506–515). Berlin; New York: Walter de Gruyter.

Kjaer, A. L. (2008). The every-day miracle of legal translation. *International Journal for the Semiotics of Law*, *21*, 1, 67–72.

Kleinschmidt, M. (2007). *Venture capital, corporate governance, and firm value*. Wiesbaden: Gabler Edition Wissenschaft.

Kocbek, A. (2008). The cultural embeddedness of legal texts. *Journal of Language & Translation*, *9*, 49–70.

Koehn, P. (2005). *Europarl: A parallel corpus for statistical machine translation*. Paper presented at MT Summit X. Retrieved from http://www.mt-archive.info/MTS-2005-Koehn.pdf.

Koehn, P. (2017). Neural machine translation. CoRR – Computing Research Repository, arXiv: 1709.07809. Retrieved from https://arxiv.org/abs/1709.07809.

Kübler, N. (2003). Corpora and LSP translation. In F. Zanettin, S. Bernardini, & D. Stewart (Eds.), *Corpora in translator education* (pp. 25–42). Manchester: St Jerome.

Kübler, N. (2004). Using WebCorp in the classroom for building specialized dictionaries. *Language and Computers*, *49*(1), 387–400.

Künnecke, M. (2013). Translation in the EU: Language and law in the EU's judicial labyrinth. *Maastrict Journal of European and Comparative Law*, *20*(2), 243–260.

Kurzon, D. (1997). 'Legal language': varieties, genres, registers, discourses. *International Journal of Applied Linguistics*, *7*(2), 119–139.

Lagoudaki, E. (2006). *Translation memories survey 2006*. London: Imperial College.

Laviosa, S. (1998). The corpus-based approach: A new paradigm in translation studies. *Meta*, *43*(4), 1–6.

Laviosa, S. (2002). *Corpus-based translation studies: Theory, findings, applications*. Amsterdam: Editions Rodopi B.V.

Lavoie, J. (2003). Faut-il être juriste ou traducteur pour traduire le droit? *Meta*, *48*(3), 393–401.

Lewins, A., & Silver, C. (2007). *Using software in qualitative research: A step-by-step guide*. London: Sage.

Lincoln, Y. S., & Guba, E. G. (1985). *Naturalistic inquiry*. Newbury Park, CA: SAGE.

LIT Search project. (2015). *Pilot project for an EU database of legal interpreters and translators*. Leuven: KU Leuven.

Logan, M. S. (2000). Using agency theory to design successful outsourcing relationships. *The International Journal of Logistics Management*, *11*(2), 21–32.

Lupoi, M. (2013). Trusts in Italy as a living comparative law laboratory. *Trusts & Trustees*, *19*(3–4), 302–308.

Maclachlan, K., & St. Clair, R. (2008, April). *Practitioner led action research adult literacy and numeracy in Scotland*. Paper presented at Practitioner Research: Can it support professional development? North West SfL Research Forum, Lancaster University.

Madsen, D. (1997). Towards a description of communication in the legal universe. *Fachsprache, 19*, 17–27.

Manganaras, I. (1996). The qualified legal translator is a lawyer trained in translation. *Lingua Legis, 4*. Retrieved from http://www.translegis.com.pl/ll_archiwum/LL_4_6.pdf.

Martin, T. (2007). Managing risks and resources: A down-to-earth view of revision. *The Journal of Specialised Translation, 8*, 57–63. Retrieved from http://www.jostrans.org/issue08/art_martin.php.

Mattila, H. E. S. (2006). *Comparative legal linguistics*. Aldershot: Ashgate.

Matulewska, A. (2007). *Lingua legis in translation*. Berlin: Peter Lang.

Matulewska, A., & Gortych-Michalak, K. (2014). Teaching certified translator candidates at the Adam Mickiewicz University in Poznan, Poland. In *Proceedings of New Tasks for Legal Interpreters and Translators in the Enlarged Europe* (pp. 246–257). Warsaw: Polskie Towarzystwo Tłumaczy Przysięgłych i Specjalistycznych TEPIS.

Mauro, J. (1988). Au carrefour des droits et des langues: La langue applicable au contrat, le risque linguistique. *Gazette du Palais, 1.214*. Retrieved from https://www.gazette-du-palais.fr/.

Maxwell Chandler, H., & O'Malley Deming, S. (2012). *The game localization handbook*. London: Jones & Bartlett Learning.

Mayoral Asensio, R. (2003). *Translating official documents*. Manchester: St Jerome.

McAuliffe, K. (2009). Translation at the Court of Justice of the European Communities. In F. Olsen, A. Lorz, & D. Stein (Eds.) *Translation issues in language and law* (pp. 99–115). Basingstoke: Palgrave Macmillan. Retrieved from http://ssrn.com/abstract=2208716.

McAuliffe, K. (2013a). Precedent at the Court of Justice of the European Union: The linguistic aspect. *Current Legal Issues, 15*, 483–493.

McAuliffe, K. (2013b). The limitations of a multilingual legal system. *International Journal for the Semiotics of Law, 26*, 861–882.

McKay, C. (2011). *How to succeed as a freelance translator*. Boulder, CO: Two Rat Press.

Megale, F. (2015). Mondialisation et traduction juridique: Nouveaux parcours de recherché. *International Journal for the Semiotics of Law, 28*, 31–52.

Melander, L., Rosell, D. T., & Lakemond, N. (2012). *Aligning goals and monitoring suppliers in new product development*. Paper presented at 13th International CINet Conference. Retrieved from liu.diva-portal.org/smash/get/diva2:547603/FULLTEXT01.

Mellinkoff, D. (1963). *Language of the law*. Boston: Little, Brown.

Menghini, M. (2012). Intertextual markers in sports-related arbitration. In V. K. Bhatia, G. Garzone, & C. Degano (Eds.), *Arbitration awards: Generic features and textual realisations* (pp. 232–251). Newcastle: Cambridge Scholars. Retrieved from http://www.uniroma4.it/?q=node/1026.

Mertz, E. (2007). *The language of law school*. Oxford: Oxford University Press.

Michaels, R. (2006). The functional method of comparative law. In M. Reimann & R. Zimmermann (Eds.), *The Oxford handbook of comparative law* (pp. 339–366). Oxford: Oxford University Press.

Milton, J., & Bandia, P. (2009). Introduction: Agents of translation and translation studies. In J. Milton & P. Bandia (Eds.), *Agents of translation* (pp. 1–18). Amsterdam: John Benjamins.

Ministry of Justice. (2015). Practice Direction 25B: *The duties of an expert, the expert's report and arrangements for an expert to attend court*. Retrieved from https://www.justice.gov.uk/courts/procedure-rules/family/practice_directions/practice-direction-25b-the-duties-of-an-expert,-the-experts-report-and-arrangements-for-an-expert-to-attend-court#IDAFGIT.

Mitamura, T. (1999, 13–17 September). *Controlled language for multilingual machine translation*. Paper presented at Machine Translation Summit VII: MT in the Great Translation Era, Singapore. Retrieved from http://lti.cs.cmu.edu/Research/Kant/PDF/MTSummit99.pdf.

Mitnick, B. M. (2013). Origin of the theory of agency: An account by one of the theory's originators. *SSRN Electronic Journal*. Retrieved from http://ssrn.com/abstract=1020378.

Mol, M. (2007). *Outsourcing: Design, process, and performance*. Cambridge: Cambridge University Press.

Molnár, O. (2013). Source text quality in the translation process. In J. Zehnalová, O. Molnár, & M. Kubnánek (Eds.), *Traditions and trends in trans-language communication* (pp. 59–86). Olomouc: Palacký.

Monjean-Decaudin, S. (2010a). *Approche juridique de la traduction du droit*. Working Paper, CEJEC European and comparative law research center. Retrieved from http://cejec.u-paris10.fr/wp-content/uploads/2010/01/smonjeandecaudin070110.doc.

Monjean-Decaudin, S. (2010b). Territorialité et extraterritorialité de la traduction du droit. *Meta*, *55*(4), 693–711.

Monjean-Decaudin, S. (2012). *La traduction du droit dans la procédure judiciaire*. Paris: Dalloz.

Monjean-Decaudin, S. (2013). Réflexion sur l'*inflexion du signifié* dans la traduction juridique de Claude Bocquet. *Parallèles*, *25*, 1–10.

Monjean-Decaudin, S. (2014). Théorie et pratique de la traduction juridique ou sur les lieux d'une rencontre. *Semiotica*, *201*, 81–101.

Montalt Ressurrecció, V., Epeleta Piorno, P., & Izquierdo Garcìa, I. (2008). Developing communicative and textual competence through genres. *Translation Journal*, *12*(4). Retrieved from http://translationjournal.net/journal/46competence.htm.

Monzó, E. (2011). Legal and translational occupations in Spain: Regulation and specialization in jurisdictional struggles. In R. Sela-Sheffy & M. Shlesinger (Eds.), *Identity and status in the translational professions* (pp. 11–30). Amsterdam: Benjamins.

Monzó Nebot, E. (2008). Corpus-based activities in legal translator training. *The Interpreter and Translator Trainer*, *2*(2), 221–252.

Monzó Nebot, E. (2015). Understanding legal interpreter and translator training in times of change. *The Interpreter and Translator Trainer*, *9*(2), 129–140.

Mossop, B. (2007). Empirical studies of revision: What we know and need to know. *The Journal of Specialised Translation*, *8*, 5–20. Retrieved from http://www.jostrans.org/issue08/art_mossop.php.

Mossop, B. (2014). *Revising and editing for translators*. Manchester: St Jerome.

Mule, J., & Johnson, C. (2010). How effective is machine translation of legal information? *Clearinghouse Review Journal of Poverty Law and Policy*, *44*(32).

Munday, J. (2008). *Introducing translation studies*. London: Routledge.

Nagy Hesse-Biber, S. (2010). *Mixed methods research*. London: Guilford.

Ng, K. H. (2014). Legal translation and the problem of heteroglossia. In S. Glanert (Ed.), *Comparative law: Engaging translation* (pp. 49–66). London: Routledge.

Nida, E. A. (1964). *Toward a science of translating*. Leiden: E. J. Brill.

Nida, E. A. (1976). A framework for the analysis and evaluation of theories of translation. In R. W. Brislin (Ed.), *Translation: Applications and Research* (pp. 47–91). New York: Gardner Press.

Nielsen, M., Johansen, W., Engberg, J., Frandsen, F., & Bhatia, V. K. (1997). On Vijay K. Bhatia: Analysing genre: Language use in professional settings, 1993. [Review of the book *Analysing genre: Language use in professional settings*] *Hermes*, *19*, 207–239.

Nielsen, S. (1994). *The bilingual LSP Dictionary: principles and practice for legal language*. Tübingen: Gunter Narr Verlag Tübingen.

Noortwijk, K. van, & De Mulder, R. (2007). *A quantitative analysis of legal word use*. Paper presented at BILETA (British & Irish Law, Education and Technology Association) 2007 Annual Conference, Hertfordshire, UK. Retrieved from http://www.bileta.ac.uk/Document%20Library/1/A%20quantitative%20analysis%20of%20legal%20word%20use.pdf.

Nord, C. (1991/2005). *Text analysis in translation*. Amsterdam: Rodopi.

Nord, C. (1997). *Translating as a purposeful activity*. Manchester: St Jerome.

Nord, C. (2007). Training functional translators. In M. Tennent (Ed.), *Training for the new millennium: Pedagogies for translation and interpreting* (pp. 209–223). Amsterdam: Benjamins.

Nord, C. (2013). Functionalism in translation studies. In C. Millán & F. Bartrina (Eds.), *The Routledge handbook of translation studies* (pp. 201–212). London: Routledge.

Northcott, J., & Brown, G. (2006). Legal translator training: Partnership between teachers of English for legal purposes and legal specialists. *English for Specific Purposes*, *25*(3), 358–375. doi: 10.1016/j.esp.2005.08.003.

Noy, C. (2008). Sampling knowledge: The hermeneutics of snowball sampling in qualitative research. *International Journal of Social Research Methodology*, *11*(4), 327–344.

O'Brien, S., & Simard, M. (2014). Introduction to special issue on post-editing. *Machine Translation*, *28*, 159–164.

Obenaus, G. (1995). The legal translator as information broker. In M. Morris (Ed.), *Translation and the law* (pp. 247–259). Amsterdam: John Benjamins.

Okumus, F., Altinay, L., & Roper, A. (2007). Gaining access for research: Reflections from experience. *Annals of Tourism Research*, *34*(1), 7–26.

Olohan, M. (2007). Economic trends and developments in the translation industry: What Relevance for translator training? *The Interpreter and Translator Trainer*, *1*(1), 37–63.

Olohan, M. (2011). Translators and translation technology: The dance of agency. *Translation Studies*, *4*(3), 342–357.

Olohan, M. (2015). *Scientific and technical translation*. Abingdon: Routledge.

Olohan, M., & Davitti, E. (2015). Dynamics of trusting in translation project management: Leaps of faith and balancing acts. *Journal of Contemporary Ethnography*, *46*(4), 391–416.

Olsen, F., Lorz, A., & Stein, D. (Eds.) (2009). *Translation issues in language and law*. Basingstoke: Palgrave MacMillan.

Olvera-Lobo, M., Castro-Prieto, M., Quero-Gervilla, E., Muñoz-Martín, R., Muñoz-Raya, E., Murillo-Melero, M., *et al.* (2005). Translator training and modern market demands. *Perspectives: Studies in Translatology*, *13*(2), 132–142.

Orlando, D. (2015). *The trials of legal translation competence: Triangulating processes and products of translators vs. lawyers*. As yet unpublished doctoral thesis. Trieste: Trieste.

Orozco, M., & Sánchez-Gijón, P. (2011). New resources for legal translators. *Perspectives: Studies in Translatology*, *19*(1), 25–44.

Orts, M. A. (2012). A genre-based approach to the translation of private normative texts in legal English and legal Spanish. *International Journal for the Semiotics of Law*, *25*(3), 317–338.

Paloposki, O. (2009). Limits of freedom: Agency, choice and constraints in the work of the translator. In J. Milton & P. Bandia (Eds.), *Agents of translation* (pp. 189–208). Amsterdam: John Benjamins.

Pelage, J. (2000, 17–19 February). *La traductologie face au droit*. Paper presented at La traduction juridique: Histoire, théorie(s) et pratique, Geneva. Retrieved from http://www.tradulex.com/Actes2000/pelage.pdf.

Pepper, A., & Gore, J. (2015). Behavioral agency theory: New foundations for theorizing about executive compensation. *Journal of Management*, *41*(4), 1045–1068.

Perrow, C. (1986). Economic theories of organization. *Theory and Society*, *15*(1–2), 11–45.

Peruginelli, G. (2006). Legal information on the web: The case of Italy. *International Journal of Legal Information*, *34*(2), 327–357.

Peruginelli, G. (2010). *Searching law in a multilingual environment*. Pisa: ETS.

Petelin, R. (2002). Managing organisational writing to enhance corporate credibility. *Journal of Communication Management*, *7*(2), 172–180.

Philip, G. (1999, June). *Computer Corpora and the law: A new approach to the translation of legal terms*. Paper presented at the International Association of Forensic Linguistics Fourth Biennial Conference. Retrieved from http://amsacta.cib.unibo.it/1134/.

Phillips, A. (2003). *Lawyers' language*. London: Routledge.

Philpott, K., Dooley, L., O'Reilly, C., & Lupton, G. (2011). The entrepreneurial university: Examining the underlying academic tensions. *Technovation*, *31*(4), 161–170.

Pickering, A. (1995). *The mangle of practice: Time, agency and science*. Chicago: Chicago University Press.

Piehl A., & Vihonen, I. (2010). *Writing for translation*. Luxembourg: Translation Centre for the Bodies of the European Union.

Pigeon, L.-P. (1982). La traduction juridique: L'équivalence fonctionnelle. In J.-C. Gémar (Ed.), *Langage du droit et traduction* (pp. 271–281). Québec: Conseil de la langue française.

Platsas, A. (2008). The functional and the dysfunctional in the comparative method of law: Some critical remarks. *Electronic Journal of Comparative Law*, *12*(3), 1–16.

Pollman, T. (2002). Building a tower of Babel or building a discipline? Talking about legal writing. *Marquette Law Review*, *85*(4), 887–928.

Pommer, S. (2005) Re-evaluating interdisciplinarity: The significance of comparative law for legal translation methodology. In *FIT Proceedings, XVIIth World Congress of the International Federation of Translators: Rights on! Tampere 4.-7.8.2005* (pp. 72–74) Paris: FIT.

Pommer, S. (2008). Translation as intercultural transfer: The case of law. *SKASE Journal of Translation and Interpretation*, *3*(1), 17–21.

Pontrandolfo, G. (2011). Phraseology in criminal judgments: A corpus study of original vs. translated Italian. *Sendebar*, *22*, 209–234.

Pontrandolfo, G. (2015). Investigating judicial phraseology with COSPE: A contrastive corpus-based study. In C. Fantinuoli & F. Zanettin (Eds.), *New directions in corpus-based translation studies*, 137–160. Berlin: Language Science Press.

Pontrandolfo, G. (2016). *Fraseología y lenguaje judicial: Las sentencias penales desde una perspectiva contrastiva*. Ariccia: Aracne.

PricewaterhouseCoopers (2012, 15 May). *Translation bureau benchmarking and comparative analysis final report*. Retrieved from https://www.google.com/url?sa=t&rct=j&q=&esrc=s&source=web&cd=2&ved=0ahUKEwjM36aCu7LbAhUqAsAKHdfhBsIQFggvMAE&url=https%3A%2F%2Failia.ca%2Fdl359&usg=AOvVaw36Q293Qchf_UthE7zvXrOj.

Prieto Ramos, F. (2014). Legal translation studies as interdiscipline: Scope and evolution. *Meta*, *59*(2), 260–277.

Prioux, R., & Rochard, M. (2007). Economie de la révision dans une organisation internationale: Le cas de l'OCDE. *The Journal of Specialised Translation*, *8*, 21–41. Retrieved from http://www.jostrans.org/issue08/art_prioux_rochard.php.

Pym, A. (1996). Material text transfer as a key to the purposes of translation. In A. Neubert, G. Shreve, & K. Gommlich (Eds.), *Basic issues in translation studies* (pp. 337–346). Kent, OH: Kent State University.

Pym, A. (2004). Text and risk in translation. In M. Sidiropoulou & A. Papaconstantinou (Eds.), *Choice and difference in translation: The specifics of transfer* (pp. 27–42). Athens: The National and Kapodistrian University of Athens.

Pym, A. (2009, March). *Western translation theories as responses to equivalence*. Paper presented at Innsbrucker Internationale Ringvorlesung zur Translationswissenschaft, Universität Innsbruck.

Pym, A. (2010). *Exploring translation theories*. London: Routledge.

Pym, A. (2014). Translator associations: From gatekeepers to communities. *Target*, *26*(3), 466–491.

Pym, A. (2015). Translating as risk management. *Journal of Pragmatics*, *85*, 67–80.

Pym, A., Grin, F., Sfreddo, C., & Chan, A. L. J. (2012). *The status of the translation profession in the European Union*. Luxembourg: European Commission.

Pym, A., Grin, F., Sfreddo, C., & Chan, A. L. J. (2013). *The status of the translation profession in the European Union*. London: Anthem.

Ralli, N. (2009). Terminografia e comparazione giuridica: Metodo, applicazioni e problematiche chiave. *inTRAlinea, Specialised Translation I* (Special issue). Retrieved from http://www.intralinea.org/specials/article/Terminografia_e_comparazione_giuridica_metodo_applicazioni_e_problematiche_.

Rasmussen, K. W., & Engberg, J. (1999). Genre analysis of legal discourse. *Hermes*, *22*, 113–132.

Rasmussen, K. W., & Schjoldager, A. (2011). Revising translations: A survey of revision policies in Danish translation companies. *The Journal of Specialised Translation*, *15*, 87–120. Retrieved from http://www.jostrans.org/issue15/art_rasmussen.php.

Rigdon, M. (2005). Trust and reciprocity in incentive contracting. *Journal of Economic Behavior & Organization*, *70*(1–2), 93–105. Retrieved from https://mpra.ub.uni-muenchen.de/2007/

Robson, C. (2011). *Real world research: A resource for social scientists and practitioner-researchers*. Oxford: Blackwell.

Rodríguez-Inés, P., 2010. Electronic corpora and other ICT (Information and communication technologies) tools: An integrated approach to translation teaching. *The Interpreter and Translator Trainer*, *4*(2), 251–282.

Rogers-Glabush, J. (2009). *IBFD international tax glossary*. Amsterdam: IBFD.

Romagnino, K. D. (2011). Nearshore alternative: Latin America's potential in the offshore legal process outsourcing marketplace. *Inter-American Law Review*, *42*(2), 367–413.

Rush, J. (2002). *Understanding and negotiating contracts: Master the small print and get a better deal.* Oxford: How to Books.

Sacco, R. (1987). Un point de vue italien. *Les cahiers de droit*, *28*(4), 845–859.

Sager, J. C. (1994). *Language engineering and translation: Consequences of automation.* Amsterdam: John Benjamins.

Salmi-Tolonen, T. (2006). From linguistic knowledge to contracting capabilities – and back again. In D. Lowe (Ed.), *International academic symposium on commercial management* (pp. 83–92). Manchester: Centre for Research in the Management of Projects, University of Manchester.

Samuel, G. (2014). *An introduction to comparative law theory and method.* Oxford: Hart.

Samuelsson-Brown, G. (2010). *A practical guide for translators* (5th ed.). Bristol: Multilingual Matters.

Sánchez Ramos, M. M., & Vigier Moreno, F. J. (2016). Using monolingual virtual corpora in public service legal translator training. In E. Martín-Monje, I. Elorza, & B. G. Riaza (Eds.), *Technology-enhanced language learning for specialized domains: Practical applications and mobility* (pp. 228–240). Abingdon: Routledge.

Sandrini, P. (1999). Legal terminology: Some aspects for a new methodology [Electronic version]. *Hermes*, *22*, 101–112. Retrieved from http://download2.hermes.asb.dk/archive/download/H22_06.pdf.

Šarčević, S. (1997). *New approach to legal translation.* The Hague: Kluwer Law International.

Šarčević, S. (2000, 17–19 February). *Legal translation and translation theory: A receiver-oriented approach.* Paper presented at Legal Translation, History, Theory/ies, and Practice. Retrieved from http://tradulex.org/Actes2000/sarcevic.pdf.

Šarčević, S. (2012). Challenges to the legal translator. In P. M. Tiersma & L. M. Solan (Eds.), *The Oxford handbook of language and law* (pp. 187–199). Oxford: Oxford University Press.

Scalia, A. (1990, 17 September). Oral remarks delivered to Colorado Bar Association. *USA Today*.

Scarpa, F., & Orlando, D. (2017). What it takes to do it right: An integrative EMT-based model for legal translation competence. *The Journal of Specialised Translation*, *27*, 21–42.

Schane, S. (2006). *Language and the law*. London: Continuum.

Schäffner, C. (1998). The concept of norms in translation studies. *Current Issues in Language and society*, *5*(1–2), 1–9.

Schäffner, C. (2004). Metaphor and translation. *Journal of Pragmatics*, *36*(7), 1253–1269.

Schäffner, C. (2012). Translation competence: Training for the real world. In S. Hubscher-Davidson & M. Borodo (Eds.), *Global trends in translation and interpreter training: Mediation and Culture* (pp. 30–44). London: Continuum.

Schroth, P. W. (1986). Legal translation. *American Journal of Comparative Law*, *34*, 47–65.

Scott, J. R. (2012). Can genre-specific DIY corpora, compiled by legal translators themselves, assist them in 'learning the lingo' of legal subgenres? *Comparative Legilinguistics*, *12*, 87–100.

Scott, J. R. (2013, November). *Training is all around you all of the time*. Paper presented at legal translation event, European Commission Representation, London, UK.

Scott, J. R. (2015a, January). *Professionalizing legal translation ... Do or die!* Paper presented at the symposium Becoming a legal translator, University of Roehampton, UK.

Scott, J. R. (2015b). How legal translation studies research might assist lawyers with best procurement practice. In G. Jacobs & G. M. Alessi (Eds.), *The ins and outs of business and professional discourse research: Reflections on interacting with the workplace* (pp. 117–138). Basingstoke: Palgrave.

Scott, J. R. (2015c). Suggestions for optimizing the agency of freelance legal translators. In G. Tessuto & R. Salvi (Eds.), *Language and law in social practice research* (pp. 224–248). Mantua: Universitas Studiorum.

Scott, J. R. (2017a). Legal translation training: A way forward for aspiring lawyers in a clogged job market? (2017). *Tilburg Law Review*, Special issue on Translating Law, *22*, 215–235.

Scott, J. R. (2017b). The pernicious effects of terms used for and by the legal translation profession. *Revista de Llengua i Dret: From Legal Translation to Jurilinguistics*, *68*, 57–75.

Scott, J. R. (2017c). Legal translation: A multidimensional endeavour. *Comparative Legilinguistics, Journal of Legal Communication*, *32*, 37–66.

Scott, J. R. (2017d). The pivotal role of legal translation practitioners in the fight against cross-border organised crime. *The European Review of Organised Crime*, *4*(2), 147–164.

Scott, J. R. (2018). Negotiating constraints on legal translation performance in an outsourced environment. In G. Tessuto (Ed.), *Law, language and communication: Negotiating cultural, jurisdictional and disciplinary boundaries* (pp. 370–392). Cambridge: Cambridge Scholars.

Scott, J. R. (forthcoming). Specifying Levels of (C)overtness in Legal Translation Briefs. In I. Simmonaes & M. Kristiansen (Eds.), *Legal translation (studies) as a challenge / Herausforderungen an das Rechtsübersetzen*. Berlin: Frank & Timme.

Seidel, J. V. (1998). Qualitative data analysis. Appendix to the *The Ethnograph v4. Manual*. Retrieved from www.qualisresearch.com.

Sela-Sheffy, R., & Shlesinger, M. (2008). Strategies of image-making and status advancement of translators and interpreters as a marginal occupational group. In A. Pym, M. Shlesinger, & D. Simeoni (Eds.), *Beyond descriptive translation studies: Investigations in homage to Gideon Toury* (pp. 79–90). Amsterdam: John Benjamins.

Shapiro, S. P. (2005). Agency theory. *Annual Review of Sociology*, *31*, 263–284.

Sharma, A. (1997). Professional as agent: Knowledge asymmetry in agency exchange. *The Academy of Management Review*, *22*(3), 758–798.

Smith, M. R. (2007). Levels of metaphor in persuasive legal writing. *Mercer Law Review*, *58*, 919–947.

Smith, R. (2009, 19–20 November). Copyright issues in translation memory ownership. *Proceedings of the Thirty-first International Conference on Translating and the Computer* (pp. 1–9). London: Aslib.

Smith, S. A. (1995). Culture clash: Anglo-American case law and German civil law in translation. In M. Morris (Ed.), *Translation and the law* (pp. 179–197). Amsterdam: John Benjamins.

Smyth, D., Barker, R., & Belcher, T. (2015). Rage against the (translation) machine. *Journal of Intellectual Property Law & Practice*, *10*(3), 153–154.

Snell-Horby, M. (1988/1995). *Translation studies: An integrated approach*. Amsterdam: John Benjamins.

Snell-Hornby, M. (2006). *The turns of translation studies*. Amsterdam: John Benjamins.

Solan, L. M. (2011a). Lawyers as insincere (but truthful) actors. *Brooklyn Law School, Legal Studies Paper No. 238*. Retrieved from http://papers.ssrn.com/sol3/papers.cfm?abstract_id=1873359.

Solan, L. M. (2011b). Linguistic issues in statutory interpretation. *Brooklyn Law School, Legal Studies Paper No. 254*. Retrieved from http://papers.ssrn.com/sol3/papers.cfm?abstract_id=1950310.

Solan, L. M. (2013). Judging language plain. *Brooklyn Law School, Legal Studies Paper No. 360*. Retrieved from http://papers.ssrn.com/sol3/papers.cfm?abstract_id=2342350.

Somers, H. (2007). The use of machine translation by law librarians: A reply to Yates. *Law Library Journal*, *99*(3), 611–619.

Spina, S. (2010). The dictionary of Italian collocations: Design and integration in an online learning environment. *Proceedings of the Seventh Conference on International Language Resources and Evaluation (LREC'10)*. Retrieved from http://www.lrec-conf.org/proceedings/lrec2010/summaries/681.html.

Strandvik, I. (2012). Legal harmonization through legal translation: Texts that say the same thing? In C. J. W. Baaij (Ed.), *The role of legal translation in legal harmonization* (pp. 25–49). London: Kluwer.

Strandvik, I. (2014). Is there scope for a more professional approach to EU multilingual lawmaking? *The Theory and Practice of Legislation*, *2*(2), 211–228.

Strandvik, I. (2015). On quality in EU multilingual lawmaking. In S. Šarčević (Ed.), *Language and culture in EU law: Multidisciplinary perspectives* (pp. 141–168). Farnham: Ashgate.

Strandvik, I. (2018). Towards a more structured approach to quality assurance: DGT's quality journey. In F. Prieto Ramos (Ed.), *Institutional translation for international governance: Enhancing quality in multilingual legal communication* (pp. 51–62). London: Bloomsbury.

Strandvik, I. (in press). Translation quality, quality management and agency: Principles and practice in the European Union institutions. In J. Moorkens, S. Castilho, F. Gaspari, & S. Doherty (Eds.), *Translation quality assessment: From principles to practice*. New York: Springer.

Strandvik, I. (forthcoming). The Eurolect Observatory Project: Research at the service of multilingual law-making. In L. Mori (Ed.), *Observing Eurolects: Dynamics of language variation in EU law*. Amsterdam: Benjamins.

Studies on translation and multilingualism: Quantifying quality costs and the cost of poor quality in translation (2012). Luxembourg: Publications Office of the European Union.

Suojanen, T., Koskinen, K., & Tuominen, T. (2015). *User-centered translation*. Abingdon: Routledge.

Sutskever, I., Vinyals, O., & Le, Q. V. (2014). Sequence to sequence learning with neural networks. *Advances in Neural Information Processing Systems*, *27*. Retrieved from http://arxiv.org/abs/1409.3215v3.

Swales, J. (1990). *Genre analysis: English in academic and research settings*. Cambridge: Cambridge University Press.

Tate, W. L., Ellram, L. M., Bals, L., Hartmann E., & van der Valk, W. (2010). An agency theory perspective on the purchase of marketing services. *Industrial Marketing Management*, *39*(5), 806–819.

Teclaw, R., Price, M. C., & Osatuke, K. (2011). Demographic question placement: Effect on item response rates and means of a Veterans Health Administration survey. *Journal of Business and Psychology*, *27*(3), 281–290.

Tiersma, P. M. (2000). *Legal language*. London: University of Chicago Press.

Toury, G. (1998). A handful of paragraphs on 'translation' and 'norms'. *Current Issues in Language & Society*, *5*(1&2), 10–32.

Toury, G. (2012). *Descriptive translation studies—and beyond*. Amsterdam: John Benjamins.

Trosborg, A. (1997a). *Rhetorical strategies in legal language: Discourse analysis of statutes and contracts*. Tübingen: Gunter Narr Verlag Tübingen.

Trosborg, A. (1997b). Text typology: Register, genre and text type. In A. Trosborg (Ed.), *Text, typology and translation* (pp. 3–24). Amsterdam: Benjamins.

Troussel, J.-C., & Debussche, J. (2014). *Translation and intellectual property rights*. Luxembourg: European Commission.

Tu, Z., Liu, Y., Lu, Z., Liu, X., & Li, H. (2017). *Context gates for neural machine translation*. CoRR – Computing Research Repository, arXiv:1608.06043v3. Retrieved from https://arxiv.org/abs/1608.06043.

US Bureau of Labor Statistics (2015). *Occupational outlook handbook, 2014–15 Edition: Interpreters and translators*. Washington, DC: US Department of Labor. Retrieved from http://www.bls.gov/ooh/media-and-communication/interpreters-and-translators.htm.

UK Ministry of Justice, Practice Direction 25B (n.d.). Retrieved from https://www.justice.gov.uk/courts/procedure-rules/family/practice_directions/practice-direction-25b-the-duties-of-an-expert,-the-experts-report-and-arrangements-for-an-expert-to-attend-court.

Vandendaele, A., Bruyer, T., & Jacobs, G. (2015). 'We never even wondered whether we trusted them or not': From freedom to mutuality in a student research project. In G. Jacobs & G. M. Alessi (Eds.), *The ins and outs of business and professional discourse research: Reflections on interacting with the workplace* (pp. 102–116). Basingstoke: Palgrave.

Venuti, L. (1995). *The translator's invisibility*. London: Routledge.

Vermeer, H. J. (1989). Skopos and commission in translational action. In L. Venuti (Ed.), *The translation studies reader* (pp. 227–238). Abingdon: Routledge.

Vespaziani, A. (2009, September). Towards a hermeneutical approach to legal metaphor. *ISSL Papers Special Issue: Dossier on Law and Literature. A Discussion on Purposes and Method. Proceedings of the Special WS on Law and Literature held at 24th IVR World Conference in Beijing, China*. Retrieved from http://www.lawandliterature.org/area/documenti/Law%20and%20Literature%20%20IVR%20WS%20Proceedings%202010.pdf.

Vigier, F., Klein, P., & Festinger, N. (2013). Certified translators in Europe and in the Americas: Accreditation practices and challenges. In A. Borja Albi & F. Prieto Ramos (Eds.), *Legal translation in context* (pp. 27–51). Bern: Peter Lang.

Vinay, J.-P., & Darbelnet, J. (1958/2000). A methodology for translation (J. C. Sager & M.-J. Hamel, Trans.). In L. Venuti (Ed.), *The translation studies reader* (pp. 84–93). London: Routledge.

Wagner, A., & Gémar, J.-C. (2015). Les enjeux de la jurilinguistique et de la juritraductologie. *International Journal for the Semiotics of Law, 28*, 1–8.

Walker, D. M. (1980). *The Oxford companion to law*. Oxford: Clarendon.

Way, C. (2016). The challenges and opportunities of legal translation and translator training in the 21st century. *International Journal of Communication, 10*, 1009–1029.

Wehrli, A. (2012, 11 May). *Language, law and power*. Paper presented at Law, Language and Professional Practice, Faculty of Law, University of Naples 2, Caserta, Italy.

Welch, C., Marschan-Piekkari, R., Penttinen, H., & Tahvanainen, M. (2002). Corporate elites as informants in qualitative international business research. *International Business Review, 11*, 611–628.

West, D. C. (1997). Purchasing professional services: The case of advertising agencies. *International Journal of Purchasing and Materials Management, 33*(3), 2–9.

What Consumer (n.d.). *It is not fit for purpose*. Retrieved from http://whatconsumer.co.uk/it-is-not-fit-for-purpose/#comments.

White, J. B. (1985). *Heracles' bow*. Madison: University of Wisconsin Press.

Williams, M., Hillage, J., Pinto, R., & Garrett, R. (2012). *Sector skills insights: Digital and Creative* (Evidence Report 49). Retrieved from the UK Government website: https://www.gov.uk/government/uploads/system/uploads/attachment_data/file/304485/Sector_Skills_Insights_Digital_and_Creative_evidence_report_49.pdf.

Winter, R. (2005). Some principles and procedures for the conduct of action research. In O. Zuber-Skerritt (Ed.), *New directions in action research* (pp. 9–22). London: Falmer.

Wiseman, R. M., Cuevas-Rodríguez, G., & Gomez-Mejia, L. R. (2012). Towards a social theory of agency. *Journal of Management Studies, 49*(1), 202–222.

Witz, A. (1992). *Professions and patriarchy*. London: Routledge.

Wolinsky, A. (1994). Competition in markets for credence goods. *Journal of Institutional and Theoretical Economics, 151*(1), 117–131.

Wright, K. B. (2006). Researching Internet-based populations: Advantages and disadvantages of online survey research, online questionnaire authoring software packages, and web survey services. *Journal of Computer-Mediated Communication, 10*(3). doi: 10.1111/j.1083-6101.2005.tb00259.x.

Yates, S. (2006). Scaling the tower of Babel fish: An analysis of the machine translation of legal information. *Law Library Journal, 98*(3), 481–500.

Yunus, K. B., & Awab, S. (2011). Collocational competence among Malaysian undergraduate law students. *Malaysian Journal of ELT Research, 7*(1), 151–202.

Zanettin, F. (2012). *Translation-driven corpora*. Manchester: St Jerome.

Zu, X., & Kaynak, H. (2012). An agency theory perspective on supply chain quality management. *International Journal of Operations & Production Management, 32*(4), 423–446.

Zweigert K., & Kötz, H. (2011). *An introduction to comparative law*. Oxford: Oxford.

Software and Electronic Tools

NVivo (Versions 9-10). QSR International Pty Ltd.

Sandvox (2011). Pasadena (CA): Karelia Software.

Sketch Engine (2011). Brighton: Lexical Computing Ltd.

Wufoo.com. Palo Alto: SurveyMonkey.com, LLC.

INDEX

Page numbers followed by *f*, *t* and *n* refer to figures, tables and note number, respectively.